REGULATORY REFORMS IN ITALY

Regulatory Reforms in Italy

A case study in Europeanisation

DIETER KERWER
*Max Planck Project: Common Goods,
Bonn,Germany*

Ashgate

Aldershot • Burlington USA • Singapore • Sydney

Published by
Ashgate Publishing Limited
Gower House
Croft Road
Aldershot
Hampshire GU11 3HR
England

Ashgate Publishing Company
131 Main Street
Burlington, VT 05401-5600 USA

Ashgate website: http://www.ashgate.com

British Library Cataloguing in Publication Data
Kerwer, Dieter
    Regulatory reforms in Italy : a case study in
    Europeanisation
    1. Transportation and state - Italy
    I. Title
    388'.0945

Library of Congress Cataloging-in-Publication Data
Kerwer, Dieter.
    Regulatory reforms in Italy : a case study in Europeanisation / Dieter Kerwer.
        p. cm.
    Rev. ed. of author's thesis (Ph.D.)--European University Institute in Florence. 1999.
    Includes bibliographical references.
    ISBN 0-7546-1690-8
        1. Transportation--Italy. 2. Transportation and state--Italy. 3. Transportation--Europe.
    4. Transportation and state--Europe. I. Title

    HE251.A2 K47 2001
    388'.0945--dc21   2001022159

ISBN 0 7546 1690 8

Printed in Great Britain by
Antony Rowe Ltd, Chippenham, Wiltshire

Contents

List of Figures and Tables

Preface and Acknowledgements

This book would not have been written, had - in the Autumn of 1994 - Adrienne Héritier not offered me a position on her research team. Working with her turned out to be more adventurous than I had expected. Italian transport policy, which I subsequently studied, seemed to me a puzzling world. What is more, only a few months after I enrolled, she accepted a chair at the European University Institute in Florence. I soon found myself moving my books and piles of photocopies from the University of Bielefeld to the EUI. This was a fortunate windfall. Since collecting empirical data became easier, the Italian case appeared more promising. The question I became interested in and which I try to answer in this thesis may be summarised as follows: what accounts for the amazing stability of Italian transport policy in the face of European challenges, given the fact that – as most national and European policy-makers readily believe – it is not capable of addressing the problems of the sector?

During the course of this research I have become indebted to many people. First of all, I have to thank my colleagues and friends Christoph Knill, Dirk Lehmkuhl and Michael Teutsch for stimulating debates, criticism, and persistent good humour. I feel fortunate for having had the possibility to work with them on a research project.

Furthermore, I would like to thank the numerous policy experts of the EU and in Italy for their patience in answering my questions. More often than not, I was impressed by their competence. I owe many discoveries and insights to our conversations. Since I promised them anonymity, I cannot mention their names here - with one exception. Dott. Filippo Strati, Director of *Studio Ricerche Sociali* in Florence, introduced me to transport policy issues in Italy. Without him, it would have taken me much longer to become oriented.

I had the chance to present the preliminary results of this research in the workshop on 'European Integration and Convergence of National Policies' at the University of Utrecht in June 1995, at the conference on 'Transport and Infrastructure Policy in the European Union' at the Max-Planck Institute for the Study of Societies in Cologne in November 1995, and at the conference 'La Réorganisation des Etats Européens' in Grenoble in September 1997. I would like to thank the participants for helpful comments.

vii

Dr Burkard Eberlein and Professor Pierre Muller read parts of the manuscript. I gratefully acknowledge their inspiring comments. Maria Elena and Francesca Manfredini provided research assistance. They were more helpful and generous than I could have expected. I would like to thank all my friends at the EUI. Due to them, my sojourn in Florence has been a rewarding intellectual and human experience. I specifically want to mention James Turpin, with whom I enjoyed all the pleasures of friendship.

This book is a revised version of the Ph.D. thesis I defended at the European University Institute in Florence in 1999. I would like to thank the examination committee, Professors Adrienne Héritier, Stefano Bartolini, Colin Crouch, and Helmut Willke, for their insightful comments and constructive criticism which helped make this a better book.

Steven Tokar and Darrell Arnold worked hard on the Continental-European style of the earlier drafts. I would like to thank them both for making me believe I actually have written an English book.

Finally, I would like to thank Tatjana Baraulina for her encouragement and for her presence during the long periods of our separation.

1 Introduction

The following study is dedicated to an analysis of the past decade of transport policy in Italy. The investigation focuses on how the two sub-sectors of surface transport, road haulage and railways, have been managed by the public and private actors involved. The development of Italian transport policy in these two sectors presents a striking puzzle even to the casual observer. Dissatisfaction among transport users is widespread, and the performance is considered to be disappointing in comparison with other industrialised nations. Furthermore, in both sectors, the policy seems to have failed, either by not having offered a remedy or by having aggravated the situation even further. Yet, until recently, no major policy change could be observed. This is surprising since such radical transport policy reform models in the form of privatisation and deregulation have been sweeping through the industrialised world ever since the deregulation movement began in the USA in the second half of the 1970s. What is even more surprising is that whenever international influence did have an effect, this led to a variety of adaptation patterns, not necessarily conforming with these influences.

A research interest in Italian transport policy risks being just as odd as Italian transport policy itself. In Italy the study of public policy in general, and even more so of transport policy, is not a well-established field outside of economics and law. Current events do not seem to offer a remedy to the situation. Rather, Italy still seems to be a good case for the study of topics which were of primary interest in the past (Bull, 1996). The Italian political system is presently going through a major transition as a new regime is being formed (e.g. Caciagli, 1994; Bull and Rhodes, 1997). It thus offers the possibility to study processes of change in the party system and the constitutional set-up. Furthermore, the widespread corruption that has been uncovered seems to offer a unique opportunity to study political corruption (e.g. Pizzorno, 1992). But why study the peculiar sub-field of economic policy called transport policy? Such a research interest does something more specific than simply add to the scarce knowledge about public policy in Italy. Rather than being an area study, I understand the following investigation to be a contribution to a very topical question. I expect that studying Italian transport policy will shed light on the wider question of how national policy-making patterns are influenced by developments in the in-

1

ternational environment. More specifically, I shall look at the influence of the European Union in this context, as a part of what is widely known as Europeanisation, i.e. the general influence of the European level upon the national one.

There are several reasons why the Italian case is suitable for an investigation about international influences on national policy-making patterns. The most important reason is that the Italian transport policy stands in contradiction with international policy developments which have occurred throughout the rest of the European Union. Italian transport policy traditionally was highly interventionist. Infrastructures such as roads, railway tracks, ports, etc., were built, owned and run by the administration. The transport services provided by these infrastructures were either directly provided by state-owned companies (railways, airlines) or by private firms subject to strict rules which tended to replace rather than shape markets (Santoro, 1977; Del Viscovo, 1990). Italy was by no means the only country that managed its transport system in such a way. In the past interventionism was the rule rather than the exception. However, this has changed in recent years. Starting in the US in the 1970s, a world-wide reform movement which has been labelled 'privatisation' and 'deregulation' began spreading throughout the industrialised nations. In Europe these reforms also affected the public utilities such as telecommunications and energy. In the area of transport privatisation and regulatory reform the role of private actors in providing services and building up infrastructures has increased. The European Single Market Programme has also begun transforming governance in the public utilities sector. Since interventionism was an obstacle to the creation of a Single Market in these sectors, the fact that these developments are in stark contradiction to the Italian interventionist policy pattern leads us to ask how these national policies are affected by international developments.

The main finding of this study is that the usual image of international influence on national policy-making patterns is too simple. There is a widespread conviction today that increasing economic integration erodes national boundaries and severely limits national policy choices (e.g. McKenzie and Lee, 1991; R. Reich, 1992; Ohmae, 1995). This general problem is magnified within the EU, because the building of a Common Market depends on making national boundaries even less relevant than they are in the international context. However, the long inertia of the policy-making pattern shows that the international effect does not *force* change upon a nation. Even within the European Union, where member states may be forced by supranational legislation and where the chance of change by coercion may thus be biggest, policy change through Europeanisation relies on translating external constraints into internal pressure to change. The resulting change occurring in this translation process is contingent on national actors and institutions; external pressure, as such, does not have an affect on political events. This has consequences for conceptualising the effects of Europeanisation.

In this introductory chapter the following goals are pursued. First, the present change in policy-making patterns is explained in more detail by contrasting two ideal types. This allows us to specify the contradiction between Italian policy traditions and the new international and European developments. The following section then explains why discontinuous second-order change has to be considered improbable. Policy-making patterns are institutionalised; that is, they shape the perceptions and preferences of the actors and are difficult to reverse. The subsequent section presents some of the hypotheses about why change due to international factors takes place. The main focus will be on a nation-state within the European Union. Two conflicting hypotheses will be developed, the first one arguing that policy transfer within the European Union has to be understood as a process of *coercion*, the second arguing that policy transfer is a process of voluntary *emulation*. Then, the research design which will test these hypotheses will be presented.

The Contemporary Transformation of the State

A logical prerequisite for studying the external impact on national policy-making is that there be an external challenge to a national political system. If this challenge is related to single decisions, this observation is trivial. Most of the time political decision-making addresses problems outside the political system in its national or international environment. Some authors even equate political decision making with solving societal problems (Scharpf, 1997). The observation becomes less trivial if not only single decisions, but the established ways of dealing with problems are being challenged. It is this challenge to *patterns of decision-making* that is of importance here. In this section, I first want to conceptualise how one may conceive of patterns of political decision-making. Then I want to introduce two ideal types of such patterns, the distributive state and the regulatory state. The present transformation of the state may be described as a trend in which the latter replaces the former. This trend puts Italian policy-making traditions under pressure because, as in most other European countries, Italy has been closely following the model of the distributive state since the Second World War.

There seems to be a large consensus that political decision making does not happen at random, but follows a recurring pattern. To lawyers this may be most obvious since – for them – economic policy making is constrained by a vast number of laws which embody an underlying philosophy, an 'economic constitution' (e.g. Joerges, 1991). In the empirical social sciences, too, propositions abound for conceptualising policy-making patterns with terms such as 'policy style' (Richardson, 1982), 'policy paradigm' (Hall, 1993) or 'industrial policy paradigm' (Dobbin, 1994). In an attempt to account for the apparent empirical repetitiveness of political decision-making, these terms try to conceptualise policy making in terms of standard operating procedures which entail a vision of the world, the salient problems and the way to tackle them. Standard operating procedures, in this sense, are not entirely static, but they do vary with a much lower frequency than the political programmes of governments that come to power. A recent proposal has been to use the concept of 'state' for this purpose. State, according to an approach that may be traced back to Tocqueville, 'denotes a specific configuration of the dominant ideas about the scope and direction of legitimate public power in society' (Skocpol, 1985, 21). The state may be seen as delineating a generally accepted definition of the dividing line between public and private goods and the way public goods should be provided (Willke, 1995). It is important to underline that this definition does not exclude political conflict and competition. On the contrary, the definition of the boundaries and forms of legitimate political action are not static, but should be seen as an outcome of ongoing political conflict (Malkin and Wildavsky, 1991). For example, the change from the classical liberal to the welfare state was only accomplished after decades of struggle by the labour movement. Furthermore, conflict does not entirely end if a form of the state is no longer directly challenged. Even during the immediate period after the war, while the welfare state was not generally called into question, conflicts ensued about how it should be structured. The acceptance of the welfare state did not preclude conflict but rather structured it in a specific way.

What is the advantage of introducing the concept of the state instead of the other terms mentioned such as 'policy paradigms' or 'policy styles'? The first advantage is that, in the version introduced here, it is not only centred around public actors, but it explicitly involves private actors as well. A further advantage will become clear when we specify at which level these patterns are situated. Whereas standard operating procedures implicitly refer to the level of organisations, state denotes a more abstract level. For the purpose at hand, I want to distinguish between three levels of abstraction in policy-making patterns. On the most general level, political decision-making is structured by what one could call state discourse, which (especially in the continental European nation-states) defines means and ends of public action (Kaufmann, 1994). Of these fundamental discourses only three major discourses may be identified which centre around the main societal and political problem to be identified: the absolutist state is concerned with legitimising state power by the fundamental task of providing internal security; the liberal state focuses on the problem of limiting the power of the state by introducing the rule of law; finally, the welfare state, which is concerned with the problem of industrialisation. A fourth stage of state discourse is discernible, which centres around ecological problems and their solution. At this level of abstraction, however, the changes of the state which we aim to analyse here cannot be captured. We are concerned about changes which are more within the parameters of the third discourse, and not necessarily split between the third and the fourth. An alternative would therefore be to look for more concrete conceptualisations. Another way of defining the state would be to equate it with the legal dimension of policy making. The state would be the sum of the policies in legal terms (Lowi, 1985). With this definition of political action it would be easy to see how specific tasks of the state are converted into patterns of political decision-making. However, this definition is too concrete. The multitude of public policies are not easily aggregated into a coherent picture of the prevailing scope and forms of legitimate political action. We therefore have to aim at an intermediate, third level of policy-making patterns. The standard operating procedures that we are concerned with here vary much less often than party programmes but change more often than the very slowly-evolving state discourse. The word 'state' is used in this sense when a more fundamental political change has to be analysed (Müller and Wright, 1994). The state is usually specified according to the formula of X-state, with an ensemble of specific political actors, strategies, organisational forms, conflicts, etc. The analysis may be more narrow, concentrating on just one aspect of the structuration, such as administrative reforms, or it may include more dimensions. However narrow or broad the analysis, the aim is always to specify a specific pattern of legitimate political action.

The advantage of the approach is also its disadvantage. Abstract elaboration that tries to blend a vast number of different aspects into a coherent picture of politics are inevitably simplistic. Therefore, if they are treated as an empirical hypothesis, they may be easily rejected, because areas will be found which are not fitting for the description. The disadvantage is that they are too general to be empirically tested; they cannot be easily falsified. However, this alone rather neglects their value as heuristic devices. The disadvantage is also a methodological advantage, which is of special relevance here. If two simple ideal types are contrasted (as shall be done below), they enable us to discriminate between first-order conservative changes which remain within one type of state and a second-order change which goes beyond one type and leads to the next. This is especially important, since in modern democracies, all policy areas can be characterised by a steady flow of decisions that modify former decisions. Change is perpetual; but it is difficult to tell what it means without a theory. Claims of fundamental change may be contested, especially in the realm of politics. A government's claim over having fundamentally reformed the administration may not be shared by the opposition.

Having clarified that the term 'state' in this context defines the form and scope of political action, we are now in a position to sketch out the fundamental transformation of the state which began in Western Europe at the end of the 1970s. Put as simply as possible, there has been a transition from *direct* to *indirect* forms of governance of the economy. This change in governance has been fundamental because it has led to new policy goals, a new administrative organisation (needed to achieve these goals), new salient actors and new conflict structures. In short, the political world has changed as a whole, not just in part.

The direct form of governance is usually described in reference to the ideal type of the Keynesian welfare state (e.g. Scharpf, 1987). The underlying belief was that a fundamental task of the state was not only to secure the functioning of the market, but to secure macro-economic achievements as well, especially full-employment. This was seen as the historical lesson of the Great Depression. The experience served to solidify the conviction that political intervention in the economy can make a fundamental difference in two (opposing) ways: in the case at hand, the wrong reactions of policy-makers at the outset of the economic crisis precipitated it; other policies, especially Roosevelt's New Deal, helped to overcome it. The Great Depression was the reason for the widespread conviction that governments not only could but also should intervene. After all, to this day, the economic crisis is seen as one cause of World War II. Furthermore, after the war, this policy was attractive because it was a political answer to the persistent class conflict. The generally-accepted belief that a capitalist economy has an in-built tendency towards crisis has resulted in a uniquely ambitious attempt at steering the economy (Scharpf, 1987, pp. 45-60). To solve the main problem, keeping inflation as low as possible and unemployment as high as possible, governments tried to stabilise the economic cycles by means of a set of policy instruments, i.e. public spending, monetary policy and influence on the wage policy of the trade unions. This presented an intellectual challenge to economists: namely, to elaborate models and conduct empirical research in order to provide the knowledge necessary for macro-economic steering. The social challenge was to convince the trade unions to moderate their wage demands. The model of the Keynesian welfare state worked fine for some time, but by the beginning of the 1980s it was in crisis. It was no longer solving its fundamental problems and was even viewed as being part of the problem that it was supposed to cure. The most important reason for the end of the Keynesian strategy was the increasing economic integration of the global market, which made attempts at macro-economic steering on the national level impossible.

The subsequent transformation may be described as a fundamental transformation of the state from a demand-side oriented policy, which aims at full employment, to a supply-side oriented policy, which aims at structural competitiveness (Jessop, 1996, pp. 61-65). For the purpose at hand, it seems to be possible to conceptualise this as a transition from the Keynesian welfare state to the 'Competition state' (Cerny, 1997).[1] The competition state is engaged in regulatory competition with other nation-states and therefore has to give up traditional ways of securing welfare (Cerny, 1997, p. 269). To continue to secure the welfare of a nation, a shift of strategy becomes necessary, away from the direct strategies of maximising welfare, of the Keynesian era, to indirect governance to increase the welfare of a nation. Political decision-making increasingly addresses the problem of providing the prerequisites for national survival in the global economy, i.e. infrastructure and education (R. Reich, 1992). A good example of this is the development of the federal R&D policy in the USA. In the past it was oriented towards defence, whereas its main purpose now is to enhance the competitiveness of the U.S. economy by promoting fundamental innovation (Willke, 1995, p. 349).

In the competition state, the welfare of the citizens of a nation is connected to the attractiveness of a territory to investors because of a competitive edge that it provides. Under these circumstances, the provision of public goods becomes strategically important. The provision of infrastructures like telecommunication, electricity and transport will influence the location of firms and the level of employment. It is for this reason that the service sector has become a major object of political concern. Admittedly, the service sector has always been subject to political intervention. For decades infrastructures have been identified as goods that would not be produced by the market and that thus justified state intervention. What is new, however, is the way these are provided. In the era of the Keynesian welfare state the essential services were often produced by the central administration or by public companies. In this sense infrastructures were public goods in the double sense that they were not only produced by state intervention but also by the state itself. In the competition state, on the other hand, privatisation and deregulation turns former public goods into 'collateral goods' (Willke, 1995). That is they are not provided by the bureaucracy, but they are produced within a web that links public and private actors.

The development towards the competition state is the cause of major changes in the service sector; given its new salience in economic policy making, these amount to profound changes (Majone, 1994; Majone, 1996;

Majone, 1997).[2] The basic line of development is simply that Western European states are becoming much more similar to the United States. With the European Union increasingly playing the role of the federal government for its member states, this involves major changes in the logic of the political game (Majone, 1997, pp. 148-159). First of all, there is a fundamental shift in the *function* of the state and the dominant *instruments* used to achieve its goals. Whereas Keynesian politics relies on monetary instruments, the competition state just corrects market failure by regulative instruments. This has implications for other dimensions of the state. According to the US-example, regulation in the public sector is conducted within the framework of 'statutory regulation' (Majone, 1996b). This implies that independent regulatory commissions are created to carry out the supervision called for in the statute. This *organisational* change is important because multifunctional bureaucracies cannot specialise in the way these agencies can. If 'deficit spending' and 'corporatist wage bargaining' turns into 'regulation by independent commissions', the *political cleavages* change and new actors move to the foreground. The main political problem shifts from redistribution to the question of who controls the regulatory process. These questions make political parties and trade unions less important *actors* and create new challenges for parliamentary committees and for regulatory experts. Furthermore, since the decentralisation of the former central bureaucracy implies that hierarchical relationships are replaced by contracts, legal litigation will increase; it thus becomes increasingly probable that political disputes are solved by legal claims.

Conceiving of political change as a distinction between two different forms of state implicitly assumes that persisting patterns of action exist over time in the sphere of politics. This has been forcefully underlined by the neo-institutionalist approach, which has become increasingly important for political analysis in recent years.[3] The fact that neo-institutionalism developed in different disciplines (especially sociology, economics and political science) and that it has been developed in a more inductive fashion, on the basis of empirical investigations, has made the theoretical message less clear than it would have been had it been developed as a coherent theoretical approach (Hall and Taylor, 1996, p. 936). The new institutionalisms, in their various forms, disagree on virtually everything, especially on what should be conceived of as an institution and what type of institutions there are (Jepperson, 1991). However, in spite of these differences, there are also areas of shared consensus, especially in the way they break with the past methods of analysing political processes. Past approaches to politics were reductionist in that they explained the outcome of political processes by exogenous factors (Thelen and Steinmo, 1992, pp. 3-7). Structural theories, like the different versions of Marxism or of structural-functionalism, explained political processes by the influence of macro-variables, such as class conflict, etc. Group theories of politics favoured micro-variables instead: external preferences and the distribution of resources determined the outcome of political conflicts. In both approaches the institutional setting was seen only as a neutral stage, which could be neglected in an explanation of political processes. Contrary to this, neo-institutionalism adopts a *holistic* approach in which the institutional structure of a political system has a profound influence on political life. The institutional structures account for the stability of institutional life over time because they do not immediately respond to changes in the environment. If there is one point that is largely shared, it is the concept that institutions are characterised by inertia (Krasner, 1988). However, this does not imply that political institutions do not change. Policy innovation and reform abound in modern Western democracies (Hogwood and Peters, 1983) and it is more difficult to oppose administrative reforms than to initiate them (Brunsson and Olsen, 1993, pp. 33-47). These changes slowly transform institutions as well. What is more, institutional arrangements within the political system are themselves a perpetual cause of change (for example, the competition between government and opposition) (Polsby, 1984, pp. 159-167). These may also cause changes in institutions. However, institutions do not change randomly. This is captured by the idea that institutional development is rarely revolutionary. Change is usually incremental. Institutional development is *path-dependent* in that 'prior institutional choices limit available future options' (Krasner, 1988, p. 71).[4] This concept of path dependency has important consequences for the conceptualisation of institutional change. First, change is not conceived of as a functional adaptation to the environment but as an incremental adaptation over time. The result is that institutional development cannot be interpreted as a process in which only the best solutions survive. On the contrary, history is 'inefficient': it may follow a sub-optimal path (March and Olsen, 1989, pp. 54-56). An institutional perspective explains many observations that a functional theory does not, e.g. why the dramatically inferior performance of Third World economies has not led to institutional convergence with the First World (North, 1990, pp. 7-9). Path-dependent institutional evolution also explains another less-frequent but well-known paradox of institutional development. Although institutions are relatively stable, it has been frequently observed that they suddenly collapse. Recent examples are the institutional orders in the former Soviet Union and in Italy. The explanation for this non-incremental second-order change is that incremental institutional adjustment in politics may lead to local optima but to the increasing obsolescence of the whole regime. Under the condition of obsolescence, the introduction of successful changes is likely to show fast improvements and may thus lead to the rapid decay of the former institutional order (March and Olsen, 1989, pp. 166-171).

The transition from one form of state to another is a second-order change, as understood by new institutionalism. The transition from the Keynesian welfare state to the competition state in the service sector inextricably involves regulatory reform of considerable scope. In Western Europe the political-reform challenge is not only concerned with the de-regulation of public utilities, as in the US, but also with the construction of markets in the first place. The example of Great Britain shows that it is a challenging task to privatise and to establish the new rules of the game (Bishop, Kay and Mayer, 1994). A further indication of a second-order change is that the economic critique of regulation in the USA already thought that deregulation was rather unlikely. The fact that public agencies had been captured was used to explain why a fundamental reform was unlikely and why the structure would persist (Stigler, 1971). Furthermore, if one thought that collusion between interest groups and the state was likely, one would arrive at the same conclusion. Modern governance in the sector of public utilities and welfare inevitably involves a combination of public and private actors who interact in routine ways, and in ways which public actors find difficult to change (Mayntz and Scharpf, 1995, pp. 27-33).

If the transition from the Keynesian welfare state to the competition state may indeed be conceived of as a second-order change in the sense of new institutionalism, then the question is: what caused this transformation in Western Europe? According to the neo-institutionalist perspective, incremental change is expected, not radical transformation. However, the approach not only poses the question, it also offers a clue as to where to find the answer. In the neo-institutionalist literature, incremental change is mainly driven by endogenous institutional factors, whereas radical change is driven more by exogenous factors (Krasner, 1988; Hall, 1993; North, 1990, pp. 89-91). In the following section, theories will be developed explaining the changes in the state, as elaborated above.

Explaining the Transformation of the State

The transformation of the state, conceptualised above as the transition from a Keynesian welfare state to a competition state, is a puzzle from the neo-institutionalist perspective, which as a rule expects a path-dependent development of political institutions. A recent study of the development of economic policy making in Western Europe, covering a wide variety of sectors in different countries, confirms the presently widespread conviction that these changes have to be largely attributed to transnational – especially economic – factors, and not to endogenous factors such as changes in national electorates (Unger and van Waarden, 1995). Internationalisation, i.e. increasing contact between nations which transcends national borders, basically comes in two versions: 'economic internationalisation means more economic contact between countries, that is, greater cross-border flows of information, financial capital, physical capital (production plants), labour, goods and services. Political internationalisation implies more political contact between nations, political ideas across borders...' (Unger and van Waarden, 1995, p. 13). The increasing mobility of the factors of production, which is at the core of *economic internationalisation*, limits economic policy options. If the classification of the three main state functions of public finance theory is used, no function of the state remains untouched. *Macro-economic stabilisation* has become more difficult because the fiscal instrument of deficit spending has been blunted by financial markets that punish national debts with currency devaluation (Unger, 1995). Rather than concentrating on the domestic economy, under pressure from international speculation, monetary policy is mostly dedicated to stabilising exchange rates (Thomasberger, 1995). *Welfare redistribution* has become more difficult because the mobility of production has made it increasingly difficult to raise the necessary taxes. The negative effect of the mobility factor on the ability to raise taxes is illustrated by the fact that over the past years the tax burden has been slowly shifting towards the least mobile production factor, i.e. labour (Kitzmantel and Moser, 1995; The Economist, 31.05.1997). Finally, *regulation*, too, is affected by economic internationalisation. Internationalisation, which results in production that is mobile, gives companies an exit option, meaning they can move from locations where regimes have a high regulatory burden to locations where they have a low one. Therefore, one would expect economic internationalisation to lead to a lowering of regulatory standards in economic and social regulation. However, under certain circumstances, economic internationalisation does not lead to competitive deregulation among nation-states, and it may even lead to a rising level of regulation (Vogel, 1995).

Next to these internationalisation factors, a second set of influencing factors come into play. In Western Europe, economic integration within the European Union has been an important influencing factor for its member states. This has become increasingly clear since European integration research has moved beyond its preoccupation with the integration process, where the primary interest was European-level policy and institutional development, and the question concerned whether these new institutions were still effectively controlled by the member states or whether they had developed dynamics of their own. The more recent research on the European Union moves away from analysing the process of integration towards analysing the working of the system (e.g. Jachtenfuchs and Kohler-Koch, 1996, Marks et al., 1996, Scharpf, 1997a). The assumption is that the institutional structure of the polity has become reasonably stable. According to this perspective, European integration appears to be a process of institutional differentiation. The European level has consolidated without replacing the nation-state (Lepsius, 1991). It is therefore justifiable to compare the European Union to the federal political system of Germany and the United States (e.g. Scharpf, 1988, Majone, 1996). Within this framework a major research question is: how and in what way does the consolidated European level affect the national level?

A first and important observation is that the European integration process does not directly challenge any aspect of the national polity. Admittedly, new members are required to meet the standards of democracy, but once these requirements are fulfilled there is no further influence, such as an obligatory administrative reform. Its main influence concerns national policies, not the organisational structure of the polity. A further important qualification has to be added: the influence of European policy making is not the same in all policy areas. Its strongest impact on national politics has been in the area of macro-economic policy making, due to the project of Monetary Union, and in the area of regulatory policy making. Redistributive policy making is much less developed. There is no European welfare state at the EU level resembling the complicated national welfare-state systems in Western Europe (Majone, 1996a). In the following we will not be concerned with the European Monetary Union but will concentrate on how Europeanisation is occurring through regulatory policy.

In the first three decades of its existence, the European Community only had limited success in promoting integration among its members. Although in some policy areas member states co-operated closely, for example, in agriculture, the major goal of a Common Market in which the mobility of the factors of production would be unrestrained by national boundaries, had not been achieved. In those first three decades no consensus was reached among the member states. This state of affairs changed in the mid-1980s when the European Community launched the Single Market Programme, a long-term policy plan specifying a strategy and a time-table for completing the Common Market (Moravcsik, 1991). In a short period of time the policies of the Single Market Programme, which attempted to reform European economies in the face of international competitive pressure, turned out to be an unexpected success (van Scherpenberg, 1996). Arguably for the first time, no major policy area was excluded from the European influence.

How was it possible that European policies became so significant for the member states? In the research on European integration this question has received much less attention than the question of the dynamics of the integration process. Consequently, there are no solid theoretical traditions, and it is still difficult to move beyond 'neofunctionalism vs. intergovernmentalism' (Caporaso, 1998). Any attempt to distinguish between different research perspectives on Europeanisation is inevitably going to be too controversial to merely refer to classical integration theory. As a first attempt to move beyond such a simple perspective, I propose to distinguish between two lines of research which differ in their views on political processes and therefore also identify different variables and causal hypotheses regarding Europeanisation. Since these lines of research differ in theory as well as in the underlying approach, they give rise to two different images of Europeanisation: namely, a *functionalist* and an *institutionalist* image. According to a functionalist view, political decisions adapt swiftly to changes in the environment: 'they move rapidly to a unique solution, conditional on current environmental conditions' (March and Olsen, 1989, p. 8). The historical status quo and the micro processes at work to achieve this change do not affect the outcome. A functionalist perspective is a typical vision of political life which assumes that decision outcomes are a result of competitive processes among political actors.[5] A functionalist image of Europeanisation implies that national decision-making will adapt swiftly to changes in European policy making and, furthermore, that the national institutional set-up will not influence the results. An institutionalist perspective, by contrast, does not expect such a spontaneous adaptation over time, but that history is inefficient and that path dependencies persist (March and Olsen, 1989, pp. 54-56).

An abstract distinction between functionalist and institutionalist analyses of political processes is not specific enough for the purpose of studying Europeanisation. To clarify how the two types of processes differ, it is useful to turn to categories developed for the analysis of policy innovation. In this context, Europeanisation causes policy innovation by *policy transfer*, 'a process in which knowledge about policies, administrative arrangements, institutions, etc. in one time and/or place is used in the development of policies, administrative arrangements and institutions in another time and/or place' (Dolowitz and Marsh, 1996, p. 344). Policy transfer processes may be distinguished by what is transferred (policy goals, instruments, ideas) and by the extent to which such a transfer happens (true copy, emulation, hybridisation with present policies) (Dolowitz and Marsh, 1996, pp. 349-51). Most importantly in this context, one may also distinguish different policy-transfer mechanisms. Policy transfer may be imposed or may be voluntarily adopted by decision makers. Three types of causes of policy transfer may be identified along this continuum (Dolowitz and Marsh, 1996, pp. 346-49). *Voluntary policy transfer* takes place when policy makers copy policy solutions in a different place. Because it is easier to justify a new policy if it has already been adopted elsewhere, policy transfer is especially attractive under conditions in which there is uncertainty about problems and solutions. *Direct coercive policy transfer* happens when policies are imposed on national policy makers. The agents of coercion may be other states – for example the US, which forced Europe to adopt American anti-cartel laws after the war – transnational corporations, which can threaten to withdraw from a national territory, and most interesting in this context, supranational institutions such as the EU, which issues and enforces regulation. *Indirect coercive policy transfer* occurs when external pressures constrain the choices available to decision-makers. This may happen for several reasons, such as close interdependence between countries (e.g. US and Canadian pollution control), technological push, economic integration (e.g. in the sector of financial services) and policy fashions (e.g. the embarrassment at having an outdated pollution-control policy). At this point it becomes possible to draw a distinction between a functionalist and an institutionalist image of Europeanisation: a functionalist image relies on transfer mechanisms working by coercion or semi-coercion, whereas an institutionalist image sees policy transfer as similar to a process of emulation.

The Functionalist Image of Europeanisation

A theory corresponding to the functionalist image has been developed as an extension of the policy-cycle model common in the explanation of public-policy making. For any policy to have an effect, the four phases of the cycle, i.e. agenda-setting, decision-making, implementation, and evaluation, need to be seen as four problems that have to be solved. It is possible to show how unlikely consequential European policy making is by pointing out its specific problems and showing how the European Union has found ways to overcome them. A first step in the analysis of the process of Europeanisation is to understand how the dynamics of the European regulatory policy can be explained (Mény et al., 1996, pp. 2-9).

The first major problem of the European policy cycle is to come to a decision about European policies in the face of large differences in the member state's interests. Decision making under the conditions of diverging interests is a common problem in politics. Indeed, a set of standard techniques to build coalitions has evolved which allows decisions to be made even when preferences are not homogenous. An example of such a coalition is a policy 'logroll', in which members of a group are largely indifferent to each other's demands but agree jointly to support each other to achieve their goals (March, 1994, pp. 151-60). The decision-making procedures of the European Union have long made it difficult to reach decisions, since every member state was initially granted a de facto veto right concerning any policy initiative that was against its national interest. This has been overcome by two basic factors: first, with the Single European Act, the de facto veto powers of every member state were abandoned and qualified majority voting was introduced; second, and maybe even more important, ambitious harmonisation and distributive policies have been excluded from the agenda.

The second problem of the European regulatory policy cycle is that of implementation. As with decision-making, implementation has long been identified as a problem of policy making in general (Pressman and Wildavsky, 1973). For European policies this problem presents itself in an aggravated form, because the implementation structure within the EU is much more decentralised than within the framework of the nation-state. European decisions have to be implemented by national administrations. In the context of the EU, implementation is a process comprising incorporation, i.e. translating Community law into the national legal order, and application, i.e. the subsequent efforts to achieve an actual change in behaviour.[6] Especially in cases where the outcome of European decision-making is regarded as unfavourable, there is ample room to avoid the negative consequences by distorting implementation. The European solution to the problem relies on powerful mechanisms of judicial review. This mechanism is strong because of the principle of the superiority of Community law and the possibility of challenging negligence in implementation through national courts. Potentially, this turns every citizen and every company into a potential watchdog of implementation.

Lawyers have emphasised the possibility of bringing about Europeanisation by implementing European law at the level of the member states. Coercive policy transfer from the Community level to the member states was impossible during most of the development of the European Community but has undoubtedly become a feature of the Community system with the Single Market Programme and the Single European act (Weiler, 1991, p. 2462 and p. 2477):

> Unlike any earlier era in the Community, and unlike most of their other international and transnational experience, member states are now in a situation of facing binding norms, adopted wholly or partially against their will, with direct effect in their national legal orders.

Policies can be adopted now within the Council that run counter not simply to the perceived interests of the member state, but more specifically to the ideology of a government in power. The debates about the European Social Charter and the shrill cries of 'socialism through the back-door', as well as the emerging debate about Community adherence to the European Convention on Human Rights and abortion rights are harbingers of things to come.

The possibility of coercive policy transfer within the European Union has to be explained by two separate developments, one legal and one political (Weiler, 1991, pp. 2409-10 and footnote 15, p. 2424). From the founding days, a continual attempt has been made to avoid the selective application of Community law, which, for its part, is much more likely than is a country's withdrawal from the Community. To cope with the risk of partial exit, in a series of decisions the European Court of Justice transformed European law from a system of public international law into a system of law that is similar to that in constitutional federal states. The most important feature in this respect is the ECJ doctrine of 'direct effect', the rule that Community law is superior to contradictory national law. This doctrine implies a fundamental difference to public international law, in that disputes about the violation of treaty obligations cannot be contained on the interstate level between the signing member states but may shift to national courts and involve domestic parties. In fact, this constitutionalisation of the EC law by a series of doctrines developed by the ECJ (of which the doctrine of direct effect is the most important one) has been backed up by an elaborate system of judicial review integrating national courts into the European Court of Justice, a system which covers not only Community law, but extends even to the verification of the compatibility of national law with Community law (Weiler, 1991, pp. 2412-24). The constitutionalisation of EC law was a successful process: '...Community obligations, Community law, and Community policies were "for real". Once adopted ..., member states found it difficult to avoid Community obligations' (Weiler, 1991, p. 2423). However, it is important to note that the constitutionalisation of the EC law did not have any immediate political consequences. During the 1960s and 70s, the period in which the main principles of constitutionalisation were developed through the Luxembourg compromise, the member states ensured that none of the European decisions flew in the face of their own interests. From this perspective, the reforms of decision-making procedures by the Single European Act, which replaced the principle of unanimity with qualified majority voting, are not, as such, the reasons for the success of the Single Market Programme. Rather, the reason is to be found in the fact that the latent power of European law has been unleashed by political developments. The SEA was not the 'big bang' creating European integration; instead, it merely unleashed the legal Prometheus of Community law. The starting point of coercive policy-transfer by the regulatory policy cycle is marked by the loss of control of the European decision-making process.

In European integration research there is now a firmly-established interest in the question concerning how European law affects the member states. In fact, a series of recent publications give the impression that the topic of 'legal integration' is expanding in scope and assuming a more important place on the agenda. The effort started by Weiler continues: namely, to understand the character of the superiority of European law and to explain why member states accepted it and the loss of national sovereignty it implies (Alter, 1998, pp. 122-23). As this framework is surpassed and other aspects of the black box of legal integration are illuminated, further issues are being considered. For one, the dynamics of implementation will be influenced by the actual decision-making of the courts. 'Fertile terrain for research thus lies in specifying the conditions under which the ECJ makes decisions that declare illegal national laws, regulations, or practices and exploring how member governments react to them.' (Garrett et al., 1998, p. 150). A related research question concerns the European Commission's approach to non-compliance (Mendrinou, 1996). Further, the dynamics of implementation will be influenced by the behaviour of national courts and individual litigants. The question is: what role do they play in legal integration (Mattli and Slaughter, 1998, pp. 184-86)? Finally, some researchers are considering the conditions under which successful legal integration (transposition) might actually make a difference for national political and economic practices (Haas, 1998).

The closure of the policy cycle is one precondition for stabilising a policy. The general problem is how this feed-back can be organised to keep the policy adaptive. This has been the topic of evaluation research. In Europe this feed-back is guaranteed because the regulatory approach of the EU gives rise to regulatory competition. Two types of regulatory competition can be distinguished: adaptive and manipulative. Adaptive regulatory competition takes place when nation-states adapt their regulative framework to counter the negative impact of mobility on their territory (Scharpf, 1996). To prevent the risk of a race to the bottom, the demand for European regulation often increases. This may give rise to manipulative regulatory competition in which various actors compete to influence European reregulation (Héritier, et al., 1996).

The mechanism of regulatory competition is at least as important as implementation. The regulatory strategy has been shifting away from attempts at hierarchical intervention by Community law. With the Single Market Programme, the Commission significantly reduced its ambitions to create coherent regulatory regimes by replacing the disparate national systems with a single Community system, i.e. by harmonising them. The new regulatory strategy follows the principle of *mutual recognition*, based on a decision by the European Court of Justice which prohibits member states from restricting the trade of goods and services when these have been produced under standards which are functionally equivalent to their own (Alter and Meunier-Aitsahalia, 1994). This principle considerably reduces the amount of harmonisation necessary to overcome national boundaries to a common market. Furthermore, they foster the further harmonisation of different national regulatory regimes by creating the preconditions for regulatory competition between them. Whenever goods and services produced under different regulatory regimes enter into competition, these regulatory regimes, too, enter into competition (N. Reich, 1992, Woolcock, 1996). 'For example, if German TV standards are less costly than French standards but consumers regard German TV sets as essentially equivalent to the more expensive French sets, French producers will lose business to their German competitors. Hence they will bring pressure on their government to modify national TV standards.' (Majone, 1994a, p. 165). Competition among different regulatory regimes creates pressure towards regulatory convergence, because economic interests will pressure their governments to change or abolish them. The outcome may well be a coherent set of rules throughout the Community. The advantage of this approach for Community decision-making is that decision-deadlocks may be circumvented and more efficient regulatory solutions may be found.

The view that Europeanisation is occurring through competition among national regulatory regimes has given rise to a substantial research agenda. The first question is: under which conditions does regulatory competition actually achieve convergence of national rules? It has been pointed out that this mechanism may be more fragile than first thought (Sun and Pelkmans, 1995). Economic interests might not react at all to differences in national regulations. They might also react not by creating political pressure to change, but by relocating to the more favourable regulatory regime. Or, finally, they might not react in a homogenous way, because differences in regulation (e.g. environmental standards) may be a competitive advantage for some firms. A second important question on the agenda is what effect regulatory competition actually has. Does regulatory competition give rise to a game in which nation-states compete in offering the lowest standards (a 'race to the bottom')? Or does it give rise to a game in which nation-states actually upgrade their regulation (a 'race to the top') (Vogel, 1995)? The empirical observation is that different regulatory policy areas such as social policy or environmental regulation are affected differently, and the subsequent question is how these differences may be explained.

This leads to a classification of different types of Europeanisation dynamics due to regulatory competition (Scharpf, 1997a). Another example is the question: in which areas does competition among rules have desirable effects and in which areas is harmonisation preferable (Majone, 1994a, pp. 170-74)?

If the regulatory policy cycle is set in motion by judicial review and by regulatory competition, then it is likely that two dimensions of the national political system will be affected by European policy. Public policies have been Europeanised in that the centre for formulating regulatory policies has shifted to Brussels. Furthermore, the operation of the European policy cycle has also had structural effects. Most importantly, it has influenced the structure of the interest intermediation. On the European level, new access points for interest groups to influence European policies have been created. Although the process of European interest intermediation is not yet well understood, this may put the corporatist policy-making traditions of many European-nation-states under strain and make the EU more pluralist, rather like the US (Streeck and Schmitter, 1991).[7] This structural effect stabilises the European policy cycle in that it secures demand on the European level. Furthermore, a more pluralist structure of interest groups may even strengthen the implementation mechanism because interest groups excluded by corporatist arrangements can try to influence decisions by activating judicial review.

Figure 1.1 The Functionalist Image of Europeanisation

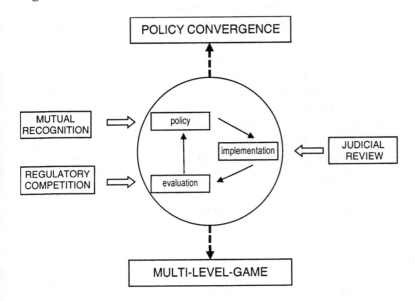

Institutionalist Image of Europeanisation

The functionalist image of Europeanisation essentially rests on two mechanisms that drive the regulatory policy cycle: enforcement of implementation by judicial review and regulatory competition. At first sight, the regulatory policy cycle seems to offer a plausible way to explain the success that European policies have had since the mid-1980s. However, the basic mechanisms underlying the functionalist image of Europeanisation have not gone without criticism. The resulting doubts arising from this criticism point to the need for developing an alternative institutionalist image of Europeanisation.

The first mechanism of Europeanisation based on the force of supranational European law is challenged by several theories which all share a deep scepticism of the possibility of hierarchical imposition by a political authority in the context of modern democratic nation-states. The empirical research on the implementation of policies (or the enactment of law) has shown that if a hierarchical relationship between policies and implementation is assumed, i.e. if policies contain goals which have to be realised by a process of implementation, the goal is often not met. Early implementation research was fascinated by the fact that implementation failure was ubiquitous, and successful implementation rather unlikely (Pressman and Wildavsky, 1973). Subsequently, even main-stream implementation research has come to the conclusion that implementation failure was an artefact of the policy-cycle model which implies a hierarchical relationship between policy decision and implementation and that this assumption has to be relaxed in order to come to a more realistic understanding of the policy-making process (Ingram, 1990, p. 478; Héritier, 1993, pp. 15-22; Carlsson, 1996). Much more radical than this is the position that concern with the implementation of prior decisions does not make sense in the policy process because the preconditions are not given. Implementation research has to assume that policy goals are given in the policy in order to have a measuring rod against which to judge implementation achievements (Mayntz, 1980, pp. 4-5). Yet, in modern democracy 'official policy is likely to be vague, contradictory, or adopted without generally shared expectations about its meaning or implementation' (Baier et al., 1988, p. 159). Policy ambiguity is an inherent characteristic of policies in modern democracies and, because it facilitates compromise between differing interests, this is not easily changed. The more contested a policy is, the more likely it is to become even more ambiguous. The greater its ambiguity, the more it needs to be interpreted, spelled out, and even changed before it can be implemented (Baier et al., 1988, pp. 160-61). The result is not a hierarchical relationship between politics and administration, but a loose coupling between the two spheres. It is important to realise that this is a prerequisite for the functioning of the decision-making process, and that attempts to introduce tight coupling might undermine decision-making capacity. If this is true for policy making within nation-states and for decision-making within hierarchical organisations, it is even more true in EU decision-making. The difficulty of decision-making under present circumstances has frequently been underlined, so one may expect the hierarchical impact of European supranational law to be considerably attenuated by ambiguity.

The second mechanism of Europeanisation developed so far is called into question by the results of research into the national political impact of international economic and political developments. Research has shown that economic internationalisation does not have a direct influence on national political decision-making. Perception influences the way these pressures are translated. A study of international deregulatory ideas on regulatory policies in Germany shows that the historical patterns of policy making have been important determinants of their impact. In Germany the state tradition in general ('*Rechstsstaat*') and the specific regulatory culture ('*Ordnungspolitik*') translates external influences in a specific way (Dyson, 1992). Another way of conceptualising the differential impact of ideas is by 'discourse coalitions' (Lehmbruch, 1997). These coalitions, which exist at a general and at a sectoral level, share certain core beliefs which structure their political action. In general, it has been argued that international developments do not impact directly on national policies but are mediated by national political institutions (Keohane and Milner, 1996). Research on the political impact of economic developments has shown that political institutions not only attenuate but may also magnify the political impact of economic developments. In fact, the present international political discourse on globalisation greatly exaggerates the constraints on decision-making due to economic internationalisation. Recent economic developments do not so radically break with the past that they justify such a development (Hirst and Thompson, 1996). The conclusion is therefore that the political consequences, in the form of new policies, are not due so much to real economic developments but rather to the discourse on globalisation itself (Cerny, 1997, p. 256). The fact that international developments may be magnified or attenuated by national political institutions shows that the international impact on national political settings is mediated by national institutions in a non-trivial way. Therefore, the functionalist adaptation image of Europeanisation does not seem to be adequate.

The critique of implementation research and research on the international influence on national political economies calls into question the functional image and calls for an institutionalist image of Europeanisation. This image of Europeanisation has been elaborated by neo-institutionalism;

in fact, it is rooted in its basic theoretical assumption. Political action is thought to be stable and repetitive because it follows routines which are endowed with meaning (March and Olsen, 1989). This is due to the fact that politics rests very much on the basis of formal organisations that rely heavily on standard operating procedures (Olsen, 1991). The organisation-centred view of political processes also implies a specific theory of institutional dynamics. First, change is overwhelmingly incremental and radical change is rather unlikely. Second, change in routines may not be imposed externally on an organisation but have to be conceived as an internal adaptation to changes in the environment. Change is always self-change, only the external pressure and constraints may vary. Therefore, from a neo-institutionalist perspective, an explanation of change rests on the way external constraints are translated into modifications of old routines. Two basic questions follow from this. First, what does the institutional structure look like? And second, by which mechanism is external pressure translated into internal change?

To conceptualise the structural setting, institutionalist theories have to move from the organisational meso-level to the macro-level of society. The polity of the European Union may be regarded as an institutionally-differentiated system along two axis. On the vertical axis, the process of European integration has led to a differentiation of two distinct levels of government: the European level and the level of the various nation-states (Wildenmann, 1991, Lepsius, 1991).[8] On the horizontal axis there are two forms of institutional differentiation which have to be distinguished. First, there is the distinction between different institutional spheres that can be said to coexist within the nation-state, the polity, economy, science, law, etc.[9] Second, these systems are also internally differentiated. Most important in this context is the acknowledgement that the political system is itself differentiated into sub-sectors of policy making which are insulated from one another and in which different structures of interest intermediation (Lehmbruch, 1991) or different governance structures have developed (Hollingsworth et al., 1994). The difference in governance structures across sectors is just as important as across countries. The type of polity that is emerging from this sketch may be called a dynamic multi-level-system of governance (Jachtenfuchs and Kohler-Koch, 1996). The various parts of this institutionally-differentiated polity have to be regarded as relatively autonomous institutional spheres, although they are loosely coupled (Olsen, 1996). This implies that they move on different paths of incremental adaptation and are not easily influenced by the outside. Because hierarchical coercive co-ordination seems to be the exception rather than the rule, the Europeanisation of nation-states has to be regarded as a highly complex process of the mutual adaptation of institutionalised action, that is, as a co-evolution (implying the absence of co-ordinated, synchronised development) of incrementally-evolving patterns of institutionalised action (Olsen, 1996).[10]

The second major aspect in the institutionalist image is the process of translation that takes place across vertically- and horizontally-differentiated institutionalised action. The concept of 'learning' has been used to portray this translation mechanism of European policy as a change in national preferences. This seems to imply a functional view of the Europeanisation process, just as the first image suggested. However, 'learning' in this context does not imply an optimal adaptation to the environment. Organisational learning from changes in the environment is common, but it is beset with problems which leave the outcome of the learning processes open-ended (Levitt and March, 1988). For example, learning might be 'superstitious' if either the wrong conclusions are drawn from past experiences or organisations are locked into limited-learning processes by optimising routines already in place instead of developing new and more adequate routines. This has been emphasised by theories which link learning to the concept of paradigm (Hall, 1993). Learning usually takes place within a single paradigm; and it is rather unlikely that one paradigm is going to be replaced by another. Another reason why Europeanisation will be a complex process is because organisational learning takes place within a politicised context. This implies that learning is not only about finding the best solution; it also always involves political strategy (Olsen and Peters, 1996). Furthermore, learning in a political context is constrained by the fact that learning may involve the admission of failure and may even lead to an enforced commitment to past decisions in order to avoid having to admit it (Staw, 1981; March and Olsen, 1989, p. 60). Another way of contextualising organisational learning theory in politics is to confine learning to explaining change within a paradigm and to assume phases of political conflict whenever a paradigm is contested (e.g. Hall, 1993).

To conceptualise Europeanisation as an organisational learning process is to expect incremental change within a single policy paradigm. Discontinuous change is more difficult to explain. Within political science and especially policy analysis, the notion of 'policy entrepreneur' (e.g. Kingdon, 1984, pp. 188-93) or 'policy broker' (Sabatier and Jenkins-Smith, 1993, p. 27) offers the possibility for an action-oriented explanation of discontinuous policy change. The experience of the deregulation of public utilities in the USA provides one example of immediate relevance to this study. The surprising fact that telecommunications, airlines and road haulage could be liberalised despite the well-entrenched interests of these industries is attributed to policy entrepreneurs. In this case, policy entrepreneurs were usually the leaders of the sectoral regulatory agencies, who used the economic consensus about widespread regulatory failure to radically change the sectoral policies. Without these entrepreneurs sectoral interests would have probably prevailed over diffuse consumer interests (Wilson, 1980; Derthick and Quirk, 1985). The importance of policy entrepreneurs for the impact of European policies on national policies has been acknowledged. Governments play this role as a two-level game, in which they use European policies to overcome national resistance to more radical policy change (Putnam, 1988; Moravscik, 1994). 'Entrepreneural politics' (Wilson, 1980) involves coalition-building to change the course of a given policy. Even more importantly, radical policy change per definition involves a change in the preferences that stabilised the former shape of the policy. Therefore, policy entrepreneurs are not just coalition builders; they are also mediators, creating new problem definitions and ways to remedy them (Jobert and Muller, 1987; Muller, 1995). Entrepreneural politics is to a large extent concerned with the elaboration of cognitive and normative frames and thus with a direct influence on the routines of policy making. One other important mechanism driving institutional dynamics - in addition to organisational learning – is entrepreneural politics.

Figure 1.2 The Institutionalist Image of Europeanisation

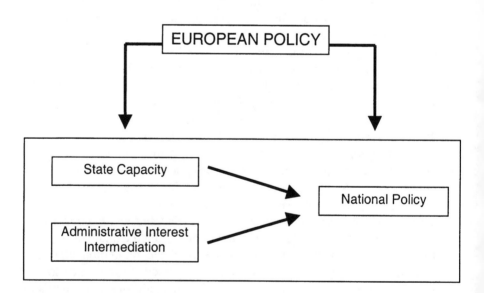

In this survey of the two main images of Europeanisation now present in the literature, a last remark cannot be omitted. In the middle-range theories developed to explain Europeanisation, elements of both are usually combined. However, most of the time there is an emphasis on one aspect. In this sense, the classification presented here is about ideal-types. For example, in the image of Europeanisation through regulatory competition the importance of European law is acknowledged, but its main emphasis is on the dynamics of regulatory regimes.

The final task in the institutionalist setting is to identify the relevant domestic institutional variables that explain the policy dynamics. Again the problem is how to delimit the large number of possible variables (Kassim and Menon, 1996). One strategy is to identify all the possible variables and subsequently test them. This strategy risks producing a complex model that is difficult to test empirically. Another strategy is to identify the major factors influencing the national policy dynamics and to take these as a starting point for inductively developing the explanatory variables. In policy analysis and political economy it is generally acknowledged that political decision-making implies intervention in sectors which are self-regulating. From this perspective, political decision-making is not only limited to the formal institutions of the state, government and the administration, it is also dependant on the co-operation of private actors to obtain the relevant information about policy problems and viable solutions for successful implementation. The type of link that is established between the 'state' and the 'sector' is the first important factor influencing the policy outcome. The type of routine co-operation between public and private actors has been conceptualised in policy analysis in the form of policy networks (e.g. Rhodes, 1990; van Waarden, 1992; Mayntz, 1992). 'Administrative interest intermediation' is a related term leading to a similar classification of forms of co-operation between public and private actors (Lehmbruch, 1991). A similar idea can be found in the realm of political economy where the concept of 'governance structure' is used to denominate the combinations of state intervention and mechanisms of self-regulation (market, hierarchy, networks and associations) that vary across countries and across sectors (Hollingsworth et al., 1994). Most of the time policy making will be influenced by such sectoral policy networks or governance structures. However, under exceptional circumstances these routine interactions may be interrupted by the attempts of the state (i.e. government and administration) to overcome routines and to introduce fundamental reforms, even against the interests of the private actors concerned. The probability of success will depend on the power of the state to overcome a sectoral status quo. This power is referred to as 'state capacity' (Skocpol, 1985; Atkinson and Coleman, 1989). State intervention which opposes sectoral interests may be an important prerequisite for more fundamental reform.

The theoretical concepts presented above have been developed in order to analyse advanced industrial nations. Although it has never seriously been questioned that Italy belongs to this category, doubts have been advanced about applying the model of policy analysis and sectoral governance to Italy. The argument has rested on the fact that Italy had a very weak government and that it was so dominated by parties that sectoral governance by public and private actors did not exist (see Dente, 1990, p. 10; Pasquino, 1989). Such claims of Italian exceptionalism have not remained unchallenged. It has also been argued that the Italian form of institutionalised capitalism should not be analysed as an exception to the rule (Regini, 1995). Second and more specifically, it has been shown that the diagnosis of *partitocrazia* only applies to the level of *politics* and that at the level of substantial *policy* private actors are routinely involved in policy making (Dente and Regonini, 1989). Furthermore, it is important to note that as the regime undergoes transition the chances that the policy process will continue to be dominated by political parties (if they ever were) is much less likely. These arguments, and the fact that policy analysis has established itself as a sub-field of political science in Italy, suggest that an attempt to apply the developed categories is justified. In the subsequent chapters I show which image of Europeanisation is best suited to interpret the process and what the outcome of the reformation of Italian transport regulation is. In the following section the methodology and the research design will be outlined.

Method

In the following I shall present a qualitative case study examining the European influence on Italian transport policy in order to examine the dynamics of Europeanisation. As a starting point, I propose a causal hypothesis about how Europeanisation influences national policy making. The case study will then expose the mechanism at work. Two policy areas shall be examined, road haulage and railway policy. Although a comparison between the two is presented, and is considered to be useful, this does not mean that this work is not best classified as a case study. The comparison contributes to a better explanation of the case. Since the cases are by no means representative of all policy situations in which Europe influences the member states, they do not offer a basis for generalisation. However, as argued below, this does not render them useless in contributing to a more general understanding of this mechanism. Therefore, before the research design is presented in detail, a few reasons shall be given concerning why I preferred a case study over other research designs, especially over a comparative design, which is widely considered superior to the case-study approach.

Research Strategies: Comparative Method vs. Case Study

In policy analysis, not all methodological problems of the empirical social sciences are debated to the same extent. Description does not give rise to methodological considerations. Descriptive case studies producing historical explanations by tracing sequences of events that explain outcomes do not need a sophisticated methodology. Methods of data collection such as interview techniques seem to be less of a problem in the examination of political decision-making than in anthropological field work, for example. This may be due to the fact that political decision-making gives rise to a lot of written documents that contain essential data. Furthermore, the debate about the superiority of quantitative over qualitative methods or vice versa seems to have become less of an issue (King et al., 1994). The methodological debate in reference to policy analysis only becomes relevant when the ambition is to go beyond a description of empirical observation to causal inferences. An influential methodological statement concerned with analysing politics soon enough comes to the conclusion that any research which is trying to establish relations of cause and effect, be it quantitative or qualitative, faces the problem of controlling these causal inferences.

The methodological debate has not yet reached a unanimous conclusion about how statements of cause and effect may be validly established, let alone about how to generalise them. In a volume on methodological aspects of policy research we find the following outspoken view about the state of affairs by a distinguished contributor on comparative method (Przeworski, 1987, p. 45):

> ... we still simply do not know how to go about studying the determinants of agricultural policies in France, for example. These policies have something to do with the economic and political situation in France, something to do with the EC as a government, something to do with the economic and political situation in other EC countries, something to do with weather, economics and politics in Argentina and Australia, and quite a lot to do with American - Soviet relations and American grain sales to the Soviet Union. Obviously, a study of French agricultural policy is feasible; but presently no methods for conducting such studies exist. These methods would constitute standard ways of doing things, ways justified by accepted canons of evidence and inference.

Why is the problem of causal inference in policy research unresolved? Policy research shares the problem with other social sciences that the best method for establishing causal relations does not work. The natural sciences rely on experiments to establish cause and effect. In the experimental method, the influence of a factor on a dependent variable is investigated by holding all other possible influences constant, manipulating the independent variable and measuring the effect on the dependant variable. In the social sciences it is often impossible for an investigator to hold all possible influences constant and manipulate the independent variable.

Admittedly, in the past there had been attempts to introduce the experimental design into the social sciences as 'quasi-experiments' (Cook and Campbell, 1979), in which model reforms were introduced in such a way as to allow research on their effects. But the cognitive and social difficulties which beset this method have prevented it from being more widely applied (Hunt, 1990). The most popular method of controlling causal inferences is the use of comparative studies. To use the example mentioned in the quote above: to test the influence of super power politics on French national agricultural politics, a second similar country could be studied to see if the effect is the same. The possible research designs were first formalised by John Stuart Mill and they have been repeated ever since. Many classical social science studies have been applying them more or less consciously in their material studies (Smelser, 1976). However, in policy research this method has not solved all the problems of causal inference. The major problem is that there are many possible influences on policy development but only very few cases in which all these variables could be tested (and potentially eliminated). Therefore it is not possible to conclude which subset of all possible influences are the decisive factors. Policy developments are inevitably overdetermined (Przeworski, 1987, pp. 38-41).

A second weakness of the comparative approach is the fact that it has to assume causal independence between the units which are compared (Ebbinghaus, 1996, pp. 409-10). In research designs comparing countries, for instance, dependent and independent variables are assumed to be operating within a country, and comparisons across countries are designed to find out which nation-specific factors account for national peculiarities, and which similarities for universal processes. In an increasingly interdependent world, the assumption of national endogenous variables is increasingly becoming questionable, and comparative research design is confronted with the following question: how many national developments have external causes? The dynamics of liberalisation, for example, may not only result from the ideology of a party; they may also be caused by an international policy fashion. In fact, referring to diffusion among populations of similar social units has become popular in explanations in the tradition of sociological neo-institutionalism.

Given the difficulties with the comparative method and the even greater problems of experimental research designs in the social sciences, one should wonder if it is possible to arrive at general causal knowledge, beyond description. From a methodological point of view, description may be safest; but general knowledge is more useful. Theory-oriented case studies offer a way out of the comparative research dilemmas (Eckstein, 1975). The study of single cases is often considered to be inferior to comparative designs, because single cases do not offer any possibility for generalisation. However, if case studies are designed as crucial cases, i.e. cases that confirm or challenge theories at the core of their predictions, case studies do contribute to the accumulation of general knowledge.

The scepticism implicit in inductive research strategies, which is at the basis of the defence of the case study, is also the point of departure for an important scholarly tradition in comparative social research. In a recent book laying the groundwork for policy research, Scharpf argues that the complexity of political decision-making calls for a shift in the discussion concerning how to do policy research (1997). The present focus on the methodological discussion is centred on procedures which are able to test hypotheses. Scharpf does not deny the importance of these methods. He argues, however, that in the face of complexity, it is doubtful if big improvements in the present state are possible. To make progress, it is important to shift the methodological discussion away from procedures that test hypotheses and towards ways of generating interesting hypotheses. From this viewpoint, the development of meta-theoretical frameworks allowing the formulation of hypotheses are of prime importance for the quality of research and should be one of the fundamental considerations in our reflections on methodology. For frameworks to be useful they have to structure the phenomena of an empirical field, they have to structure the questions, they have to denominate factors with a high explanatory power and they have to specify the kind of data necessary to confirm or disconfirm a hypothesis. Furthermore, in contrast to implicit research strategies, such frameworks allow the comparison of results and approaches. Presently, a research strategy based on frameworks is rather popular in policy research. A few examples of such frameworks are the 'garbage can model' (Kingdon, 1984) the 'référentiel-model' (Jobert and Muller, 1987), the 'policy paradigm model' (Hall, 1993), the 'advocacy coalition framework' (Sabatier and Jenkins-Smith, 1993), and 'actor-centred institutionalism' (Mayntz and Scharpf, 1995a and Scharpf, 1997). Frameworks of this kind differ from attempts at a unitary characterisation of a national policy style (most notoriously, 'pluralism' or 'corporatism') in that they are more general in their applicability. Often they are frames that allow the integration of different approaches and theories according to the needs at hand.

Research Design

The research design will follow the major methodological prescriptions previously developed. The major explanatory hypotheses tested will be developed in reference to the theoretical discussion about the transformation of the state and the causes for it. The theoretical discussion above is part of an attempt to do more than merely comparatively test random conjectures about causal hypotheses, and thus to avoid the risk of overburdening the comparative method. After the disciplined generation of hypotheses, comparative testing is used to eliminate explanations wherever it is considered useful. Since I want to test two different causal mechanisms, transferring them from the international to the national level, no general explanatory hypothesis is able to be offered in the introduction. Such hypotheses shall be developed in the respective chapters. The only general assumption that needs to be mentioned here is that there is indeed a discernible European influence.

Choice of the Case

The case study presented here is dedicated to the analysis of the influence of European policy on Italy in the transportation sector. Transport is an interesting policy to study for several reasons. A first, pragmatic reason is that transport policy gained momentum about ten years ago, and as such, enough time has lapsed for consequences to be felt at the national level. Furthermore, transport is part of the Single-Market Programme and thus connected with a set of policies widely perceived as rather successful. Additionally, European transport policy has encountered long national traditions in this field. In many European countries the origins of transport policy date back to the last century. In fact, it has been argued that railway construction offered the first experience in economic management for the modern nation-state (Dobbin, 1994) and that carrying out transport goals was often closely linked to the more general project of nation-building; it served to unify a territory by supporting its defence and increasing the mobility of the citizens. This link to nation-state building has secured a place for transport policy at the national level; and the aim of territorial consolidation has led to a contradiction between the traditions practised by the nation-states and the European ambition to create an integrated transport infrastructure. For this reason, it is interesting to examine the European impact on the national level in reference to transport policy. Given that a presumably vigorous European policy is encountering strong national traditions the question is: what does the impact look like?

One further restriction important for this undertaking has to be justified. Since transport policy is vast, the analysis has been restricted to the area of surface transport, i.e. road and rail. However, unlike air transport, for example, in these policy areas globalisation – at least considered as a movement of increased economic competition on a global scale – is not such an important force. Surface transport resembles a laboratory situation in which European pressures may be observed in isolation.

In order for the analysis of the European influence on national policy-making patterns of a country to be suitable, a possible influence must be visible. This is only the case if the means and ends of national policy making differ from those at the European level. This is true for many other countries but especially for Italy. Italian economic policy has been highly interventionist. As with other late industrialisers, in Italy the process of industrialisation was state led. In transport a highly-interventionist policy developed which was opposed to the European policy of introducing competition on a European scale. Given this contrast with the general European model, any European influence on Italy in this area should lead to a visible change in policy making. Furthermore, it is something of a crucial case with respect to the influence of Europe because Italy has a long record of being at the periphery of the European decision-making processes.

Thinking about the Italian case, however, some methodological disadvantages come to mind. Public policy research in Italy is not well developed. It is limited to legal scholarship (mostly dedicated to making sense of complicated legislation) and to a lesser extent to abstract economic modelling. It does not often include the analysis of political processes and institutions. In fact, policy research in political science is poorly developed (Bull, 1996, pp. 34-36).[11] This general condition leads to greater difficulties when collecting data. And while this means that it is very hard to find any study relevant for the analysis of political processes, especially in transport policy, the research is still important: at the very least, research on Italy can serve to reduce the bias towards the three major members of the EU: the UK, France and Germany.

A second potential disadvantage turned out to be less important in the final analysis. In the past few years, the political landscape in Italy has changed. Due to a wide-spread corruption scandal, the party system was swept away and with it the logic of post-war politics. One might think that these national developments risk eclipsing any (necessarily) weaker European influence, and that such developments would jeopardise the starting point of this study. This preoccupation turned out to be unfounded. At the beginning of the period under study here, transport policy was controlled by a closed policy community, which did not follow the logic of party government; thus the steps towards a new political regime in Italy did not heavily affect transport policy. As will be shown, however, in fact the development was quite to the contrary: the national political developments enhanced rather than diminished the European influence.

The third potential disadvantage of using the Italian case is the poor implementation of European legislation; in fact, this might throw the entire assumption of a European influence into question. If Italy agrees to everything but never implements anything, the question of the European influence in the area of transport policy seems to be irrelevant. Not denying the poor implementation record of the past, the situation of implementation has improved a great deal. Some procedural improvements accelerating transposition in Parliament and other institutional developments have increased the opportunities for real European influence.

Notes

1   For a history of ideas on the 'competition state' in general see McKenzie and Lee (1991: chapter five) and for federal states see Dye (1990).

2   The term 'regulatory state' is not in opposition to the term 'competition state'. The choice of terminology just stresses the most important change from a public policy view, the change from distributive policies involving money to regulatory policies involving law.

3   For reviews see Powell and DiMaggio (1991), Scott (1995: chapter three and four), Thelen and Steinmo (1992), Hall and Taylor (1996).

4   See also March and Olsen (1989: chapter four), North (1990a: 364ff.) and Hall and Taylor (1996: 939); for economic history see North (1990: chapter eleven).

5   In European integration research the term 'functionalism' is already in use to label the normative theory of regional integration developed by David Mitrany (Mutimer, 1994: 21-26). In contrast to the federalist theory of European integration that aimed at creating a European federal state, functionalism proposes as an alternative way to integration via intensification of co-operation in different policy areas by international organisations. To emphasise that this type of co-operation is organised along tasks and did not involve political institution-building, it was termed 'functional'. 'Neo-functionalism', its successor, shared the conviction that co-operation among states should be developed along functional lines but expected that by 'spill-over' these would inevitably lead to political institution-building at a regional level (Mutimer, 1994: 26-33). In contrast to this tradition the usage of 'functionalism' here does not refer to a certain logic of integration but to a basic view of political processes.

6   The terminology concerning implementation in the European context is not homogenous. 'Implementation' has been used as a synonym for 'incorporation' (Krislov et al., 1986: 62). Contrary to this definition, here 'implementation' is used for the entire process of incorporation and application (see also Siedentopf and Hauschild, 1988: 26). A distinction between incorporation and application is often introduced, yet sometimes 'incorporation' is called 'transposition'; 'application' is sometimes called 'compliance' if the stress is on the behavioural outcomes rather than the action to achieve it (Haas, 1998).

7   For the discussion on European interest intermediation see, for example, Greenwood and Grote and Ronit (1992); Mazey and Richardson (1993), van Schendelen (1993), Eichener and Voelkow (1994).

8   This view of the integration process stands in contradiction to the supranational image of European integration which saw the integration process as a vertical shift of competencies from the national to the supranational level. It also contradicts the intergovernmental view, which denies that the supranational level could be more than the agent of the EU member states. The implicit zero-sum game between the levels is not assumed in the institutionalist model.

9   For this argument with respect to Europe see Olsen (1996) and Jachtenfuchs (1995). For more general arguments see Mayntz (1988) and Luhmann (1977).

10 Olsen attaches two meanings to the term Europeanisation. One is the institutional differentiation of a genuine political system at the political level, the other is the effect of this process on the nation state. Here, I would like to restrict the definition of Europeanisation to the second meaning only. The first process I would call the process of institutional differentiation.

11 For first statements see Lange and Regini (1989); Dente (1990), and Regonini (1995).

2 European Transport Liberalisation

The founding document of the European Community, the Treaty of Rome, assigned top priority to the issue of transport, which was thought to be vital to physically integrating the Common Market. Nevertheless, a Common Transport Policy (CTP) was left undeveloped for a long time. Only in the mid-1980s did the CTP finally gain momentum. This is not to say that no decisions whatsoever regarding transport had been made at the Community level before that. However, until about a decade ago European transport policy did not significantly change the way transport was dealt with in Europe: it continued to treat it as a national issue or as an issue to be settled within bilateral agreements among member states. Academic observers (e.g. Lindberg and Scheingold, 1970) and commenting practitioners (e.g. degli Abbati, 1987, Erdmenger, 1983) were extremely disappointed in the poor shape of the CTP.

Over the past decade, the CTP has become ever more significant and consequential for the member states. The dynamics of the Single-Market Programme, enforced by the procedural amendments of the Single European Act, have secured transport a firm place on the European agenda. My research question is concerned with how this European transport policy influences national transport policy.[1] For reasons presented above, I have chosen to examine the process of Europeanisation by an in-depth case study on Italy. In this chapter, I shall present the case to be interpreted and explained. First, I want to give a brief overview of some basic concepts of transport policy. Second, I want to present the development of the CTP in order to find out how the development of the European transport policy created pressure to adapt at the national level. In the following chapter, I want to map the development of Italian transport policy. The resulting developments on the national level are surprising. The developments in the Italian transport policy cannot simply be seen as a consequence of European transport policy making.

A Brief Introduction to Transport Policy

To the newcomer, transport is likely to be a confusing area of public-policy making.[2] First of all, there is no single integrated system of transport. The four basic transport systems or modes of transport - rail, road, shipping and air transport - are only very broad indications of diverse systems and activities. For example, rail transport may be about transporting goods over long distances, as is common in the U.S., or it may be about high-speed trains transporting (mainly) passengers between major cities, or it may be about local commuter trains transporting passengers to their workplaces and back. Therefore, transport systems and activities are often distinguished according to the type of 'object' transported – i.e. passengers or goods – and their range of operation. A further important distinction for transport systems is between infrastructure and operation. To continue using the example of rail, infrastructure may be defined as all the hardware that has to be in place before trains can operate, i.e. railway tracks, signalling systems, stations, depots, etc. But the distinction between infrastructure and operation may not be as clear cut as this. Increasingly, infrastructures themselves are being split along the lines of infrastructure and operation. To given an example, for harbours to be an effective infrastructure for the shipping of goods, loading and unloading has to be organised. This service, although part of the infrastructure, may be regarded as the operational dimension of this specific infrastructure. From these distinctions, an impressive classification of transport systems could be built across the four transport modes. From an organisational point of view, ownership of transport enterprises may be public or private. Furthermore, if the economic activity of transporting goods is considered, the important intermediate figure of freight forwarders, who organise sometimes complex chains of intermodal transport for their customers, has to be mentioned. Since all of these areas are subject to political intervention, transport policy itself is complex.

Next to the real life heterogeneity of the simple activity of moving physical entities across space, a second factor that makes transport policy difficult to grasp is policy making itself (Button, 1993). Since public intervention started in the last century, it has influenced transport in various ways: governments influenced the costs of various modes of transport by taxes and subsidies, they protected the functioning of the market with competition law and consumer protection, they regulated the access of enterprises to the market by licensing, they used moral appeals to increase road safety ('don't drink and drive!'), they influenced the long-term development of the sector by promoting or carrying out research and development, they provided information on transport activities such as official statistics, they influenced transport via other policies such as energy and environmental policy, and sometimes they even produced services, for example state-owned railways. The list of goals that government intervention tried to achieve is just as long and can be analysed according to different types of market failure: governments intervened to contain the monopoly power of railways, to control excessive competition between hauliers, to reduce negative external effects such as environmental damage by air and noise pollution, to provide public goods that would not be produced by the market (roads), to provide accessible transport for all, to promote regional development, and to improve the co-ordination between different modes of transport, etc. Even more difficult than producing an exhaustive list of means and ends and a satisfactory classification of each, is to create a link between them. The effect of transport policy measures is not well understood. What is more, it is not clear which type of measure contributes to which goal. More often than not, conflicting goals call into question the justification of a specific policy measure (Button, 1993, p. 245). For example, policies to contain externalities may have the effect of increasing costs, and thus have an adverse effect on accessibility.

Fortunately, for the present case study it is not necessary to clear up this messy conceptual area. To reduce the potentially vast area of transport to manageable proportions, European policy developments are only considered here in two modes of transport: *rail* and *road*. The investigation will focus on what are called *operations*; only those aspects of infrastructure are included which are relevant for the operational dimension. Furthermore, the focus will be on freight transport rather than on passenger transport. However, it is easier to make these distinctions in road rather than in rail transport. Due to the present technical characteristics of rail transport, infrastructure and operation are tightly linked. Whereas lorries run on virtually any type of road, trains have to fulfil specific requirements to be able to run on a certain track. Trains have to be of the same gauge as the track they run on, they have to be able to receive the signals guiding their trip, and if they are powered by the electricity, they have to be adjusted to the type of power provided (Befahy, 1995). For lorries, technical infrastructure compatibility is much less of a problem. Also, the distinction between passenger and freight transport is blurred within the highly-integrated system of railway transport. Being the more profitable business, passenger transport is usually favoured in the allocation of track capacity and efforts towards technical improvement. Therefore, to understand what is happening to freight transport, passenger transport has to be included.

The second type of limitation concerns the type of government intervention considered here. Of all possible types of intervention, this study will only be concerned with *market regulation*, that is, measures that are adopted to protect the proper working of the market. Negative externalities such as adverse effects on the environment or the provision of public goods that are not produced by the market are not considered here.

There are many types of justification for market-regulatory measures. From the point of view of the goals pursued by political actors it is difficult to delimit the concerns of this policy area. Concentration on the *policy instruments* employed in transport policy making simplifies the problem. If we imagine market regulation on a continuum from the lowest to the highest degree of intervention, the most drastic form of market regulation is public ownership (Majone, 1996c, pp. 11-15). In this borderline case, it is not entirely correct to speak of regulation because the market is replaced by a natural monopoly, that is, an industry which, due to its specific characteristics, is most efficient when there is only one producer. In this case, direct regulation is replaced by hierarchy. In the transport sector, railways have come closest to this case. However, as is shown by the case of the US, natural monopolies such as railways have also been regulated.

Between the extremes of public ownership, on the one hand, and a complete lack of government intervention, on the other, the instruments of market regulation are applied to ensure the functioning of the market (Baum, 1993, pp. 160-61). Since they are important in order to understand the subsequent European and national policy developments, it is helpful to introduce them here. The first set of instruments regulate who may offer transport services. This *market-access regulation* entails both quantitative and qualitative measures. *Quantitative* market-access regulation limits the transport capacity available in the market. An upper limit on the available capacity is enforced by issuing only a limited number of licences for the market. The common justification emphasises that it prevents so-called 'cut-throat competition'. *Qualitative* market-access regulation is concerned with the ability of firms to offer services of acceptable quality. Firms willing to offer transport services have to demonstrate a good reputation (no serious criminal offences and no record of continual infringements on safety or driving regulations, etc.), appropriate financial standing and professional competence (Commission, 1997, p. 12). Qualitative market-access regulation is more basic and less intrusive than quantitative restrictions.

The second set of instruments for market regulation are aimed at setting the price of the services offered, replacing the mechanism of supply and demand. There are different systems for establishing the *tariffs* at which transport services have to be supplied. That tariff with the least interventionist system is the *reference tariff*, a recommended price for a certain service that is not legally binding for the contracting partners. The *bracket tariff* is more intrusive: it sets a legally-binding price for a service. However, contracting partners may negotiate within the bracket, that is, an upper and a lower boundary for the set price. The *fixed tariff* is the most intrusive: it is legally binding and does not allow for any margin of discretion.

The two basic sets of market-regulatory instruments were used to build regulatory regimes of considerable complexity. Market access regulation may be differentiated according to different types of markets (Maresch, 1987). For example, in the past countries such as Germany, France, and Italy distinguished between the market for short- and long-distance road haulage, between own-account transport and professional road haulage, and so forth. For each market different quantitative and qualitative access criteria applied. Tariffs, too, may be classified according to different markets. These are usually set out in long tables that differentiate the price according to different distances and types of goods transported. Furthermore, separate tariffs have often been established for special categories of goods such as petroleum products, chemicals, cars, etc. This complexity may be further increased by spreading competencies over several levels of government, especially in federal systems.

As has been mentioned, *public ownership* in the transport sector, a widespread phenomenon in Europe, may be regarded as the functional equivalent of regulation. This makes sense when one takes into consideration the trend towards privatisation. If proponents of privatisation want to avoid the worst case – i.e. converting a public monopoly into a private monopoly – some form of competition has to be introduced. This, in turn, calls for market regulation. This has been the case with railways.

Finally, transport is influenced by *taxes* and *charges* (Baum, 1993, p. 161). In Italy, for example, there are more than 100 transport-related taxes and charges across all the modes of transport. These may be related to the different phases of market regulation. Market access is covered, for example, by vehicle charges, market operation by taxes on fuel and road-user charges.

Although in transport policy the relationship between policy instruments, the effect of their application, and the justification may be elusive, two broad patterns of transport policy in which these are routinely linked can be distinguished (Button, 1992, p. 35). The *Anglo-Saxon approach* views transport as just another economic sector trying to improve the efficiency and limit negative external effects. The range of policy instruments is usually smaller and justification less elaborate. There is a tendency towards laissez-faire. The *continental-European approach*, on the other hand, tends to see transport as an infrastructure for the wider economy and society as a whole. Transport policy is more concerned with goals such as regional development and the provision of public transport for its citizens or environmental protection (good railways stimulating the choice of less polluting modes of transport). For this reason the continental European approach is more interventionist and applies a wider range of policy instruments.

Building a Common Transport Market

One of the main objectives if not *the* main objective of European transport policy has been to build a common market for transport services.[3] However, the objective of unifying the diverse national transport systems has proven to be no easy task. The typical Community method of liberalisation, i.e. introducing the four freedoms, has proven to be difficult in the transport sector. This was not only due to the nature of the sectoral or economic problem but also to institutional, decision-making problems within the EU. This has one important consequence for the outcome of Community policy.

The Problem of European Transport Policy

In being concerned with the most effective management of transport, European transport policy is similar to national transport policies. An important difference between the two is that the European perspective also involves the question of integration. The EU policy aims to solve transport-related problems with reference to the EU as a whole. One of the main goals of the EU has been to create a Common Market for transport, which would hopefully lead to a more efficient transport system for Europe as a whole and create a better means for tackling transport-related problems. Yet, the goal of a single transport market stands in flat contradiction with the post-war policy traditions in transport in many countries. In the following paragraphs the CTP's problem in establishing a Common Market shall be presented in a rather schematic way. This exposition precisely describes the situation in road haulage, which has been at the centre of European policy efforts for many years, but in a modified way it also applies to railways.

Markets in post-war Europe, and also in the member states of the EEC, were previously organised along national lines. The qualitative and quantitative market-access criteria and price regulation differed from country to country. These different national regimes only applied to national road hauliers. Sensibly, these regulations did not rule out the cross-border movement of goods. International transport was regulated by bilateral agreements between states that were involved in this operation. The central element of these international regulatory regimes were the quotas by which transport capacity was allocated to each country on an annual basis. Foreign hauliers did not have access to the national transport market. In the jargon of transport economics, they did not have the right to carry out *cabotage*, that is, they were not allowed to transport goods between two points within a foreign country (Gröhe, 1996, pp. 1-3). One of the aims of the CTP was to merge the numerous national regulatory regimes and their international supplements into a single borderless market. A road-haulage firm registered in one of the member states would be able to provide services anywhere throughout the Community.

Political Conflict

The negotiations of the EC-Treaty in 1957 established transport as a major concern for joint-Community action. Two phases of transport policy may be distinguished for the purpose at hand: namely, before 1985 and after.[4] These two phases were characterised by a particular Commission strategy towards the CTP and a dominant constellation of interests (Erdmenger, 1983; Whitelegg, 1988). In these different periods, the problem of market making – which was the major concern in this context – was approached in different ways. But measures were primarily aimed at the road-haulage sector.

In the first phase, from 1957 to 1985, no progress was made towards a common market for road-haulage services. This was due to the opposition of the big European countries of Italy, France and Germany. There are several reasons for this, the most obvious being the straightforward interest in protecting their domestic road haulage industries. For the proponents of liberalisation – especially for the Netherlands – liberalisation entailed a host of new business opportunities, whereas for the opponents – especially Germany – there was a risk of attracting competitors to their large markets. However, mere economic interest is not enough to explain the policy deadlock that existed for such a long period of time. Another factor which made liberalisation difficult was that opponents were followers of what has been termed the continental European philosophy of transport policy, which maintains that transport is a vital economic and social infrastructure which requires state intervention (Button, 1992, p. 35). Furthermore, there was no pressure that would have made delaying the decision excessively harmful. As mentioned above, cross-border transport in the Community did not depend on a Community solution because functionally-equivalent arrangements existed in the form of bilateral and multilateral agreements. And finally, an important institutional factor contributed to the deadlock in decision making. The *de facto* unanimity principle made it easy for the opponents to oppose progress towards liberalisation if they perceived that it was harmful to them.[5]

The modest policy outcome mirrored these problems.[6] Neither the liberalisation of cabotage nor the harmonisation of taxes was achieved, nor was technical harmonisation. Progress was only made in addressing the social regulation for drivers, which was a mere secondary problem. Designed as a step towards an eventual liberalisation, the Community introduced a regulatory regime for trans-border Community transport, comprising quotas and even a bracket tariff system. However, this system never really challenged the significance of the traditional quota system (Kiriazidis, 1994, p. 12). It was perceived to be of symbolic value only.

The situation changed in the mid-1980s. The general trend towards deregulation and privatisation called the continental-European approach into question, thus undermining the legitimisation of the opponents resistance to transport liberalisation (Kiriazidis, 1994, pp. 10-11). More specifically, by coincidence the European Parliament chose to assert its presence on the European stage by taking the European Council to court, maintaining it had infringed on the EC treaty by not developing a common transport policy. The resulting verdict of the European Court of Justice held this accusation to be correct, thus causing a problem for the opponents of progress in transport policy. Finally, in 1985 the Single Market Programme was adopted; this aimed to achieve in many other sectors what had been attempted for road haulage (Sleuwaegen, 1993, p. 216). This was supplemented by procedural changes introduced by the Single European Act in 1987, where the unanimity principle was replaced by a principle of qualified majority voting for the matters included in the Single Market Programme, hence covering the liberalisation of transport regulation (Kiriazidis, 1994, p. 2).

Due to this coincidental combination of factors, the CTP took off. However this does not imply that consensus was easily reached on the way forward. According to the EU-Treaty, the decision-making process in the area of the CTP involves the Commission, as the initiator of new policies, and the Council, as the final decision-maker, with the European Parliament becoming more important over time (Erdmenger, 1996, pp. 44-45). The European Council is the crucial obstacle to the decision-making process. For most of the EU history, the principle of unanimous decision-making allowed any member state opposing progress to veto new policy proposals. Although this rule has been replaced with the principle of qualified-majority voting for legislation in the Single European Act, for transport the principle of unanimity is still in force whenever there are unfavourable consequences for regional development and the operation of transport systems. Although this does not imply a right to veto, member states can still insist on unanimity (Erdmenger, 1996, pp. 46-47).

The decision-making story, although taking place within the same institutional framework, differed slightly in the case of road and rail. For road haulage the decisive question remained: what level of harmonisation is required by liberalisation? Beyond discussion, the underlying objective was to craft a common market. In railway policy, by contrast, the fundamental question was: is the objective of building a market acceptable?

Reaching an Agreement on Road-Haulage Policy After 1985 two different coalitions in the Council opposed each other on the issue of the proper relationship between liberalisation and harmonisation. These different positions mirrored the different implications of the EU policy for the national road-haulage industries.[7] The group of small member states, the Benelux countries and Denmark, advocated the liberalisation of cabotage because they held a large share of the international road-haulage market. The U.K., too, supported liberalisation, but mainly because of an ideological preference for deregulation. Its share of the international market was low because of its geographic separation from the continent. By contrast, the governments and industries of Germany, France, Italy and Spain all resisted liberalisation because their declining shares in the international road-haulage market reflected a declining competitiveness.

Although all the opponents of liberalisation had enough votes to block progress under qualified-majority voting, liberalisation was finally achieved (Young, 1994, pp. 10-11). The threat of a possible direct application of the EC-Treaty, which would have implied direct and unconditional liberalisation, may have created the will to compromise in this camp. Under these conditions, a compromise was reached. Liberalisation was phased in over several years, and some minimum harmonisation was included as well. Germany, the major opponent to liberalisation, gained some fiscal harmonisation in exchange for having to accept the liberalisation of cabotage.

Reaching an Agreement on Railway Policy[8] In the case of the (fundamental) railway reform a consensus may have been sought in order to secure the procedural possibility of formally reintroducing unanimity in transport policy (see above). In the past the different actors performed the following roles: on the one hand, the Commission, supported by the European Parliament and the European Court of Justice, were promoting the creation of a Single European Market in transport; on the other hand, the Council built up its impressive record of resistance against policy initiatives. In the case of railway policy, Parliament deviated somewhat from its earlier record when it adopted the view of the Community of European Railways (CER): namely, that it is not essential to separate the infrastructure manager from national railway companies institutionally (Interview CER, April 1996). But overall it did conform by condemning the Council for its attempts to hamper efforts to ease the access of new railway enterprises (Agence Europe 22.03.1995, p. 13). The following section shows that, in the case of the CRP, the Council also conformed to its tradition of opposing liberalisation. As the next section will show, because of a pro-liberalisation consensus in the Council, this strategic veto point has still not been overcome.

Subsequently, I shall explain why the decision-making process has not been stalled anyway.

The fact that the Council's decision to adopt a new railway policy passed unanimously does not imply that there were not divergent interests in the new policy. Quite to the contrary, two broad *coalitions* may in fact be distinguished (Kiriazidis, 1994, Interview Commission, March 1997, Agence Europe 28.03.1991, p. 7). The first coalition consisted of Britain and the Netherlands. This group may be seen as unconditional supporters of liberalisation. During the negotiations both countries had already planned railway reforms going beyond the requirements discussed. However, they had no specific interest in exporting their reform plans to other European countries. Apparently, Britain did not need the support of a European reform to overcome national resistance, and the Dutch, until recently, had not assigned a major priority to railway policy (Lehmkuhl, forthcoming). The second coalition was comprised of conditional supporters of the new railway policy. These countries identified different problems that would be generated by the proposed liberalisation, especially technical compatibility and security of operations (Agence Europe 28.03.1991, p. 7). The position of Germany, France and Italy, the three remaining countries under study in this volume, are representative of the second coalition and may be described as follows: the German representatives in the Council were generally in favour of the new railway policy but had difficulties in developing clear preferences because the domestic German railway reform had not produced any conclusive results (Teutsch, forthcoming). The Italian representatives conformed to their usual behavioural pattern and did not develop any clear preferences at all. In fact, there does not seem to be a continual dialogue between the Commission and the Italian representatives (Interview Commission March 1997; Interview European Freight and Logistics Leaders Club, March 1997). France was most sceptical about railway liberalisation in Europe (Douillet and Lehmkuhl, forthcoming). It opposed both elements of liberalisation: the division between infrastructure and operation and free access to the national railway network by non-national enterprises. This has even been demonstrated again quite recently, when France opposed the creation of European freight freeways. The basic principle seems to be to slow down liberalisation as much as possible. The French position is not merely defensive; it tries to promote a different reform vision by stressing co-operation between different (national) railway enterprises. Technical compatibility between different national networks has become a major concern in their perspective. Furthermore, in contrast to the European market view of railways, France has tried to reassert the definition of railways as a public service. France seems always on the verge of leaving this coalition and resorting to outright opposition to the Community policy trend.

The position of the national governments in the Council is roughly the same as the position of the national railways within the Community of European Railways, the main lobbying association at the Community level. This association cautiously welcomes the liberalisation policy and tries to solve the new problems and moderate the pace of the reform (Community of European Railways, 1996). Within the CER, the French railways are the only railways that fundamentally oppose liberalisation. They therefore continually seem to risk isolation.[9]

This brief overview of the preferences of the major players in the decision-making process shows that considerable resistance to the liberalisation of railway policy would have been possible. The majority of member states belonged to the coalition of conditional supporters, and France was on the brink of outright opposition. Why then was a decision about a fundamental change of the CRP reached in a relatively short period of time? The general momentum of the Common Market Programme may have played a role.[10] However, the two major factors that explain the surprising consensus are the following. First, the directive was successful in changing the preferences of the decision makers. The new perspective on rail, described above in terms of an expanding market of railway enterprises, which replaced the former view - that the railway was an infrastructure - was attractive because it offered a reform perspective. It was successful in revising the terms of the debate about the railway reform. 'If the directive was a success, it wasn't so much a success with what it did directly, but what it did indirectly, and that is to create a new thought process to be applied to the railways, to think again about what railways were supposed to be doing, how they were supposed to be run' (Interview Commission, March 1997).

Policy Outcome

In road haulage as well as in railway policy, reaching agreement on a common policy was no easy task. It is commonplace in the analysis of political decision-making that solutions to problems depend very much on the interests involved and the institutional setting in which decision making is embedded; the solution adopted also often deviates from the solution that is perceived to be the best. What do the compromises look like in the policy areas investigated here?

Road Haulage The series of decisions regarding road haulage which have been adopted since the inception of the European transport policy in the mid-1980s shares the bias of many Single Market policies. They are strong when it comes to abolishing restrictions to the 'four freedoms' – the free movement of labour, capital, goods and services – but they tend to be much weaker in creating new European rules to replace the former national rules (Scharpf, 1996).

As described above, the creation of the Single Market for road haulage depends on merging three formerly distinct markets into one European market and developing a coherent regulatory regime for the common market. The first decision made on the European level concerned *cross border* transport within the Community (Council Regulation 1841/1988).[11] In 1988 it was decided to phase in liberalisation by increasing the Community quotas, thus enlarging the market beyond the international quotas agreed to by member states. From January 1993 onwards there were no more quantitative restrictions for cross-border road haulage between the members of the EU. Any road-haulage firm that wanted to offer cross-border transport services could do so, as long as it fulfilled the qualitative access criteria specified by the Community.[12]

The second decision regarded the possibility of *cabotage* transport within the EU, i.e. the possibilities for road hauliers to operate throughout the Community, irrespective of their country of origin (see above). Liberalisation on this issue was even more of a problem than it was in the area of international transport. Therefore, liberalisation was phased in over an even longer period of time. In 1989 a limited number of licences for cabotage transport were introduced within the EU to test the consequences of permitting cabotage. Since the immediate competitive threat did not seem to be so large, in 1993 cabotage was completely liberalised, with no quantitative restrictions. Only qualitative market access criteria were to apply. From 1993 onwards the number of licences issued for cabotage steadily increased. In July 1998 all quantitative restrictions on cabotage were abolished.

These two decisions have, after a lengthy delay of several decades, created the Single Market for road haulage. However, they have not created a coherent regulatory regime for the entire market. The distinction between the national and the European market is still relevant. National market regulation may still differ from cross-border market regulation within the EU. As we shall see later, this results in pressure on the national market regulation.

Whereas the liberalisation of the market has been a success, the harmonisation of competitive conditions has been less successful. Admittedly, the important area of technical regulation has been dealt with rather successfully (Kiriazidis, 1994, p. 13). However, the harmonisation of taxation is the most important element for creating a level playing field. Two decisions have been reached in this area. In 1992 a minimum level for fuel taxes was set (Council Directive 1992/82). In 1993 a minimum level for vehicle taxes was fixed, and those member states not using tolls for the usage of motorways were allowed to introduce annual charges for the use of the road infrastructure (Council Directive 1993/89). Although these decisions were important for increasing the acceptability of liberalisation, they have not been very successful in levelling the playing field. A Commission report saw some progress in the area of vehicle taxes and road-user fees. There has been some adjustment towards the minimum level in all countries, but most of the member states now apply vehicle tax rates above the minimum. However, significant variations remain, ranging from an annual level of 4,000 ECUs in the U.K. to below 1,000 ECUs in Spain, France, Greece and Italy (Commission, 1997, p. 63). Finally, in the important area of road-user charges, some harmonisation has occurred. A common charging system has been introduced for the primary roads in several member states such as Germany and the Benelux countries, which, unlike member states such as France and Italy, did not have a system of road-user charges in place. The so-called 'Eurovignette' allows the national government to charge foreign users of national motorways up to 1,250 ECUs per year. This aspect of the CTP for road haulage is essential for introducing the 'polluter pays' principle in transport and is likely to be an important issue in future. It also reveals how difficult it is for the EU to set new rules for liberalised European markets. The Eurovignette system is a very modest pricing scheme, and very crude, too, because it is not connected to the actual distances travelled. The member states strongly oppose the proposals to introduce a road pricing system which would allow modestly higher charges (Commission, 1995c). Therefore future prospects for improving performance and correcting the external effects of the market do not seem to be good.[13] To sum up, the EU road-haulage policy is biased towards market liberalisation but less capable of creating equal conditions for competition or providing means to counter external effects of transport policy, especially on the environment.

Railways[14] In the beginning of the, 1980s there was a widespread feeling that the European railways had entered into a profound crisis. In 1985 the European Conference of Ministers of Transport (ECMT), which represents 19 European states, called for urgent measures to improve international rail-transport service, because 'European railways are at present in a particularly difficult competitive situation which could become almost desperate unless vigorous action is taken immediately' (1985, p. 8). The sense of crisis was based on the observation of a steady decline of the railway's share in the passenger and freight-transport market.

The unfavourable situation of railways in intermodal competition, especially with respect to road haulage, was considered to be one of the reasons for this development. It was believed that important reasons for the poor economic performance of the railways were government interference, which resulted in the imposition of social-service obligations and a low degree of management autonomy, and the fact that railways had to bear infrastructure construction and maintenance costs. However, what may have even contributed more to the widespread diagnosis of crisis was the fact that there were structural impediments internal to the railways, impediments which prevented them from adapting sufficiently to the new demand for transport services, which for its part puts a higher value on flexibility and reliability than on quantity. These structural impediments can be attributed to the railway as a technical system, which is inevitably a rather inflexible mode of transport, better adapted to low-quality/high-quantity transport. A further disadvantage of railways is the low level of international integration of the various railway systems, resulting from the fact that railways were developed in a national framework (European Conference of Ministers of Transport, 1985, pp. 48-49). A low degree of technical compatibility in signalling systems in areas such as power supply increase the costs of trans-border freight transport. The quality is further reduced by administrative differences, which prevent the development of single tariffs and door-to-door services. The international fragmentation of railways is a major obstacle to their intermodal competitiveness because it hampers long-distance hauls, where railways enjoy a competitive advantage over road transport. According to the European Commission the crisis of the European railways contributes to a general crisis of mobility because the loss of shares in the transport markets (to road haulage) increases accidents and reduces environmental sustainability in Europe (Commission, 1996, p. 5).

Despite these symptoms of crisis, the railway policy of the EC shared the fate of the CTP in general. Until the mid-1980s it never surpassed its very modest initial stage, and when the first attempts to shape an integrated CTP were finally made, it included all transport modes except railways (Ross, 1994, p. 193). Of course, railway policy wasn't entirely neglected by the EC, but it was not integrated with other policy measures.[15] The main aim of the early railway policy was to reduce the disadvantages of railways in intermodal competition due to state intervention and to increase the transparency of the financial relationship between the state and the railways (Erdmenger, 1981, p. 88). This approach was not very successful. Ten years later social-service obligations had not been reduced, and state aid to railways had increased. Only the transparency of the financial relationship between states and railways had increased (Erdmenger, 1981, p. 89). Until the mid-1980s this situation remained unchanged (Whitelegg, 1988, p. 58). The policy only conceived of the railways as a financial problem, ignoring any broader context. It was argued that the CTP did not offer any constructive proposals but only 'financial imperatives dressed up as transport policies' (Whitelegg, 1988, p. 56).

In the second half of the 1980s the Community tried to relaunch a Common Railway Policy. One could have expected the policy to seek a possible solution to the poor economic performance of the railways by scaling down their activities to the economically-successful areas (Befahy, 1995, p. 15). These measures could have significantly reduced the financial burdens on the member states, most of which had to subsidise their railways heavily. However, in its action programmes and its legislative proposals the Commission pursued quite a different strategy. It was above all the various national projects for High Speed Trains (HST) which permitted the Community to design a *growth strategy*, this had the advantage of increasing the political viability of the Community's railway reform.[16] This may be the reason why 'the EC's "rediscovery" of rail policy since the mid-1980s has been led by a Commission newly intent on assuming a much more activist and multifaceted role in HST planning, development and funding' (Ross, 1994, p. 193).

Since directive 91/440 the Common Railway Policy (CRP) has been extended to all major areas of railway policy, and despite the rhetoric of subsidiarity no significant area of railway policy has remained in the exclusive competence of the member states.[17] A recent Commission White Paper offers a comprehensive outline of 'A Strategy for Revitalising the Community's Railways' (Commission, 1996). The policy problem that is to be addressed by the Community is expanded. Whereas the earlier policy identified the financial crisis of the railways as the main problem, this is now seen to be a mere symptom of the decline of this mode of transport, caused by the rise of other modes, especially road transport (Commission, 1996, pp. 7-9). According to the Commission, however, the decline of the railways is not taken as evidence of the fact that this mode of transport is outdated and should be given up. Railways could compete with other modes of transport, if its disadvantages in intermodal competition such as social-service obligations or higher infrastructure costs were removed,[18] and even more importantly, if railways were offering services which were better tailored to the demand of the users (Commission, 1996, p. 10). It is the Commission's firm belief that the establishment of a market will be an important means for creating new transport services by attracting new operators and increasing the efficiency of the former monopolies. The strategy of revitalising the railways in the medium run therefore aims at creating a Single Market for rail services in both passenger and freight transport. The

Single Market is created by two connected measures. Given that both road and rail have to bear the internal and external costs for the usage of their respective infrastructures, it is hoped that the services offered by rail allow it to compete with road transport.[19]

The core goal of the European CRP is to reverse the decline of the European railways by introducing competition among different railway companies. Intermodal competition, especially with road transport, is to be supplemented by *intramodal competition* on a *European scale*. This implies that any European company may provide any service throughout the European Union. This is a radical idea, which challenges the widely-accepted policy belief that for technical and economic reasons railways are natural monopolies and that they have to be protected from intermodal competition.

There are several reasons to assume that intramodal competition constitutes the core goal of the CRP. First, this goal is in line with the Single Market Programme in general and especially with the policy pursued in other network utilities such as telecommunications and electricity, where the principle of competition between different suppliers from the same infrastructure has also been applied. Furthermore, as shall be shown below, most of the recent decision and the obligations that have thus far arisen have been concerned with the introduction of intramodal competition.[20] The programmatic declarations of the Commission propose advancement on this track. Finally, the other goals associated with the CRP, especially the goals of achieving technical compatibility between the different national railway systems ('interoperability') and of increasing the environmental sustainability of transport may be subsumed under the market-building project. 'Interoperability' is a precondition for competition on a European scale, as well as a contribution to environmental sustainability, because growth in the railway sector will divert traffic away from road transport, which is inherently more polluting.

The European railway reform concentrates on four different aspects of railway administration.[21] First, new principles about *railway management* have been adopted. According to the CRP, the current practice in which the administration can perpetually interfere should be abolished and be replaced by management that operates according to the principles of any private enterprise. Railways should be free to determine their investment and business plans, have the possibility to establish international consortia with other railway companies, make decisions on staff and public procurement, expand their market share and establish activities in fields associated with railway businesses. Eventually, tariffs could be abolished to allow railways themselves to determine the price for services offered.

Secondly, the *financial regulation of railways* covering aspects internal to the railways as well as aspects of the financial relationship between states and railways was adopted. Until the end of 1992 railways were exempt from the Community rules on state aid. From 1993 onwards these rules were introduced, with member states being obliged to make the application of these rules viable: member states are obliged to reduce debts so as to make financial management according to economic criteria possible and to improve railway finances.[22] Any state aid granted to reduce these debts or to cover operation losses has to obtain authorisation from the Commission. Authorisation, as a necessary precondition, usually involves a subsidy linked to a restructuring programme that aims at increasing competitiveness. Compensation for social-service obligations and exceptional social costs such as early retirement schemes are still excluded from the state aid rules. Furthermore, infrastructure investments are legitimate as long as there is no distortion of competition (Commission, 1996, p. 18).

Another set of obligations aims at establishing the rules for a future transport services market. They determine the conditions for market access and the rules for market processes. The following obligations resulted from the Community legislation. First, since January 1993 access rights for railway enterprises have been granted, albeit in a very limited way and only for specific enterprises and for specific markets segments.[23] Furthermore, the conditions of access rights such as licensing, the allocation of infrastructure capacity, and charging for the infrastructure were specified, but only entered into force in June 1997.[24] Until now, co-operation agreements between railways to exploit the new rights to access in international passenger transport and in combined transport have been exempted from European competition rules by the Commission.

Closely connected with the previous measures is the separation of the rail infrastructure and rail-operation management. Here, only the separation of accounts is compulsory, and cross subsidies between the two areas are prohibited. Organisational separation (the creation of a subdivision for infrastructure within the organisation) or institutional separation (the creation of a different company for infrastructure management) are optional. This provision is believed to be necessary in order to increase the financial transparency and establish competition, since the financial separation of the network from the operation is a prerequisite for allowing the calculation of the infrastructure usage costs, which for its part is a precondition for other railway companies' access to the railway infrastructure. These four aspects of the CRP may be summarised into two different dimensions. The principle of granting managerial autonomy to former state railway companies and making contracts to govern the financial relation between the administration and the railways are part of the *organisational reform* of the railways;

the principle of separating the rail infrastructure from the operation of services and the introduction of rules for access are part of the *regulatory reform.*

The analysis of the European policy development shows that the new CRP is an ambitious policy that aims at fundamentally changing how the railways are organised in Europe. However, it is important to note that this policy has thus far only resulted in modest binding obligations. This observation is not only based on the fact that the CRP is largely implemented by directives, which according to the EC treaty only specify goals and grant member states leeway in implementation, but also on the fact that the regulatory reform dimension has not advanced very far either. The liberalisation of market access is restricted to 'groupings of railway enterprises to operate international services between the member states where the constituent enterprises are established and the right of the enterprises offering international combined transport to operate throughout the Community' (Commission, 1996, p. 15), and it only became binding in June 1997 (Commission, 1997b, p. 5). The Commission proposal to extend these access rights to all freight transport and to international passenger transport (Commission, 1995a, p. 19) had still not been accepted two years later (Commission, 1997a). The European Parliament therefore proposed to limit the next step to the liberalisation of rail-freight transport (Commission, 1999, p. 3). In the mean time, the Commission decided to liberalise access rights on a voluntary basis by proposing 'trans-European rail freeways for freight' (Commission, 1997b, pp. 7-8). The underlying idea is that member states would agree to certain rail corridors which all operators could access and where the use of the infrastructure would be simplified (for example, by simplifying access or using a transparent charging system). Consistent with the principle of keeping binding legal requirements to a minimum, it was decided that 'the definition of a Freeway and their subsequent implementation by member state railways must respect Community law. Nevertheless, Freeways will, *on a voluntary basis*, take a number of issues further than the requirements of Community law'(Commission, 1997b, p. 9; emphasis added).

Furthermore, the separation of the infrastructure and the operation has been limited to the area of accounting; it has not been extended to organisational separation. The Commission now believes that in order to safeguard the access to rail networks, the management of the infrastructure and of the provisions of services should be carried out by two different business units (Commission, 1996, p. 19). In its first amendment proposal of the core railway directive, 91/440, the Commission still refrained from turning the organisational separation of network management and the provision of services into a legally-binding requirement (Commission, 1995a, pp. 21-

23). Only after the European Parliament had endorsed this measure did the Commission muster up the courage to do so (Commission, 1999, pp. 2-3). The voluntary nature of the CRP is illustrated well by the fact that the single member states apply the rules in their national context in quite different ways and to different extents, without infringing Community law.

Conclusion: Pressure for National Transport Policies

The analysis of the recent progress in European transport policy development in this section was carried out with a specific purpose. Traditional analysis of European integration pursues questions concerning how the Community manages to acquire competencies in policy domains that were once primarily a national concern. This is not the fundamental concern here. In most of the policy areas that were formerly exclusively associated with nation-states, the EU has acquired some competency (Schmitter, 1996, pp. 11-13). The urgent question now seems to be how member states are influenced by this development. The natural starting point for investigating this influence is European policy making. It may be assumed that European policy making can influence national policies to a different degree, thus putting a limit to the range of available leeway at the national level. The analysis of the two transport sectors, road haulage and railways, has exposed the aims of the European transport policy and its constraints on the member states.

To summarise the results very briefly, in road haulage the main thrust was liberalisation, and therefore concerned with abolishing old rules. Now, member states no longer have the possibility to limit capacity and to set rates in international transport. Furthermore, it is no longer possible for them to exclude foreign hauliers from their domestic markets or to put a quantitative limit on how many enter. Less important in this context, qualitative market access rules and technical standards have been standardised throughout the Community. It is important to note that the regulation of domestic markets has not been touched by the European policy: member states may still employ quantitative market access regulation and price regulation in their domestic markets. If a tariff system is in place, it will also apply to any foreign hauliers operating in that specific territory.[25]

The CRP also aims to create a common market for railway transport services. Compared to road haulage, market building in this sector involves a much more constructive effort to create a market. Creating a new regulatory regime that determines the conditions of market access and the prices paid for railway infrastructure usage is a demanding job. The analysis has shown that so far the binding measures have been phased in slowly and that binding obligations have remained rather modest. In the area of railway policy it is important to note which areas are excluded. Although CRP seems to be closely linked to privatisation, there is no obligation to privatise the whole enterprise or any part of it. The only obligation is to ensure access to the railway network.

The analysis of the CTP has shown that transport has been firmly established on the European agenda. One of the central CTP concerns is building a common transport market in the sectors examined here: road haulage and railway policy. This expansion of the European policy agenda has several consequences for member states in general and for Italy in particular. Two types of consequences for national policy making may be distinguished.

First, the CTP may cause *implementation pressure*. Member states have to comply with legal obligations created by the European policy, for example, the rules regarding the qualitative criteria for market access in road haulage or the rules regarding non-discriminatory access to the railway network. If the national *status quo* does not conform with the European rules, compliance necessarily involves implementing these. If the *status quo* within a country already conforms with European rules, compliance is possible without changing national rules. Because the consequences of the CTP depend on the national *status quo*, the impact cannot be predicted from the European policy but is a result of the difference between the European and the national policy.

The second type of consequence of the CTP is more elusive than the first. The CTP's legal obligations omit some areas of transport policy; from a legal point of view these areas remain exclusively within the range of national competencies. For example, member states are free to decide if they want to retain the tariff system for road haulage operation on their territory. Or they may chose to preserve public ownership of their railways if they find ways to reconcile this with free access to the railway tracks. However, whenever national rules are *de facto* (not *de jure*) poorly compatible with the European rules, or not compatible at all, the CTP builds up *adaptation pressure*. The liberalisation of market access in the road and the rail sectors have generated adaptation pressure for rules which are beyond the formal reach of the CTP.

The *liberalisation of cabotage* in *road haulage* may stand in contradiction to the transport regulation *status quo* (Commission, 1997, pp. 41-43). Market access restrictions which exclude foreigners are in outright contradiction to this principle and would have to be abandoned. But this jeopardises other components of traditional transport regulation as well. If market access for foreigners is free, any quantitative access limit to national hauliers is discriminatory towards national hauliers. Foreigners could expand their capacity as they wish, nationals could not. Furthermore, national tariffs are also being called into question. Enforcement, already notoriously difficult within a closed market, is even more difficult with ready access to foreign hauliers. Since these are more difficult to control than tariffs designed for closed national markets,[26] there is a risk that they will be turned into a discriminating device. The liberalisation of cabotage would thus call all the major elements of the national market regulation into question.[27]

Liberalisation also calls the instruments of traditional market regulation into question and with it the way European nation-states manage transport in order to achieve economic and social goals. Liberalisation also affects the road-haulage tax regime. Road haulage is subject to taxes on gasoline, for example, and charges on road usage, which differ across countries. This raises the question concerning whether a liberalised market would be a level playing field., i.e. whether road-haulage firms are competing on the basis of efficiency of their services without being disadvantaged by a higher level of taxation than their counterparts. Liberalisation risks exposing road hauliers in Europe to unfair competition, leaving those that have a lower tax burden better off and not necessarily those that are more efficient (Kiriazidis, 1994, p. 15). Within the European policy process, an important question is: how much *harmonisation* is necessary to create a level playing field?

A simple solution to the regulation and taxation problems connected with the liberalisation of national regimes would be to replace the diverse regulations with a single coherent European system valid for all the countries throughout the Community. However, up till now this has proven to be politically impossible. Across the member states, different policy traditions exist - indeed different views on transport prevail - so that no agreement on such a coherent regime has been able to be reached. In the subsequent section it shall be shown, however, how an acceptable solution was found and what effect this had on the outcome of the compromise.

The pressures that it is possible for the CTP to exert on railways are more complex than in the case of road haulage. Since the beginning of the 1990s, the goal has been to create a common market for railway transport services as well. However, the point of departure is entirely different for rail transport. Throughout post-war history, with very few exceptions the road haulage sector has been structured like a market, although it has been highly regulated in many countries. The question therefore was how to merge national markets into a European market. Railways, by contrast, were organised as hierarchically-integrated single organisations in charge of maintaining their infrastructure and providing services. Therefore, the most pressing question for the CTP has not been market merging, but *market building*. This involves solving the intricate puzzle concerning how to organise competition between different operating companies on a single railway track. For the tightly-integrated railway system it has become just as common to assume an exclusive operator as to assume that roads would be used by many uncoordinated operators. The question is therefore: how can national and foreign companies access a network which was formerly reserved exclusively for one national operating company? However, once solutions to the technical problem of organising intramodal competition are found, the subsequent questions start to look similar to those that arise in road haulage. What type of market regulation is necessary to organise competition on a European scale? Which taxes and charges should be levied and by whom? What is an appropriate non-discriminatory price for the usage of the rail infrastructure? Is the level playing field distorted by subsidies that governments grant their railway companies, etc.?

To conclude, the CTP has created numerous adaptation pressures in the road and rail sectors. European liberalisation questions various aspects of national market regulations, taxes and subsidies. The rise of the CTP may be expected to have an impact on any national transport policy. Subsequently, the question is, if the rise of the CTP did influence the national transport policy in Italy, in which way and to what extent did the national policy react to this European influence? To answer this question it is necessary to analyse the national policy with respect to Europe in order to judge whether the national policy development shows traces of such influences. The two types of influence to be distinguished have been developed above. In the case of *implementation pressure*, one may encounter *implementation success* or *failure*. In the case of *adaptation pressure*, it is important to emphasise that the issue is not whether a member state performs according to its legal obligations, but rather, whether there is conformity between national and European rules. A national development increasing the conformity between national and European rules is an episode of *convergence*, whereas the opposite is *divergence*.[28] A third possibility, namely of a *neutral* development with respect to the European development, may be termed *persistence*. In the following sections I shall consider which pressures for implementation and adaptation have been created in Italy and which aspects of Italian policy development may be seen as a reaction to it.

Notes

[1]   Another important question is how the development of a European transport policy has been possible after such a long time of inertia. This would be in line with the focus on the European level of European integration research (Mutimer, 1994: 13). I want to take for granted that a CTP has been firmly established and has become consequential for na-

tional transport policies. The explanation of the European policy development is only of secondary importance.

2   For an overview with an Anglo-Saxon bias see Banister and Button (1991) and Button (1993), for a German perspective see van Suntum (1986) and Wolf (1992), and for an Italian view Santoro (1977) and Del Viscovo (1990).

3   The exaggerated concern with liberalisation is a standard criticism of EU transport policy (see Wolf, 1992; Whitelegg, 1988: 7; Weidenfeld, 1992: 16).

4   On the history of the CTP, see Santoro (1974), Erdmenger (1983), degli Abbati (1987), Button (1992), Kiriazidis (1994), McGowan (1994).

5   Some initial strategic mistakes by the Commission were less important: attempting a comprehensive liberalisation approach covering all modes of transport, it even managed to arouse the opposition of the most favourable proponent of liberalisation, the Dutch representatives. Because aspects of this approach were against their interest, too (Lindberg and Scheingold, 1970: 167). But even when the Commission switched to a more incremental and piecemeal approach to rally support, no real breakthrough was achieved.

6   For an overview of the development of the CTP in road haulage before its take off in the second half of the 1980s see Whitelegg (1988: chapter five).

7   The following is based on Young (1994), who conducted a large number of interviews with decision-makers on the European level shortly after the decision was made to liberalise the EU road-haulage markets.

8   No detailed analysis of the development of the CTP for railways yet exists. Therefore, the analysis will be more detailed than in the case of road haulage.

9   The risk of isolation may be illustrated by the fact that the positive opinion of the CER about the latest railway policy initiatives of the Commission is only opposed by France. This is more remarkable in the light of the fact that the CER usually does not launch an initiative if there is disagreement among its members (Interview Community of European Railways April 1996).

10 Since 1988 the Commission has justified its liberalisation directive with Art. 90 of the EC-Treaty thus implying that certain public monopolies infringe the EC treaty. A few month before the decision of the Council to adopt the railway reform, the ECJ confirmed the Commission strategy (Taylor, 1994: 322-326). The threat of Art. 90 liberalisation, however, did not seem to play a role in the decision to adopt the new railway policy.

11 To distinguish between transport operations among EU member-states from operations between member states non-member states, the term 'cross border transport' is used for the former, whereas 'international transport' is used for the latter. Thus the transport market between Italy and Germany, for example, is called cross-border, whereas the transport market between Italy and Switzerland is called international.

[12]   For the specification of these qualitative access criteria see Council Regulation 1992/881, Council Directive 1996/26, and an amendment proposal by the Commission (1997a).

[13]   The important topic of road pricing will not be dealt with in this study, because Italy already had its own system of motorway tolls in place. It was therefore not affected by the Eurovignette and its associated problems.

[14]   Compared to other modes of transport railways are tightly-coupled systems. They need a high degree of vertical co-ordination between infrastructure, traffic control and services and between different services (Baumgartner, 1993: 36-38). This is the reason why railway policy cannot easily distinguish between passenger and freight transport. The following discussion of European rail-freight transport development therefore has to be presented in the general context.

[15]   The Community's early railway policy may be summarised by three regulations concerning railways which date back to 1969 and 1970. Regulation 1969/1191 had the objective of reducing the public-service obligations of railways to improve the situation of the railways in intermodal competition. Regulation 1969/1192 was an attempt to render the financial relations of the state to the railways more transparent by making state-imposed compensation payments for public-service obligations mandatory and by prohibiting other types of financial aid which would distort intermodal competition. The circumstances under which state aid may be granted are specified in regulation 1970/1107. Other regulations regarding intermodal competition were more programmatic in character (Schmuck, 1992: 41).

[16]   The political viability of the new railway policy was enhanced in two ways: national railways find a growth strategy more attractive than downsizing their activities, and resistance on environmental grounds is much more difficult, because rail is environmentally friendlier than road transport.

[17]   This does not mean that member state discretion in implementation is negligible; on the contrary, Council Regulation 1991/440 explicitly calls upon the member states to adopt the legislation needed to implement the directive.

[18]   In principle the Commission's policy is to expose rather than protect railways from intermodal competition. In a proposal to the Council, the Commission proposed to prevent member states from denying access to international bus transport of passengers because it would seriously affect a comparable rail service (Commission, 1996: 15, FN7).

[19]   At the present stage of research whether the railways would be able to survive on a level playing field in intermodal competition seems to be an open question. First of all, infrastructure pricing is a problem. External costs are difficult to objectively calculate for both rail and road, and for railways even internal costs seem to be a hard task for transport economists (Dodgson, 1994: 239). But even if the presumptions of the pricing models are not contested and the prices for services could be estimated, uncertainty about the determinants of the choice of transport users would prevent a prediction about a possible future share of rail in the transport market.

[20] See Council Directives 1991/440, 1995/18 and 1995/19.

[21] The most important legal provision is Directive 1991/440.

[22] The railways' exemption from state aid, which was granted by the Regulation 1970/1107, was abolished, and the obligation of financial normalisation was introduced by Directive 91/440/EEC.

[23] Directive 1991/440 'has created the right of access for *groupings* of railway enterprises to operate *international* services between the Member states *where the constituent enterprises are established* and the right of enterprises offering *international combined transport* to operate throughout the Community' (Commission, 1996, p. 14, emphasis added).

[24] Council Directives 1995/18 and 1995/19.

[25] Council Regulation 1993/3118, Art. 6, for commentary see Gronemeyer (1994: 271).

[26] This may be due to language problems or the fact that foreigners are registered elsewhere and effective sanctioning depends on cooperation between different national authorities.

[27] This indirect effect is a common aspect of Community liberalisation policies. In the legal literature it is discussed under the label of 'reverse discrimination' (see e.g. Graser, 1998).

[28] The distinction between convergence and divergence is usually applied to comparisons of different units of the same hierarchical level, for example, specific national economic systems (Unger and van Waarden, 1995; Crouch and Streeck, 1997). In contrast to this usage, the distinction here applies to units on two hierarchically different levels: national and European transport policy. This allows us to distinguish the hierarchical relationships from the indirect influence, which is also important for national policy development.

3 Italian Transport Policy in the European Context

Italy promises to be an instructive case for the examination of the impact of Europe, since its transport policy tradition differs substantially from the European Common Transport Policy (CTP). The Italian approach relies on extensive public intervention that reduces or replaces the market mechanisms in this sector. It is therefore not compatible with the long term goal of the CTP to build a common market for transport services. The fundamental question of Italian policy developed out of this contradiction. Are we witnessing an instance of policy convergence, i.e. the introduction of policy instruments and policy goals that conform with Europe? Or is it rather divergence, i.e. defensive reactions to European policy initiatives which actually increase the difference between the ends and means of national and European transport policy?

In the case of Italy, the prospects for policy convergence seem to have improved considerably over the last decade or so for several reasons. One reason for this is an apparent favourable change in the national patterns of economic policy making in general, and in the transport sector in particular. For most of the post-war period, the Italian economy was characterised by a vast public sector (Anselmi, 1994, Sorace, 1994, pp. 784-89). State holdings such as the *Istituto per la ricostruzione industriale* (IRI), the *Ente nazionale per l'energia elettrica* (ENEL) and the *Ente nazionale idrocarburi* (ENI) dominated the industrial and the service sector. The transport sector was characterised by ubiquitous state intervention. The provision and operation of infrastructure such as roads, railroad terminals, ports, airports and the actual transport of passengers and freight in the various modes were all publicly controlled, being either owned or regulated by the state. Railways have been nationalised for most of the century. The crisis-ridden Italian air carrier, *Alitalia*, is also state-owned and heavily dependent on state subsidies. For most of the post war years, shipping to the Italian islands has been dominated by state enterprises such as *Tirrenia*. The promotion of *intermodal transport* via a network of railroad terminals offers a more recent example of the strong tendency of state interventionism. However, over the last ten years, there have been signs of a change in the intervention style in many areas of the economy, which may have improved the prospects for Europeanisation. Italy has also been affected by the world-wide movement towards privatisation and deregulation (Cassese, 1995; Macchiati, 1996; Cavazzuti, 1996; Bellini, 1996, chapter six). A long tradi-tion of interventionism by means of state ownership and detailed regulation is increasingly being undermined by the privatisation of public enterprises and the introduction of new rules for competition. In the transport sector this tendency was especially visible in the privatisation of the state-owned railways in 1993. In addition, *Alitalia's* monopoly as provider of air-transport services on the most important domestic routes was abolished in 1996. Furthermore, there are also projects to privatise the operating compa-nies of airports and air traffic. Similar signs of change in the style of intervention may be also seen in the area of shipping. Infrastructure opera-tions are being privatised as well. The port authorities, who formerly were in charge of providing the whole range of services in a port, now have to limit their activities to the task of long-term planning and controlling the services offered by private companies. The transport sector abounds with examples of privatisation and deregulation. A change in the intellectual debate concerning the role of state intervention in the economy mirrors this development (e.g. Reviglio, 1994, Necci and Normann, 1994, Sylos-Labini, 1995). However, it is still doubtful if the present redefinition of the Italian 'economic constitution' (Cassese, 1995) translates into a 'neo-liberal turn' (Jobert, 1994). An adequate evaluation of the changes made will entail a detailed examination of the changes in the relationship between the state and the different sub-sectors of transport. Until this is carried out, it would be hurried to interpret these developments as having already accomplished policy convergence with European policies. However, they do seem to offer the basic prerequisites for the effective influence of European poli-cies.

There is an improved prospect for policy convergence if two addi-tional factors which contribute to the influence of European policies are taken into account. First, it has often been observed that the EU has been extraordinarily successful in the area of market liberalisation. The Single-Market Programme launched in the mid-1980s is generally believed to be a success story. In this area, once the centre of policy formulation shifts to the European level, it is likely to bring about policy convergence and even the structural adjustment of the political system (Mény et al., 1996). As has been shown above, the CTP closely follows the principles of the Single Market Programme. Therefore, it may be expected to be a success, too. A second factor that is likely to increase the influence of European policies in Italy is the logic of Italian Community membership. In the past the Com-munity has characteristically been used to externally justify internal policy changes (e.g. Dyson and Featherstone, 1996). Since there is a wide consensus on the necessity for reform in both of the transport sectors examined here, European policy may be seen as supplying a welcome solution to a national problem.

If it is correct to assume that the prospects for the convergence of Italian transport policy have improved, the results of the empirical investigation presented here are puzzling. The two case studies show that in Italy, despite improved preconditions, the dynamics of national policies for road haulage and railways are largely characterised by inertia. Decision making in the last decade has remained traditional. On the whole, Italian transport policy in the sector of road and rail has been 'going through the motions'. Old routines dominate, although dissatisfaction is widespread indeed.[1] How has this been possible in spite of the advent of the CTP? Any current successful steps in sectoral reforms which might mark the start of policy convergence, nevertheless pose the question: why has the reaction to European policy come about so late? Since European and national developments seem to be only loosely coupled, in subsequent chapters the mechanism through which the Europe influences the national level will be investigated.

Road Haulage

Italy was not well prepared for a single road haulage market. As the declining share in the international transport market has shown, Italian hauliers were not ready for competition with their Community rivals (Ministero dei Trasporti, 1992, p. 16). Furthermore, the administration of the road-haulage sector had always been heavily biased towards interventionism. The established regulatory framework, with its strict control of market access and fixed prices for transport services, was not well adapted to accommodate intra-European competition.

The Community reform project was thus a formidable challenge to Italy. Transport enterprises would have to devise strategies to adapt to the new competitive situation. The challenge, however, was also political. The liberalisation of road haulage presented a unique opportunity for Italy to reform the administration of the sector which, even according to reports of the Ministry of Transport, never achieved its major sectoral goals of balancing the modal split and preventing cut-throat competition among hauliers. An adaptation to the rules of the common road-haulage market could have been accompanied by measures to improve the low productivity of the road-haulage industry. Surprisingly, Italy did not react to road haulage liberalisation in this way. Instead of introducing widespread regulatory reform like countries in a comparable situation such as France and Germany, Italy opted for regulatory inertia; and instead of adopting an effective industrial policy like the Netherlands, the Italian government opted for fiscal benefits which were not even designed to improve the productivity of the sector. As a result, an ever-widening gap now exists between the Italian road haulage policy and the European CTP. How did it happen? Why is Italian road haulage policy still drifting away from Europe despite the European effort to establish a CTP? The following sections will offer an explanation for this phenomenon by identifying the factors which contributed to policy inertia on the national and the European level. At the national level, a low state capacity, due to fragmentation and the structure of the interest mediation favouring anti-liberal forces, contributed to institutional stability. The European influence, on the other hand, has not yet contributed to convergence and has even had the effect of increasing the divergence between national and Community road-haulage policy.

A Decade of Road-Haulage Policy

The following paragraphs will show that the development of regulation and fiscal instruments led to a continual increase in state intervention, with protectionist tendencies increasingly eclipsing market co-ordination within the road-haulage sector. This line of development is surprising, because state intervention steadily increased despite perpetual regulatory failure[2] and despite the ambitions of the CTP. In the subsequent chapters an explanation for this is offered.

Regulation The history of road-haulage regulation in Italy started in 1935. Two instruments to control market processes were provided (Fontanella, 1974, p. 138). Qualitative standards for market access were defined. A firm that wanted to offer transport services had to prove technical and financial soundness and personal reliability. Furthermore, a licensing procedure was introduced that permitted the administration to control the number of vehicles circulating and thus the transport capacity of road haulage. By the 1960s it had become clear that the market was not under effective control. A liberal company policy of granting licences and strategies to overcome access restrictions led to cut-throat competition (Santoro, 1974, p. 212). Subsequently, in 1974 regulatory reform in the road-haulage sector was introduced, significantly shifting the regulatory framework towards increased interventionism.[3] The major change in the range of instruments was provided by the introduction of a system of compulsory bracket tariffs, which fixed the maximum and minimum prices for transport services.[4] The determination of the price due according to the tables of this tariff system has turned out to be so complicated that most of the transport users employ a simplified version of their own to arrive at a price which they propose to the haulier (Interview CONFINDUSTRIA, May 1996).

No less than nine years elapsed from the time the decision was made to introduce the tariff system in 1974 to its actual implementation in January of 1983. In this period a substitute to the bracket tariffs evolved for certain types of goods such as cement, petroleum products, liquid chemicals, containers and vehicles (Cozzi and Govoni, 1989; Interview ANITA, March 1996). These were called 'collective economic agreements' (*accordi economici collettivi*), which – unlike the rates of the compulsory tariff system – were influenced by shippers as well as by hauliers. These agreements were within the framework of the law, 298/1974, and in 1983 they were formally recognised as legitimate exemptions from the tariff system. Each of them is an arena for negotiating the rates with the transport industry. Their significance lies in the fact that they favour the hauliers in their struggle with the transport using industry.[5] These arenas are not completely independent from one another; instead, they inter-link. The result of the collective agreements is also relevant for the general compulsory tariffs.[6] The determination of the prices is thus a result of a multitude of different negotiation systems which offer opportunities for the interest groups involved to show their usefulness. They indicate a strong politicisation of the sector, leaving little room for market co-ordination of activities.

The reform was only moderately successful in controlling prices in the road-haulage market, although the instruments were employed in quite a harsh and rigid way. By 1985 market access had become very difficult because the Ministry of Transport decided to freeze the transport capacity at its then present state. It did not issue any new licences. Therefore new enterprises could only access the market by buying a licence from a firm which was leaving the market.[7] Market access was further hampered by the new EC regulation of qualitative access criteria. From the beginning, the tariff system suffered from a lack of compliance. Most of the time prices for transport services were well below the lower limit of the tariff system. The legal sanctions that were provided for this kind of infringement did not change the situation, because it was too difficult to detect fraud. In 1993 an attempt was made to enforce compliance with two measures (law 162/1993). The range of validity for the tariffs was extended to include contracts which contained other services apart from transport. Furthermore, a possibility was created for the road haulier to claim a potential difference between the price that was set in the contract and the minimum of the tariff bracket, should it be lower.[8] In the aftermath of the regulatory revision of 1993, the role of market processes became less and less important in the control of transport operations. To sum up, the regulatory reform of 1974 and its subsequent amendments led to a sharp rise in regulatory intervention.

The introduction of the compulsory bracket tariff system was the main reason for an avalanche of detailed regulation.

Fiscal Measures To decide if the development of road-haulage taxation has led to convergence with the reform model of the EU, a different criterion is needed than the one used to evaluate regulation, i.e. evaluating whether there has been an increase or decrease in state intervention is not a sufficient criterion. Taxation and charges are better adapted to the situation of a liberalised Community market when they are levied according to the principle of territoriality rather than of nationality (Rommerskirchen, 1985, pp. 217-218). The principle of territoriality implies that road hauliers are subject to the taxes and charges of the state in which transport takes place, whereas the principle of nationality implies that hauliers contribute to the revenue in their country of registration. To give an example, roads in Germany are mainly financed through vehicle taxes which only apply to vehicles registered in Germany. The principle of nationality implies that foreign road users do not contribute to financing the infrastructure. Other countries such as France and Italy have a system of motorway tolls, which allows the application of the principle of territoriality. Motorway-users are charged irrespective of their nationality. The viability of a common market for road haulage increases with the shift to the principle of territoriality because this decreases the distorted competition between hauliers of different nationalities.

When the first consequential Commission proposal to establish a single market for road haulage was made in 1986, the Italian system of taxation and charges was already quite well adapted to liberalisation. This was because the major taxes and charges were levied according to the principle of territoriality. Motorway tolls had been introduced when the first motorways were built. Furthermore, taxes which arise under the principle of nationality, e.g. mainly taxes for the acquisition and ownership of vehicles, were low in comparison with taxes on petroleum products. Table 3.1 shows the salience of the principle of territoriality in the Italian system of taxes and charges. Market entry, registration and ownership add up to one quarter of the revenue, operation comprised the last three quarters.[9] The comparison between 1983 and 1994 shows that there was a further minor shift to the principle of territoriality, since the share of the operation increased slightly from 75.75% to 77.35%, whereas the taxes and charges for market entry – vehicle registration and ownership – were all roughly reduced by half.

Table 3.1   **Distribution of Tax Revenue in Road Transport**

Principle	activity	1983	1994
Nationality	Market entry	16.6%	8.5%
	Registration	0.4%	1%
	Ownership	7.3%	13.1%
Territoriality	Operation*	75.7%	77.4%

* operation includes taxes on fuel, lubricants, and road user charges; road user charges as such are excluded

Source: Centro Europa Ricerche, 1995.

To sum up, the general system of taxation was compatible with the EU policy from the start of the reform process in the mid-1980s. The minor changes that were introduced confirmed the principle of territoriality. The structure and development of road-haulage taxation differs from that of regulation. Contrary to the latter, there has been no divergence from the reform project of the EC, but on the contrary, a minor convergence.[10]

This system of taxation is modified by another fiscal instrument that is employed in Italy. Since 1990 *tax credits* have been granted to professional road hauliers. From 1990 to 1994 a yearly budget ranging from 422 to 725 thousand million lire was provided for the purpose of compensating for fuel taxes on the road hauliers.[11] Road hauliers who wanted to benefit from this scheme had to calculate their expenditure on fuel and lubricants for each of their vehicles. A benefit was granted as a certain percentage of that expenditure, which they could deduct from other taxes, namely, income tax, municipal tax or VAT. This tax credit scheme was the object of repeated intervention by the Commission and led to the initiation of an infringement procedure at the European Court of Justice in 1995. Because it has discriminatory consequences for non-Italian hauliers of the Community, the European Commission considers the tax-credit scheme to be illegal state aid (Commission Decision 9.06.1993).[12] Despite this intervention, the practice was continued in 1996 as a modified scheme (Decree-law 20.02.1996; Il Sole 24 Ore 20.02.1996). The introduction of the tax-credit scheme is the most extreme case of divergence from the European model. As opposed to the regulatory framework, the tax-credit scheme is thought to infringe on Community law.

Fiscal instruments have also been employed for the purposes of industrial policy. A first attempt to improve the economic structure of the transport sector was made in 1980. The Government provided a contribution to small hauliers for the purchase of new vehicles. Since these measures were contested by the Commission, payments were stopped and a new law was introduced to more closely link payments to hauliers to their efforts to restructure their firms (law 404/1985; Interview Ministero dei Trasporti, January 1996, No 2). This law which was replaced by a more ambitious project in 1992 (law 68/1992), offered financial aid to encourage mergers, consortia and co-operatives; it favoured the introduction of electronic data processing, and encouraged enterprises with only one vehicle to leave the market (Stornelli and Battistoni, 1994, pp. 61-79). Although the law contained detailed procedural provisions, it was never applied, because of the Commission's doubts that the incentives for retirement could reduce the market capacity (Interview Ministero dei Trasporti, January 1996, No 2; Interview CONFCOOPERATIVE, February 1996). The contentious procedure initiated by the Commission, which led to a recent ultimatum, seems to offer strong evidence of a further element of divergence. [13] However, EC state-aid rules allow subsidies as long as they are not provided in order to assist operations, but are part of a credible effort to restructure an industry or to further regional cohesion (Bellamy and Child, 1993, p. 926; Interview Commission, DGVII, April 1996). Unlike the Italian tax-credit scheme, which was not tied to any obligations for the profiting enterprises, the measures to restructure the sector are not contrary to the treaty *per se*. [14] Considering this, the attempt to restructure the sector is a rather minor divergence from the CTP.

Viewed separately, the instruments of Italian transport policy differ to the extent that they diverge from the CTP. Divergence is low in the case of industrial policy, medium in the case of regulation, and high in the case of the tax credit scheme. [15] However, this conclusion does not take into consideration that the various instruments are employed at the same time and correspondingly influence each other. If they are seen as components of a system of governance, then the policy is thought to be *protectionist, in the interest of the hauliers and against the interest of the collectivity* (Munari, 1994, p. 904). This is so for two reasons: first, the fact that the official tariff minimum is always well above the market price is an incentive for new hauliers to enter the market and a strong disincentive to leave the market (907f.); second, the tax-credit scheme increases the revenue for hauliers irrespective of the market and thus acts in the same way as the mandatory tariffs. The fate of the industrial policy confirms that protectionism has a negative effect on road-haulage policy. It failed not only because of the resistance of the Commission, but also because hauliers simply did not take advantage of the benefits supplied to firms which intended to merge (Interview Ministero dei Trasporti, January 1996, No 2). There is a strong reason to believe that the government contributed to the lack of the sense of urgency amongst hauliers by sheltering them from national and international competition. If this view is correct, then the verdict for protectionism may well be the same verdict that will be reached for a whole range of instruments that aim to govern the road-haulage sector in Italy.

More recent policy developments seem to contradict the general trend towards increasing protectionism which have been identified so far. By the beginning of 1998, the fundamental parameters of Italian road-haulage administration had been called into question. Already in 1997 the Government had announced that future *subsidies* to the sector would not be issued by *ad hoc* decrees but only within the framework of the yearly financial law. Furthermore, it stressed that these would only be issued in accordance with EC-law. By the beginning of 1998 these announcements had become true: the financial law had reserved 1.8 Billion for the sector over the next three years, approximately the average that had been issued in each of the previous years. Furthermore, the laws determining the mode in which these were to be issued was closely co-ordinated with the European Commission. Second, negotiations started between the government and the interested parties concerning the reform of the *tariff system* and the function of the *national register of professional road hauliers*. Finally, in February 1998 the Council of Ministers approved a legislative decree regarding market access in the road haulage sector.[16] All the enterprises that already held a licence could immediately double their transport capacity. Complete abolition of quantitative market access restrictions was planned for 1 January 2000 (Il Sole 24 Ore, 7.02.1998, p. 12). Given the history of Italian road haulage, these developments have surprised participant and non-participant observers. The government abolished the practice of *ad hoc* subsidisation, which it had initiated in 1990. The liberalisation of market access is most remarkable, since this is the true cornerstone of any protectionist market order. To recall the previous stand of things: since 1985 no new licences had been issued on a regular basis; and since the mid-1980s the administration had decided to hold the transport capacity of the market constant. Given the general trend to increase demand, this was harsh intervention.

At the time it seemed that the governmental reform efforts introduced in 1998 promised a watershed year in Italian transport policy. However, with hindsight, change was not as far reaching as could have been expected. Road-haulage *subsidies* are now co-ordinated with the EU so that they stand the test of Community law (Il Sole 24 Ore, 27.05.1999). Whereas the Commission condemned the financial support handed out from 1990 to 1994 for contradicting Community law, it officially approved of the later scheme[17] after some adaptations had been made (Commission 2000).[18] Still, the allocation of the funds primarily serves to reduce the high operating costs of Italian hauliers (Il Sole 24 Ore, 24.05. 1999; La Repubblica, 21.06.2000). Thus, legal changes in the wake of European law have not substantially changed the character of road-haulage subsidies. More importantly, the initiated process of liberalisation has not made any substantial progress. The compulsory bracket tariffs have not been abolished, so transport users have recently reiterated their demands for its abolition (Confindustria, 1999, p. 84). In case bracket tariffs are abolished, it is more likely that they will be replaced by an alternative tariff system rather than complete liberalisation (Il Sole 24 Ore, 22.04.1999). Finally, and most importantly, the national licence regime has not been liberalised, except that it now allows existing firms to double their capacity. The legislative and ministerial activity has been restricted to specifying the technicalities of this operation.[19] The decisive step towards liberalisation still has to be taken. Since the one-time measure to increase transport capacity only benefits incumbent firms, it does not contribute to a true liberalisation of the sector. Thus, it can be concluded that the traditional path of Italian road haulage, i.e. of increasing protectionism, has not yet been interrupted. A more incisive future reform is necessary to bring about such a change.

The result of the development of the road-haulage regime stands in stark contrast to the developments in other member states of the EU. The U.K. abolished market-access regulation and tariffs in 1968 (Knill, forthcoming). Even countries closer to the Continental-European tradition have given up market interventionism: Germany in 1994, and France as early as 1987 (Kerwer and Teutsch, forthcoming). In the Netherlands market liberalisation was accompanied by an industrial policy that genuinely aimed at boosting the competitiveness of the sector (Lehmkuhl, forthcoming). Thus convergence towards the liberal EU model is widespread. Given this, another question arises: why did the Italian policy develop along a path which steadily increased the divergence between the national practices and the Community model? This question shall be dealt with in the subsequent chapters. Before an explanation is offered, however, I shall present the railway policy.

Refusing the European 'Railway Ragout'

The European influence on Italian railway policy is more complex than in the previously-analysed road-haulage sector. In Italy the European Common Railway Policy (CRP) encountered national railway reform that had already started in 1985. An analysis of the impact of this previous reform effort raises questions about their relationship. In the first section we ask whether the national reform contradicted the goals of the European reform or whether they had a common strategy and common goals. The analysis will show that during the last decade a difference between the two policies has existed and that this difference has not been substantially reduced. European policy has not caused policy convergence with regard to its most fundamental concern: the introduction of competition between different railway companies within and between member states. In Italy the organisational fragmentation of the railways implied by this policy has been called 'railway ragout' and has been rejected by the trade unions and the railway management. Once again, as in the case of road haulage, government and administration have been too weak to overcome these well-entrenched interest groups.

Italian and European Railway Reform Projects Compared

At a first superficial glance, the Italian railway policy seems entirely different from the policy in the road-haulage sector. The Italian railway reform project seems to have undergone the spontaneous convergence of national and European policy. In contrast to road haulage, the railway sector in Italy seems to be characterised by political reform rather than policy inertia. However, important differences remain, so the question of policy convergence is once again posed.

Recent reforms aim to significantly diverge from the way railways have been run in Italy for most of the century (Ministero dei Trasporti, 1996, pp. 27-30). In 1905 the three main private railway companies were nationalised and moulded into the *Ferrovie dello Stato* (FS). Ever since, the railways have been a part of the public administration, and it has been left to the state to develop and maintain the railroads, and run the trains. In the post-war period, mainly as a reaction to the increasing financial difficulties, the legal status of the state railways has been changed several times. These reforms have been concerned with the problem regarding how much of autonomy the state railways ought to have.[20] The general tendency was to increase the railways' autonomy from the Ministry of Transport. This process has accelerated since the beginning of the 1980s. In 1985 the FS acquired the status of '*ente pubblico economico*' and was thus granted new management competencies. In 1993 the state railways were privatised. Although the public administration is still the sole owner, the railways now have the status of a joint-stock company. After almost 90 years, railways in Italy are now no longer part of the public administration.

On a formal institutional level, the change in the legal status of the railways has had two types of consequences for railway administration. Firstly, *hierarchical co-ordination* has been abolished. Management and administration competencies have been re-specified to increase the decision-making powers of the management and to limit the public administration (the Ministry of Transport and the Treasury) to a merely supervisory role. Secondly, hierarchical co-ordination has been replaced by *contractual co-ordination*. Within the general framework of an 'act of concession' which gives the FS exclusive rights to run the railways, two contracts define mutual rights and obligations for a shorter time period. The 'programme contract' defines investments in the rail infrastructure and in rolling stock. The 'service contract' defines the services that have to be provided by the railways.[21]

The analysis of the legal development leads to the conclusion that the reform efforts of the last decade gradually reversed the nationalisation process that had occurred at the beginning of the century. Signs of economic dynamism in the railway sector give a stronger impression that political reform is significant. On several occasions the FS has modified its organisational structure to boost its performance. Some measures were adopted to promote the freight transport unit, which is generally believed to be among the biggest problems of the FS. These have been supplemented by initiatives in the area of intermodal transport. Finally, the most visible sign of progress is the development of the high-speed railways.[22] The FS has initiated the development of new trains, and have begun upgrading the infrastructure to form a high-speed rail network. These elements of economic dynamism are most visibly reflected in the new organisational structure of the railways. Whereas the activities of the railways were integrated into a single organisation before the legal privatisation of 1992, the FS now has become a holding which consists of over a hundred separate firms active in diverse operations in transport, tourism and more.

The analysis so far has shown that reform has been attempted in the railway sector. However, the reform was entirely focused on the organisational dimension. The redefinition of the relationship between the state and the railway and the internal re-structuring were attempts to improve performance. In contrast to the Italian railway reform, the CRP moves a decisive step beyond that. If there is a core idea that characterises the CRP, it is the idea that railways are to be reformed by introducing intramodal competition.[23] Intramodal competition is a radical idea, since it contradicts the widely-accepted belief that – for technical and economic reasons – railways are natural monopolies, i.e. sectors which by their basic characteristics cannot be organised as competitive markets, and which are in need of protection from the competition from other modes of transport, especially road transport. As has been pointed out above, the aim of intramodal competition is pursued by organisational changes and the establishment of market rules. Therefore, if it is correct that the Italian railway reform revolves around the question of how to reconcile autonomy with institutional control, then the Italian reform does not simply have the same aims as the

CRP, or stand in contradiction to it; instead, it is a subset of the CRP. One important precondition for the market-making ambitions of the European policy is that the relationship between the administration and the railways be newly defined. In the area of organisational reform, mutual reinforcement of the two reform programmes makes progress on the national level more likely. However, the market-making ambitions of the CRP do not have a counterpart at the national level. Here, success depends on the implementation of the Community obligations. In the following section, the organisational reform and, then, the progress thus far made towards a market will be analysed in more detail in order to find out if the national policy has converged with the European policy.

The Impact of the Railway Reforms on Italy

The comparison of the European and the Italian reform programmes leads to the expectation that the different components of the European policy will have different sorts of impacts. In the area of organisational autonomy, policy congruence already exists. The question here is if the two policies are implemented in such a way that the governance of the railways changes. Although this seems rather likely because mutual reinforcement of the European and the national policy may be expected, the contrary is true: the market-building ambitions of the CRP are not supplemented by a national policy. The question in this area is whether policy convergence comes about and national policy-makers embrace these goals as well, or whether the European impact remains restricted to formally transposing the European directives. Should the former be true, the common railway policy is likely to induce more changes than if the latter is true. The first of the following sections will be dedicated to an analysis of the impact of European policy on the organisational autonomy. This will be a study of implementation of congruent intentions. The second section will deal with the consequences of European policies for market-building in the railway sector. Here, the analysis of the implementation of the European programme is supplemented by the question of whether policy convergence will take place.

Organisational Autonomy

Various aspects of organisational autonomy have been a concern of both the European and the Italian reform projects. My contention is that despite policy congruence in this area, the administrative practices have not changed significantly from the outset of the reform. Two facts make this especially clear: for one, the management is no more independent than at the outset; for another, the financial relations have only been re-defined in a superficial manner.

The railway reform of 1985 was the first attempt to enhance the decision-making power by redefining the organisational structure and the competencies of the railway management (Correale, 1989, p. 2). However, these reforms did not change old decision-making routines. The fact that the reform has remained symbolic can be illustrated in an important area of decision making; namely the determination of the price of railway fares. Traditionally, in contrast to private firms, the FS did not enjoy the right to freely determine the price of its services. For passenger transport they had to adhere to *compulsory tariffs*, fixed by the administration (Di Miceli, 1985).[24] Before the reform of 1985 the criteria by which they were calculated, the decision-making procedure by which they were fixed, and the general policy pursued, all enshrined a low degree of managerial independence in this area. The only opportunity to freely set prices was - and is to this day - limited to the freight transport sector. The 1985 railway reform did introduce some changes which significantly increased the complexity of the tariff system but they did not lead to managerial autonomy, as required by the Community and the national law (Di Miceli, 1985, p. 360). The new procedure for determining tariffs foresees the introduction of an 'economic tariff' by the railways, which would cover the costs of the service provided. However, compensation for lower 'political tariffs' was no obligation. Furthermore, for political reasons the new procedure did not lead to any change in the actual policy of modestly increasing tariffs. This is still the case at the time of writing. Often, even the increases agreed upon in the service contract have not been given (Il Sole 24 Ore, 3.09.1996, p. 13). A recent reform proposal does not include an increase of decision-making autonomy in this area (Interview Ferrovie dello Stato, March 1997).

A second dimension of the railway reform concerns the redefinition of financial relations between the state and the railway. In the past, in most European railways this relationship was structured in a mutually unsatisfactory way. The railway management was obliged to make decisions that were not justifiable from an economic point of view, such as procuring goods or services from specific national industries and maintaining unprofitable lines, without any clear compensations. The government had to finance ever increasing losses. The problem is that this arrangement blurs financial responsibility. It is not possible to know if a loss is caused by the low productivity of the railways or if it is caused by political interference. In an attempt to solve this problem, Italy, like many other European countries, introduced contracts to regulate the relationship between the administration and the railway management, the hope being that this would increase financial transparency (Amati, 1991, p. 232). According to the first contract of this kind, the intention was to restructure the railways and make them economically viable. Tariffs were to be raised to a level that would cover the costs and the compensation paid for any unprofitable social services offered, such as building maintenance and the operation of unprofitable lines. The long term objective was to reduce state transfer payments to the amount of the public-service obligations.

These contracts only represent a very modest move towards the increased financial transparency and responsibility envisaged by the CRP (Pezzoli, 1995, p. 226). They only remove the former system of indiscriminate cross subsidies between infrastructure financing, on the one hand, and the operation of services, on the other. However, they did not effectively enhance profit-making considerations because the contracts did not provide the FS with any form of sanction for negative business results. This made it possible for the FS to increase its investments in recent years (especially to develop its high-speed railways) in spite of its impressive debts (Mondo Economico, 29.04.1996, pp. 86-88). Furthermore, the contracts do not prevent interference in the economic decision making of the railways. The Italian Parliament stipulated that its approval of a contract would be dependent on a long list of detailed amendments, mostly concerning the maintenance, but in part even the construction of unprofitable lines that are only of regional importance (Corte dei Conti, 1996, pp. 44-47). This clientelistic intervention on behalf of the Italian parliament ran counter to the objective of contractualising the relationship between the administration and the railways (Corte dei Conti, 1996, pp. 48-49).

Given the modest results concerning management autonomy and contractualisation, it seems safe to conclude that, despite the congruence of national and Community reform, they did not achieve the organisational autonomy that they were aiming at. The following section will show that this also holds true for the more radical market-building goal of the Community policy.

Market-making

Transforming a country's rail system from one dominated by a monopoly to one following market principles requires that any European railway enterprise be granted access to any railway network in Europe. As with other network utilities such as telecommunications and energy, in the case of railways the liberalisation of network access is also pursued in two steps. First, the CRP prescribes that infrastructure management should be separated from the provision of services. This aims to prevent the former monopolies from discriminating against new competitors by erecting obstacles to network access. Second, the conditions for market access and market operation have to be specified. Under what conditions may a new company gain network access, and how may it provide its railway services?

Building a European Market for Railway Services? In Italy, the separation of infrastructure management and operation management has been implemented merely by organisational reform. After the conversion of the FS into a joint-stock company, infrastructure management and operation management were assigned to two separate divisions within a common holding.[25] Further steps towards separation have not yet been taken. The division managing the infrastructure (*area rete*) does not yet charge the division supplying the service (*area trasporto*) for its use of the railway network.[26] Compensation is paid according to estimations (Interview Ferrovie dello Stato, Area rete, February 1997). A system of cost calculation is in an experimental stage, but has not yet been implemented in the FS. It will take at least a few years to completely separate the accounts for the railway network and those for the provision of services (Il Sole 24 Ore, 15.03.1997, p. 9).

The other element of the CRP, the implementation of market regulation, is even less developed. In Italy, during most of the 1990s it was not possible for an enterprise other than the FS to access the railway network. According to European rules, a hypothetical enterprise planning to offer railway services in a member state would have to take a series of steps to gain access to the market. Italy has been particularly slow in introducing the necessary prerequisites (Communauté des Chemins de Fer Européenes (1995), 75-77; Interview Ferrovie dello Stato, Area rete, February 1997). A new enterprise, independent of the FS, wanting to offer railway services would not be able to get a licence that would certify that its rolling stock, the qualification of its personnel, and its security standards were up to the required level. Furthermore, it could not buy railway line capacity, or gain access to installations such as depots. After considerable delay all the Community directives were only transposed.[27] Furthermore, a national legal barrier to competition has been abolished. The exclusive right to deliver railway services formerly granted to the FS is about to be replaced by a legal regime which can accommodate a plurality of service providers.[28] However, it is still not clear whether formal transposition will actually introduce market principles.

The backwardness in relation to European developments is mainly to be attributed to a lack of initiative on the part of the management and political supervision, rather than to technical problems. A system of cost calculation for train paths was developed after the first railway reform in 1985 at a stage when this had not been discussed at the European level (Interview Ferrovie dello Stato, Area rete, February 1997). A further sign of reluctance may be seen in the fact that no independent authority has yet been established to distribute infrastructure capacity. Thus, the probability of finding a balanced treatment for this problem is reduced. Instead, the railway still claims to be a co-ordinator, not just an operator (Beltrami, 1995, p. 11).

The prospects for intramodal competition in the near future are not clear. One cannot consider the independent railways that are mainly engaged in local passenger transport to be potential competitors of the FS. Their economic condition is so precarious and their management capabilities so low that since 1997 they have been assigned to the FS for a three-years period of organisational reform (Il Sole 24 Ore 29.09.1996). Even the most successful of these, the *Ferrovie Nord Milano*, will not be able to be considered a possible competitor in the near future (Interview Ferrovie dello Stato, Area rete, February 1997).[29] However, the policy-community in Italy considers the advent of intramodal competition in the near future a very likely scenario. Competitive pressure is expected to be highest in long- and medium-distance passenger transport and in freight transport (Spirito, 1995, p. 34). Frequently cited examples of the genesis of a market in freight transport are, first of all, a US company's access to the market in Great Britain, where it now offers rail transport services and, secondly, two consortia that plan to offer intermodal transport services to and from the ports of Northern Europe, especially Rotterdam (Spirito, 1996, p. 4; Interview Italcontainer, March 1997, Interview Ferrovie dello Stato, Area Rete, February 1997). An airline company's interest in investing in an operator in the passenger sector is considered to be one of the first, modest signs of the establishment of new operators in that sector is. One group argues that the advent of a market is inevitable and urges an active rather than a passive strategy (e.g. Spirito, 1996, p. 5). Others think that the development is still dependent on the way the European reform is implemented: especially it is thought to be dependent upon whether the French model, excluding competition, prevails or whether the British model, allowing for a wide margin of competition, dominates (Beltrami, 1995, p. 9).

The analysis of the two dimensions of the CRP - i.e. organisational autonomy and market-building - leads to the conclusion that although some progress on the formal level has been made in both cases, real changes in decision-making routines have been modest. The tendency for reform to remain symbolic is most evident in the case of the contractual relationship between rail and administration. From a legal point of view this entails a fundamental change because it replaces a hierarchical structure with a contract between equal subjects. However, the analysis above has shown that in actual fact, decision-making routines have not changed fundamentally but have been accommodated by the new structure.

So far, this analysis has not distinguished between the activities of passenger and freight transport. Yet it is important to do so because there is reason to believe that the lack of any progress towards the CRP may mainly be due to difficulties in passenger transport. In this area, public intervention to keep tariffs low and to keep unprofitable lines operational is justified by arguing that the railways are a 'public service'. For freight transport, however, these types of considerations are irrelevant. Although transport is a vital infrastructure for the economy, the customers of freight transport services are firms, not individuals. The CRP thus has a greater probability for success in the area of freight transport, and – as would be expected – European liberalisation has also advanced further in the area of freight transport than in the area of passenger services. Rail freight may be considered a crucial case: if the freight transport industry does not develop into a market there is little chance that passenger transport will. The following section will be dedicated to an analysis of the reform of the FS's rail-freight activities.

Reforming Rail Freight: Towards a Competitive Market? Shortly after the first reform of the FS, at the beginning of 1986, a major reform of its freight activities was undertaken. In this period freight transport experienced great difficulties all over Europe, but in Italy the problems were especially severe. Although geographically Italy is a favourable country for rail transport[30] and a rather extensive and well-developed infrastructure exists,[31] its share of the freight transported is well below the European average.[32] Railways in Italy offered a type of service that did not meet the market's demand. Rail freight was of poor quality. For example, no timetable for freight trains existed. Therefore it was impossible to know exactly when the goods would arrive.[33] The aim of the reform was to remedy this situation. The underlying belief was that the FS should not just offer rail-freight transport, it should also become a link in a chain of *intermodal transport* (Interview Italcontainer, March 1997; Pinna, 1997; Ferretti, 1996, pp. 375-76). In Italy this idea made sense because of the barrier presented by the Alps, which apart from being a natural barrier are also a formidable political barrier since both Switzerland and Austria have adopted measures to curb road transit through their territories.

To re-launch the freight sector of the railways, a strategy was developed which was called *'societarizzazione'*; this involved changing a formerly homogeneous organisation into an organisational network. This strategy was implemented in two different ways. The first was to organisationally separate freight-transport activities from passenger transport; and the second was to look for strategic alliances in other modes of transport to facilitate intermodal co-ordination (Eurolog, 1996, p. 1). The organisational separation of freight from passenger transport was believed to be an important precondition for ending the discrimination between freight and passenger transport. There is a long list of disadvantages for freight in the Italian railways (Interview Italcontainer, March 1997; Gelosi, 1995, pp. 23-24): when a freight timetable was finally established, freight was still subordinate to passenger transport. Furthermore, investment in freight-specific infrastructure and rolling stock was only considered after passenger transport. For example, the Italian High-Speed Train, involving major investments in infrastructure and rolling stock, was not designed to include freight transport until quite recently. Another example is the fact that locomotives operating in the freight sector are often those that are considered too old for passenger transport. The fact that their technical characteristics made them less suitable for freight trains did not matter so much. The hope was that an independent freight company would be able to remedy this situation more effectively because it could defend its interest better (Interview Italcontainer, March 1997). Furthermore, it was hoped that the introduction of industrial accounting would increase the efficiency of the freight division.

In the second attempt at increasing the freight business of the FS intermodal transport was launched by creating independent companies and establishing alliances with independent companies involved in multi-modal transport. These companies were partly owned by the FS, but private capital was also involved. The aim of this strategy was to offer intermodal services which could compete at the European level (Ferrovie dello Stato, 1996, pp. 17-18). These services required different collaborative efforts with companies that were considered important for intermodal transport. A good example is *Cemat*, a group of terminal operators for the combined transport of road and rail. This is a public-private joint venture of which the FS is the majority share holder (Pinna, 1997, p. 4). Another example is the alliance with *Sinport*, a company engaged in running container terminals in harbours (Barbati, 1992). The strategy of engaging in alliances with operators was supplemented by the establishment of the *Freight Leaders Club*, an exclusive organisation grouping together the most important clients of the railways and those interested in intermodal services, with the aim of involving the users in the development of combined transport (Necci, 1992). The strategy of *societarizzazione* led to a complex network of continually-changing alliances. However, it was believed that these manoeuvres served to facilitate intermodal transport and increase the share of the railways in this sector.

How are the results evaluated nearly a decade after the reform was initiated? Transport users seem to respect the effort undertaken and acknowledge the structural limitations due to the infrastructure and the rolling stock. But they are less enthusiastic about the accomplishments: railways are still not customer-oriented enough (Interview Confindustria May 1996). Furthermore, the reformers themselves have reasons to be disappointed. The new accountancy system has not been introduced, and what is worse, freight has still not been organisationally separated from the rest of the railways (Interview Italcontainer, March 1997). The first problem was to set up an independent company for freight. Although some progress has been made in increasing the autonomy, the final step of establishing a sub-holding has not been taken.[34] At the beginning of 1996, *Eurolog* was created as an independent company, the first step towards a future rail-freight company. However, the second step – i.e. transferring the whole of the freight division to the railways – has never been undertaken, and there is no prospect of this happening in the near future (Eurolog, 1996, p. 11). One of the main prerequisites for strengthening the relative weight of freight in contrast to passenger transport has therefore not been realised. The second aspect of the strategy, the system of strategic alliances, has become discredited because the financial transactions of one of these alliances triggered the political affair that led to the downfall of the former head of the FS. The new management has therefore announced a return to the core business, which seems to exclude the expansive strategy of the former *societarizzazione*, without, however, clearly specifying what the new reform is to look like. According to one of the main protagonists of the '*progetto merci*', this jeopardises the reform plan to convert rail freight into a part of intermodal transport (Interview Italcontainer, March 1997):

> If the present railway management and the present Transport Minister do not realise that they have to separate the freight division from the other activities and face competition on a European level, the Italian railways will be marginalised. Transport policy will then be about local transport, about who will do the public works, about who gives money to the road hauliers. But it will not be about a system of logistics. At the present time we lack a fundamental strategy.

How does the experience of Italian freight transport relate to Europe? Certainly there can be no doubt that European reforms have been invoked by the reformers to justify their strategy. On the one hand, Europe's favourable statements about intermodal transport were used to justify the orientation towards intermodal services (e.g. Eurolog, 1996, p. 9). On the other hand, the possibility of competing on a European scale was highlighted (e.g. Spirito, 1996, Interview Ferrovie dello Stato, ASA Rete, February 1997), indicating that inertia seemed to be riskier than reform. Undoubtedly, references to Europe have also been used by opponents of the radical reform, who, for example, have emphasised that privatisation was not being mandated by European decisions and that less radical adaptations, like those carried out France, were possible (e.g. Beltrami, 1995). Furthermore, the Italian Antitrust has had doubts about the FS forming alliances on the national level to compete on a European scale, expressing the opinion that alliances with a company of another mode might decrease the possibility of another company competing with the FS in intermodal transport (Pezzoli and Venanzetti, 1996, p. 4). The overall impression is that amongst the policy community there is considerable controversy about how the experience relates to Europe.

The standard for evaluation proposed in the beginning considered that convergence occurs when a member state embarks on a process of reforming the railways to look for new opportunities by facing the challenges of competition. If this standard is acceptable, the Italian experience in the freight sector shows the strong influence of Europeanisation. However, two very important deficits have to be acknowledged, deficits which modify this judgement. First, no stable solution has yet been found. *Eurolog* has become an independent company, but it remains an empty box. The reform stopped halfway, and it is thus difficult to draw any conclusions from the Italian experience. There neither seems to be an irreversible development towards a new type of rail-freight service nor has an independent company been set up. Secondly, even the rationale of the strategy is increasingly being called into question by the new managements' emphasis on the need to return to the core business.

Conclusion

In the previous sections the Italian railway policy was analysed. In contrast to the case of road-haulage policy, the national rail policy shared some of the general European policy objectives. This is true for both dimensions of the Community reform: i.e. regarding the objectives of organisational autonomy and of market-building, albeit for the latter less than for the former. In both cases the analysis allowed us to conclude that changes have remained merely formal. Interference in the 'railways' business' has not been reduced substantially; nor has there even been a significant development towards free-market practices in the area of freight transport.

The Puzzle of Italian Transport Policy

The analysis of the development of Italian transport policy offered here has focused on the aspects which have been affected by the pressure exerted by the EU. For the period under study there was a surprising resistance to the external pressure generated by Europe's CTP. For most of the time, Italy's transport policy was simply going through the motions. The development in road haulage is peculiar because, for the time under consideration here, it is a case of divergence from the CTP. Whereas the European policy liberalised the markets, national policy has become ever more protectionist. The development in rail is peculiar, too, because of its inconclusiveness. Although the rail sector had already embarked on a national reform process well before the take-off of the CRP, it did not adapt in a way that would prepare Italian railways for a future competitive market. The failure in the case of freight transport is especially telling in this respect. In both road and rail European policy dynamics have not been matched by national adaptation. The conclusion suggested by this analysis is that Italian transport policy has not been influenced by the European policy!

The impression that Europe's CTP is irrelevant for understanding the dynamics of the national transport policy seems to be confirmed if the two cases analysed are compared more closely. The pressure that European policy exerts on Italy differs in both cases. It is much higher in the case of road haulage than in the case of rail. In road haulage, the liberalisation of the Community market became a reality in 1998. Obligations to implement new policies are high because any application of a national rule that curbs liberalisation is illegal.[35] Cabotage transport already challenges formerly-insulated national markets, creating pressure for Italy to adapt. Railway policy is not yet so advanced. The legal obligations have remained rather limited. One place where this is clear is in reference to the separation of infrastructure management and service provision. Although vital for the development of competition in the sector, it is still not mandatory to separate them into two independent companies. More important still, in the area of rail there is still not as much pressure to adapt. The closest approximation to the liberalisation of *cabotage* in rail transport is the voluntary agreement that a limited number of member states have signed to liberalise some routes for particular kinds of transport services. These so called 'freight freeways' do not have the same potential to create adaptation pressure as the total liberalisation of cabotage in road haulage.

If it is correct to maintain that the pressure originating from the CTP is greater in the case of road haulage than in the case of rail, then the development of Italian transport policy is even more surprising. Above, the development in both areas was described as simply having followed old routines without having successfully adapted to Europe. This is true when the metre applied to each case is the respective European policy. However, when the two policies are compared to each other, national rail policy has been much more adaptive than national road-haulage policy. In the analysis above it was shown that Italy has taken some steps towards reforming its railways in the European spirit, at least formally. Furthermore, in the area of rail freight, substantial reform has been undertaken, even though it was aborted prematurely. The comparison of the respective European pressures and the national implementation and adaptation strategies leads to a surprising observation; namely, in Italy, the more powerful European policies meet with greater national divergence, whereas less powerful European policies meet with weak national policy convergence. The comparison between the two policies leaves the impression already suggested by the two policies when viewed in isolation, i.e. that national policy developments cannot be explained simply by referring to European policy developments.

The conclusion of this chapter is that in transport policy there is no simple co-variation allowing us to explain the national policy as a reaction to CTP pressure to implement or adapt to European policy. Therefore, it is not plausible to short-circuit European and national policy developments. One possible conclusion resulting from this is that the CTP did not influence the member states at all. However, given the significance of the EU as a policy-maker, especially in matters concerning the Single-Market Programme, this conclusion would be premature. The analysis has thus far been dedicated to mapping the European and the national policy development and assessing their relative developments. Since the relationship is not a simple one of stimulus and response, we have to more closely examine the way European policy has actually influenced the national policy. We can only establish to what extent and in which ways Europe has influenced national policy developments once we have discovered the mechanisms and patterns of Europeanisation. In the subsequent sections we have to test the images of Europeanisation presented in the introduction.

Notes

[1] A reform of the road haulage sector started at the beginning of 1993. This reform seems to contradict the analysis based on the decade before (see chapter six for details).

[2] In the past, several internal reports of the Ministry of Transport came to the conclusion that the transport sector was in crisis (see Ministero dei Trasporti, 1977; no date a; no date b).

[3] See law 298/1974. For a recent overview see Lepore (1993).

[4] Other changes involved improving the effectiveness of instruments already in use, such as a revised distinction between own-account operators excluded from restrictive market access regulation and professional hauliers, and the issuing of licences according to

transport capacity instead of according to the number of vehicles (Ministero dei Trasporti, 1977: 127-129).

[5]   Transport of petroleum products is much more sensitive to strikes than transport of glass. The different bargaining power of the small hauliers varies accordingly (Interview ANITA, March 1996).

[6]   The representatives of the haulier associations who sign the collective economic agreements also negotiate the mandatory tariffs (Dani, 1994: 16).

[7]   In 1996 a licence for a medium-sized vehicle for professional road haulage cost about 40.000.000 LIT (Interview CONFINDUSTRIA, May 1996).

[8]   In the short period of time that has elapsed since the law entered into force several court claims by road hauliers have made use of these possibilities. Because of the extension of the period of validity, the industry has been sued for considerable amounts of money (Interview Ministero dei Trasporti, May 1995). But other provisions of the law, such as the fact that only written contracts have been valid as a basis for claiming the legal price from 1993 onwards will restrict this possibility in future (Interview ANITA,   March 1996).

[9]   This conclusion has to be treated with caution, since the taxes for operation are not all levied according to the principle of territoriality. Foreign road hauliers have the possibility of obtaining a reimbursement of the VAT on petroleum products whereas domestic hauliers do not. Furthermore fuel is not always bought where it is used. These considerations are important when comparing the difference in costs that Community road hauliers might have when competing with each other (Rommerskirchen, 1985: 235f.). Another disadvantage of the table is the fact that it does not only include freight transport but also public transport by road. The table therefore is only sufficient to illustrate the salience of the principle of territoriality.

[10]   This conclusion is only true for market regulation, not for the incorporation of environmental considerations into taxation.

[11]   Ministero dei Trasporti, decree of 19.10.1990 and decree of 15.02.1991.

[12]   O.J. No. L 233, 9.06.93, p. 10.

[13]   The recent extension of the period of validity of law 68/1992 and the assignment of a yearly budget for 1995, 1996 and 1997 (article 3 of law 11/1996) has been challenged by the European Commission which threatens to pass a decision on this aid scheme if no further justification is supplied (Il Sole 24 Ore, 1.05.1996).

[14]   The case of the Netherlands shows that a proactive industrial policy in the road haulage sector is not necessarily in contradiction to EU-competition law (see Lehmkuhl, 1998).

[15]   General corporate taxes valid for all enterprises are excluded here for the sake of simplicity.

[16]   *Decreto-legge* 85/1998.

[17] *Legge* 454/1997.

[18] *Decreto-legge* 484/1999.

[19] *Decreto-legge* 85/1998, *Decreto* Ministry of Transport 23.12.1998. Other activities in this period regarded international transport licences for members of the European Conference of Ministries of Transport. They did not have an effect on either the EU or the Italian domestic regime.

[20] This has been a general concern ever since nationalisation in Europe has become more widespread. The question was how the railways could be oriented towards goals such as regional development and the provision of mass transport for the citizens, while operating efficiently. The answer was that the desired trade-off between social goals and economic efficiency should be institutionalised by a correct balance between the influence of the administration and the autonomy of the railways (see e.g. Witte, 1932).

[21] Reform has also been started in the area of local rail transport. By definition this type of transport (mostly commuter transport) is provided by small private companies which are not part of the FS. As a first step to increase their economic viability, the management of these companies has been assigned to the FS, which aims to restructure them. Subsequently, the plan is to reorganise local transport at a regional level (Spirito, 1996a). The reform of local transport is excluded from the analysis in this chapter, since it is not a main concern of European railway reform.

[22] For a description of the high speed train in Italy see Strohl (1993: chapter six).

[23] See chapter two for details about the European railway reform.

[24] For freight transport the determination of tariffs was free before and after the reform. Economically this activity is much less important for the railways.

[25] A new accountancy system that accorded with industrial norms made it possible to separate the infrastructure management and the provision of services into two distinct units (Fiorentino n.d.: 32-33). It allowed the FS to take the first step towards organisational separation by separating the accounting for the two activities (Bilancia, 1992: 4). For a detailed description of the FS's transformation into a holding at the end of 1992 see *Collegio Amministrativo Ferroviario Italiano* (1996).

[26] The programme contract for 1994-2000 obliges the FS to adopt a system of infrastructure pricing that acknowledges the separation of infrastructure and operation in the following accounting year (see Corte dei Conti, 1996: 37). Due to a lengthy debate in parliament, however, the programme contract entered into force only in March 1996 and was thus only binding from January 1997 onwards (Ferrovie dello Stato, 1996b: 9).

[27] See *Decreto Presidente della Repubblica* 277/98 regarding the liberalisation of network access, *Decreto Presidente della Repubblica* 146/99 regarding allocation of infrastructure capacity and pricing and *deliberazione* 180/99 regarding infrastructure pricing issues.

[28] See *decreto-legge* 70/2000, article 5.

[29]   For a list of these enterprises and their economic performance see Ministero dei Trasporti (1994).

[30]   Given that Railways have a structural advantage over long distances, they can compete well with road transport for the long hauls between the North and the South of Italy and between Italy and Northern and Central Europe.

[31]   The total length of the railway lines in 1994 was about 16,000 km. It is roughly equal to the U.K. (16,500km) while considerably longer than that of Spain (12,000km) and smaller than that of pre-unified Germany (26,000 km) (Ministero dei Trasporti, 1996: 299). For a critical appraisal of the Italian railway network see Strati (1996: 77-78).

[32]   In the period from 1970 to 1990, the Italian railways share of transported goods was reduced by a half, from about 18% to 9% (Strati, 1996: 79). In 1990, the Community average of transported goods was still equal to 18%. This wide margin between the European and the Italian average was reduced in 1994 by a decrease of the European average to 14% (see Commission, 1996: 41).

[33]   Another indicator of the poor level of services – albeit of a more anecdotal nature - may be seen in the fact that until recently the FS accepted only cash, not even cheques. 'The user had to go with a little suitcase full of money to pay for his service' (Interview Confindustria, May 1996).

[34]   The railway reform may be interpreted as having steadily increased the autonomy of the production of rail-freight services. Immediately after the railway reform of 1985, the FS was organised in a functional way: the production of freight and passenger transport was included in one unit (Fragolino and Rossi, 1987). In 1990 the production of services was organised according to market segments, and passenger and freight transport became two separate divisions (Bilancia, 1992: 4). After the conversion into a joint-stock company in 1992, further reorganisation ensued, but the two separate divisions were still part of the Area Trasporti that was distinct from the Area Rete (Ferrovie dello Stato, 1993: allegato 4). In 1996 freight was put on the same level of hierarchy as passenger transport and infrastructure management (Ferrovie dello Stato, 1996a). The minor organisational changes introduced at the beginning of 1997 by the new head of the railways, Cimoli, mainly regarded the holding but not the individual subdivisions. At the same time there is an attempt to put an end to decentralisation by defining more precisely the mission of each of the units (Il Sole 24 Ore, 20.02.1997: 9).

[35]   For the exception of the crisis mechanism, see the description of the EU road-haulage policy above.

4 Linking Italy to Europe: Improving Prospects for Europeanisation

The informed observer is hardly going to be surprised by the mismatch between the European and the Italian policy described in the last chapter. In fact, it has frequently been noted that the transmission belt between Europe and Italy was not very effective in the past. Several general factors constituted a serious handicap for effectively translating European decisions into national ones in all policy areas. Throughout Italy's post-war period, governments changed frequently, and they were not effective policy makers. Furthermore, they usually pursued economic policies at odds with Community objectives. Parliament also slowed down the translation process. Already overwhelmed by national legislation, it was not effective in transforming European directives and regulations into national law. Finally, the Italian central administration has been notoriously unprofessional and inefficient. This has led to ineffective pre-decision co-ordination and to poorly translating the European rules into national ones. This has resulted in the consistently poor implementation record in comparison to other member states, and a record number of decisions against Italy by the Commission and the European Court of Justice.

The present chapter aims at modifying this view of Italy for the period under consideration, roughly the decade after 1985. There are reasons to believe that Italy's Community link has improved noticeably. However, this is not easy to detect, since the factors traditionally impeding Community decisions that make a difference in Italy are still in place, albeit with less negative effects. The strengthening of the Community link in Italy is due more to institutional innovation than to institutional reform. It is my contention that the founding of the Italian Antitrust Agency has considerably improved the impact of Community decisions, and especially the impact of the Single Market Programme. In the following I shall first analyse traditional aspects of the links between Italy and the Community (as approached by Italy and as they are currently influencing Italy). A more detailed analysis is dedicated to the Italian Antitrust Agency in order to substantiate the argument that this is an important development for Europeanisation. The analysis presented here concentrates on the puzzle that has been mentioned above: why is there no convergence between European and national transport policy when at the general (as opposed to the specific sectoral) level the translation mechanism for decision-making has improved?

Linking Italy to Europe: The Central Administration

The link that member states have formed with the EU differs from the link in the conventional model of 'international relations' between states, where governments representing their state negotiate treaties which in turn are ratified by parliament and implemented by the administration. In contrast to this neat separation of the decision-making process into a two-level game involving national and international politics (Putnam, 1988; Moravscik, 1993, 1994), the decision-making process within the EU is often described as a joint policy-making process. The national level participates extensively in Community-level policy formulation; and *vice versa*, the Community level also plays an important role in the national implementation process (Scharpf, 1988; Wessels, 1992). This difference has an important consequence for the distribution of power among the actors participating in the translation process. In a strict two-level game the international and the national level are mediated by the parliament. By ratifying a treaty the parliament translates it to the national level. Within the EU, the *central national administrations play a pivotal role* in the whole policy process: in Community decision-making as well as in the national implementation process, and in the transposition of Community decisions into national rules and their application (Siedentopf and Hauschild, 1988, pp. 44, 59; Bach, 1992). The central role of the national administration in applying rules is least surprising, since this is the traditional role of the administration. However, the central administration increasingly plays a role in transposition as well. Frequently, Community rules are not translated by national laws adopted by the parliament but by autonomous decisions of lesser importance in the legal hierarchy, i.e. administrative acts (Siedentopf and Hauschild, 1988, p. 55; Franchini, 1993, pp. 124-29). If Community law is transposed by a formal legislative procedure, it is a rare exception when parliament critically examines and changes the draft prepared by the administration (Siedentopf and Hauschild, 1988, p. 35). Surprisingly, the pivotal role of the administration extends to the policy-formulation stage as well. The influence depends on the fact that national experts of the administrative units concerned are intimately involved in drafting European legislation. Their search for adequate solutions to problems which are acceptable to all the parties involved mainly takes place in the very large number of committees that have formed around the European Council and the Commission (Wessels, 1996, pp. 142-44). Only in cases of exceptional national interest do these national experts, who are continuously partici-pating in the Community decision-making process, co-ordinate themselves to formulate the common national interest. In all member states, the formal structures devised to improve this national co-ordination have become less important over time; consequently governments and foreign ministries are no longer the exclusive gate-keepers between the national and the European level.[1] Compared to conventional international relations, parliaments are less powerful in the implementation phase, and governments less powerful in the policy formulation phase. The resulting dominance of the central administration is one reason why decision-making within the EU has been characterised as 'bureaucratic politics' (Peters, 1992).

In comparison with other Community member states, the administra-tive capacity in Italy is at the bottom end of the scale. This is due to a series of structural problems, which have proved highly resistant to any of the numerous post-war reform efforts. The first problem, inherited from fas-cism, concerned the recruitment procedures (Bilotta, 1983). Until recently, members of the Italian administration have mainly been recruited from Southern Italy, the primary objective being not to secure highly-qualified and motivated personnel but to reduce the notoriously-high unemployment rate. This pattern continued throughout the post-war period, and led to high numbers of poorly-paid, poorly-qualified and unmotivated employees, while at the same time making the Italian administration very inefficient. A second problem concerns the administrative structure. The enormous ex-pansion of bureaucracies during this century has been commonplace, espe-cially given that the post-war development of the welfare state has created a highly-differentiated organisational structure, a structure which leads to co-ordination problems (e.g. Mayntz, 1985, pp. 102-107). In Italy, this prob-lem of differentiation and the subsequent integration is mainly relevant on the horizontal level. Until recently, regional decentralisation in Italy has remained modest; thus vertical co-ordination is not a major issue (Cassese, 1993, p. 319). The central bureaucracy is highly fragmented. More than in other European countries, the definition of ministries is not based on their functions, but is oriented towards the necessity to provide coalition mem-bers with a seat in the cabinet (Hine, 1993, p. 226). Their competencies overlap and often lead to inefficient problem solving. In 1993, for example, economic policies were handled by four ministries, and five ministries had responsibilities in the agricultural sector. Traditionally, no less than six ministries were responsible for transport, the Ministries of Transport, Pub-lic Works, Merchant Navy, Defence, ANAS (*Azienda Nazionale Autonoma delle Strade*) and the state railways (*Ferrovie dello Stato*) (Cassese, 1983,

p. 234). The horizontal fragmentation is further increased by two tiers of semi-public bodies that perform different administrative and economic functions, some of which are a more independent part of the ministry and some of which have a more autonomous status. These 'autonomous enterprises and administrations' (*amministrazioni e aziende autonomi*) and public bodies (*enti pubblici*) constitute a vast sector, which in the mid-1980s was estimated to consist of up to 40,000 entities (Cassese, 1985, p. 9). A third problem that makes co-ordination more difficult and reduces efficiency is that the administration is highly insulated from the level of political leadership. In Italy, a tacit agreement of mutual non-interference prevails. Those active at the political level agree not to tinker with the career pattern of civil servants in exchange for the complete political neutrality of the administration (Cassese, 1985, p. 21). Finally, partly due to the strict political neutrality, the Italian administration is extremely legalistic and not oriented towards problem solving (Lewanski, 1999, p. 101). This further reduces the effectiveness of the Italian bureaucracy.

Taking into consideration the numerous general structural problems of the administration, on the one hand, and the pivotal role of the administration in linking a member state to the Community, on the other, the Italian difficulties resulting from its Community membership are not surprising. It has often been observed that Italy has a problem co-ordinating the parts of its administration that are involved in a specific issue at the Community level.[2] There have been numerous institutional experiments to improve the co-ordination of domestic policy (Franchini, 1990), but the results to date have been disappointing (Franchini, 1993, p. 88). The result is that Italy has failed to participate at the Community level. Italian representatives at various levels of the Community decision-making process have great difficulties influencing the decision-making process. This has had a detrimental effect on the implementation record for two reasons. First, a lack of influence might lead to Community legislation that does not adequately take into consideration the specific circumstances of the Italian situation; implementation is thus rendered more difficult (Morisi, 1992, p. 15).[3] The second reason is that failing to participate means that they receive less information and a that there is less time for the Italian administration to anticipate Community developments. Furthermore, there may be little motivation to implement unfavourable decisions when there is no compensation for this requirement. To gain compensation of this sort by striking bargains requires an efficient bureaucracy as well (Hine, 1993, p. 290). As the complexity of the matter being decided increases, the side payments have to be organised over increasingly heterogeneous policy areas.

The lack of co-ordination in defining the national interest at the Community level is only one cause for the problems in the subsequent implementation stage. It has to be supplemented by the logic of Italian Community membership, which is frequently invoked to create Community-level obligations in order to overcome national resistance. Considering that most of the decisions at the Community level require a *de facto* high level of agreement, Italy could have reduced its implementation deficit by slowing down European decision making. However, Italy generally assents to most Community initiatives. Italy's poor implementation record has been contrasted with the its willingness to expand the sphere for Community decision making (Giuliani, 1992). This behaviour may be explained by the logic of Italian Community membership. The Italian government has been employing European legislation to promote reforms that would have no chance as mere domestic projects. The Italian government has been using the Community to 'tie its hands' (Hine, 1993, p. 285; Dyson and Featherstone, 1996).[4] This strategy inevitably leads to strains in the implementation process.[5]

A second observation is that the administration is often slow to transpose EU rules. Application is often ineffective because of the legalistic emphasis of the Italian administration. (Siedentopf and Hauschild, p. 63) For these reasons, bypassing the legislative process has not led to a higher level of conformity with Europe.[6]

The pivotal role of the administration does not imply that the other major actors, especially the parliament, do not play a role at all when Community decisions become relevant at the national level; however, they are of less importance. Apart from the administration, the Parliament's slow transposition has been one of the major causes of difficulties in translating Community decisions into national rules: its generally cumbersome legislative procedures are too slow to transpose Community law into national law at an adequate pace. The core of the reform which tried to improve the implementation deficit therefore centred on introducing a new legislative procedure for transposition. Instead of treating each measure individually, an annual European bill is prepared that contains all the necessary legislation that has to be passed to fulfil the Community obligations (Ronzitti, 1990, p. 41; Morisi, 1992, pp. 34-36; Grottanelli de Santi, 1992: 185-86). In terms of accelerating the legislative process, the experience of the first *legge comunitaria* has been a failure. A delegation was created by the government to specify the details and then pass the legislation, but the large majority of the single laws were not actually passed. The *legge comunitaria* actually increased the complexity of the legislative process because it included the government to a greater extent than before (Morisi, 1992, pp. 41-42; Franchini, 1993, pp. 121-22, footnote 84).[7]

In Italy the difficulties in translating Community decisions into national rules has lead to an implementation gap which has been among the highest of all the member states (Hine, 1993, pp. 288-90; Morisi, 1992, pp. 5-14). Furthermore, with each successive step in the Commission's infringement proceedings and the European Court of Justice, the gap between Italy and the other member states has been widening in absolute terms (Mendrinou, 1996, pp. 4-11):[8]

- Italy is the member state that, together with Greece, has received the highest number of 'Letters of Formal Notice' from the Commission signalling an infringement of Community law.
- Following from the poor response rate to the 'Letters of Formal Notice', Italy is the member state in which the Commission has most often followed up the 'Letters of Formal Notice' with 'Reasoned opinions'.
- Italy holds the record for cases that have been referred to the Court of Justice; most infamously, it also has the highest number of cases with rulings against them. This indicates that there was no adequate response throughout the enforcement cycle.

The exceptionally poor Italian implementation record has been analysed before; thus, the major results of these analyses are only summarised here. However, the question is whether this analysis holds true for the whole period under consideration here. Doubt could arise from the fact that Italy has been undergoing a regime transition since about 1992, which for its part has been leading to reform efforts in many policy areas. It is therefore important to ask if the prospects for the Community policy to influence the national policy have improved. At first sight the answer seems to be rather negative because the administrative reform has not yet successfully tackled any of the problems listed above. Until the administrative reform legislation is implemented, the Italian Civil Service will at best be an 'administration in transition', moving towards a more efficient future (Lewanski, 1999). Given the failure to streamline the transposition of Community law, no fundamental improvements can be detected. However, in the following sections it shall be shown that the analysis summarised here may still be valid, even though it is no longer the complete picture. The prospects for implementation have been improved by developments elsewhere!

Linking Italy to Europe: The Italian Antitrust Agency

The above analysis of the Italian mechanism for translating Community law into national law points out a series of structural weaknesses. From this perspective, it may be expected that European decision making does not translate easily into national changes. The lack of convergence between the national and the Community development therefore seems to be a logical consequence of the weak link between Italy and the European Community. However, the explanation of Italian policy dynamics may not be as simple as that. In fact, there is strong reason to believe that the analysis of the implementation mechanism, which centred on the pivotal role of the national administration, has to be supplemented in order to make an adequate assessment of its capacities. My contention is that the Italian antitrust law, creating an independent Antitrust Agency, has improved the general conditions for the enforcement of Community regulation. To substantiate this hypothesis, a more detailed analysis of this development is required. In fact, the relevance for the enforcement of Community law is not self-evident. On the contrary, the primary function – i.e. protecting the market from anti-competitive practice – does not seem to give the Italian Antitrust Agency any role in the enforcement of Community law.

The Role of Antitrust in Regulation

For the Italian Antitrust Agency to able to play a part in the enforcement of Community law it has to get involved in the business of regulation (i.e. reregulation on the national level). In the orthodox world of the classical theory of economic regulation it seems to be impossible for an antitrust agency to play a role in regulation. In this tradition, regulation and antitrust are presented under the common label of 'economic regulation'. They both try to influence behaviour with legal norms and thus with coercion rather than with economic incentives, in contrast to taxation (Viscusi et al., 1995, p. 3). But the two differ fundamentally because they pursue different aims. Antitrust is usually defined as a policy 'to enhance competition in the economy by means of regulations that undo practices that restrict competition.' (Lane, 1995, 138). In contrast to this, 'economic regulation typically refers to government-imposed restrictions on firm decisions over price, quantity, and entry and exit' (Viscusi et al., 1995, p. 307) which restrict competition. This difference implies a choice between either antitrust or economic regulation; and antitrust rules are the preferable alternative whenever possible because they ensure the functioning of the market by enhancing competition rather than restricting it (Breyer, 1990, p. 21). The explanation of the mutual exclusiveness of antitrust and regulation is that they react to different forms of market failure: the former to the failure of markets to sustain competition by preventing *monopolies*, and the latter to the failure of markets to guarantee efficiency in the case of *natural monopolies*. Antitrust legislation requires rules that restrict anti-competitive practices; regulation requires rules which guarantee efficient production when competition is not viable. In short, the first requires an antitrust law enhancing competition, the second a regulatory policy restricting competition (Spulber, 1989: p. 624). For this reason, the classical theory of regulation seems to suggest the mutual exclusiveness of antitrust and regulation and seems to exclude the relevance of an antitrust agency for regulatory reform.[9]

Despite the theoretical distinction between antitrust and regulation, in economic analysis it is acknowledged that they may co-exist in the same sector. The essential insight that closely links the two policies is that regulation by definition never replaces the market completely (Viscusi et al., 1995, p. 307). Therefore antitrust issues, such as the appropriate degree of horizontal and vertical integration of firms, also remain salient for regulated public utilities (Kahn, 1971, chapter six). It has been observed that this intimate relationship between antitrust and regulation in the USA has led to a situation in which it has become impossible to clearly link organisations involved in economic regulation to specific functions (Spulber, 1989, pp. 624-632). In the future the three functions in economic policy making – regulation, antitrust enforcement and judicial review – might not be performed by the organisations endowed with the tasks – i.e. regulatory commissions, antitrust agencies and courts. Deregulation policy has turned regulators into promoters of competition. They have thus become involved in antitrust policy (Spulber, 1989, p. 624). On the other hand, antitrust enforcement has become involved in the complex supervision of industry conduct. Rules and guidelines that reduce decision uncertainty, such as merger guidelines or rules for the identification of predatory pricing, have the same role as regulations: they aim to shape industry conduct (Spulber, 1989, p. 623). Furthermore, the example of telecommunications in the US shows that courts have done more than merely provide judicial review. Courts and the Department of Justice were involved in monitoring the implementation of equal access to local networks by different telephone companies and were involved in assessing the competitive impact of access agreements between firms. Therefore, 'the courts became involved in matters of regulation and antitrust policy' (Spulber, 1989, p. 629). This development in which the link between functions of economic regulation and organisations is loosened may be termed 'institutional blurring'.[10] This trend suggests how the new Italian antitrust law could be important for domestic regulatory reform in general and for the transport sector in particular.

To sum up, economic regulation theory does not defy expectations that antitrust could influence on regulatory reform in Italy; rather, although they address different market-failure problems, combining them in different sectors makes sense even from an economic point of view. In the end, the institutional set up determines how the integration of antitrust and regulation is dealt with. Either a specific public utility is granted exemption from antitrust and the issues of regulation are dealt with in the regulatory statute, or antitrust laws apply directly. Even the economic theory of regulation acknowledges that these questions have to be clarified by an institutional analysis.

In the following sections an institutional analysis is offered. First, I want to demonstrate that the Italian Antitrust law has endowed the Antitrust Agency with considerable resources; second, that the Antitrust Agency has become a major player in regulatory reform; third, that this role of promoting privatisation and deregulation is dependent on European legislation, especially the legislation implementing the Single Market Programme; finally, it shall be demonstrated that the Antitrust Agency's activity is centred on the service sector in general and on transport in particular. The chapter concludes by summarising the ways in which institutionalising the Italian Antitrust Agency ought to strengthen the influence Europe exercises on Italy in spite of the poor performance of the public administration.

Competencies and Powers of the Italian Antitrust Agency

The new Italian competition law is enforced by an agency designed specifically for this purpose, the *Autorità Garante della Concorrenza e del Mercato*. This contrasts with the *status quo ante* where the question of the legality of restrictions on competition was settled by the ordinary judiciary (Pavesio, 1989, pp. 571-72). The Antitrust Agency consists of about 200 members who have specific legal and economic training in the field. The antitrust is shielded from political interference by the autonomy of its decision-making powers and from economic intrusion by strict rules about additional professional engagement. It is one of the few public institutions of considerable prestige in Italy, maybe comparable to the standing of Banca d'Italia. Recently, this agency has been strengthened by a task force of the *Guardia di finanza*, the Italian tax police. This enhances the future opportunities for obtaining sensitive information from enterprises (Autorità Garante (1997), 252).

As such, these characteristics of the Italian Antitrust Agency show that a serious attempt has been made to set up a working agency, and that it has been successful. The real significance of this is that the antitrust law is not enforced by the ordinary judiciary anymore, as was suggested in one of the two bills that were discussed prior to the adoption of the antitrust law.[11] The suspicion that the enforcement of the antitrust law by the ordinary judiciary would have failed is well founded (Giurisprudenza Commerciale,

1991). Not only the notorious delays of the Italian courts, but also the high level of technical knowledge required for antitrust decisions would have presented serious obstacles to enforcement. Past experience has shown that effective regulation requires intimate knowledge of the regulated sector (Majone, 1996c, pp. 9-10) and that specialised regulatory agencies have proven to be very effective in acquiring knowledge, either by recruiting professionals to enhance in-house expertise or by organising external advice (Majone, 1996c, pp. 15-16). An antitrust decision, too, may require a vast amount of technical information. A prime example is the decision regarding the relevant market for evaluating the presumed anti-competitive effect of certain economic behaviour. Therefore, in most countries that adopt antitrust legislation, a specific specialised body is provided to enforce it (Bentivoglio and Trento, 1995, pp. 50-51). It will be shown below that this form of institutionalisation has led to a substantial number of decisions; and as such, the claim that there is virtually no antitrust jurisdiction in Italy (Pavesio, 1989, pp. 572, 574) is no longer true.

The Italian Antitrust Agency is well endowed with competencies. The core of its powers are aimed at enforcing competition law. The Italian law, like most antitrust laws, classifies events that restrict competition into three categories (Bentivoglio and Trento, 1995, pp. 49-50). These three areas are: agreements between firms (e.g. to set a common price for a product); the abuse of a dominant position by a firm within a certain market (e.g. by preventing other competitors from entering the market); and finally, mergers between firms. The Antitrust Agency decides if competition has been restricted. Unless a decision is successfully contested via the administrative courts, it is binding for the firm or firms in question, and if it is ignored it may lead to various sanctions (Autorità Garante, 1996, p. 16).

These powers to enforce competition law are supplemented by additional competencies that well supersede them and imply a competition-policy mandate. In fact, the agency does not only apply the law, it also performs legislative and regulatory functions (Autorità Garante, 1996, pp. 12-13). It has the power to notify the Government, the Parliament, and the public administration of any law (planned or implemented) that restricts competition beyond the degree necessary for the achievement of public interests. It also has the right to suggest specific remedies. This power is used whenever any provision limits competition in favour of the already-existing firms in a field. Furthermore, Article 24 of the antitrust law specifically asks for studies on how to reform the sectors of public works, commercial distribution and concessions.[12] Finally, the Antitrust Agency must be heard before any regulatory reform in the public utilities is pursued. It is important to note, however, that all the consultation activity is non-binding.

The non-binding character of consultation raises a question about whether the competition policy mandate given to the Italian Antitrust Agency has made any difference. According to its first President, the significance of the advisory powers is underestimated because it is usually not viewed in connection with the decision-making power. Their effectiveness is enhanced whenever advisory activities are co-ordinated with the making of binding decisions (Saja, 1991, p. 459). After a few years of activity, two high-ranking members of the Antitrust Agency are of the opinion that the use of advisory powers has been a success and that its views are increasingly taken into consideration in the legislative process (Gobbo and Salonico, 1995, pp. 506-7). The number of references to it in the discussion of laws has increased and so has the demand for the *ex ante* opinions of the antitrust authoritiy. The following section will offer a detailed analysis of the decision-making and the advisory activity to date.

As has been mentioned above, the Italian Antitrust Agency has been designed as an 'independent regulatory agency', 'independent' meaning that it is shielded from direct interference in the decision-making process by political and economic actors. However, this does not imply the absence of any form of influence on the decision-making process. Decisions may be challenged by the two tiers of the administrative judiciary: the *Tribunale Amministrativo Regionale del Lazio* and the *Consiglio di Stato*. This implies that the process of judicial review has to be included when evaluating the action capacity of the *Autorità Garante*. The most radical challenge to date originated from an antitrust procedure in the insurance sector. In 1994 the Antitrust Agency decided that a group of 11 large and well-known Italian insurance companies had violated the competition law, and it imposed a heavy fine on them (Ghezzi et al., 1996, pp. 227-28). These companies had met at regular intervals from 1991 to 1993 to share their data and to co-ordinate the types of risks that they would ensure and at what price. The *Tribunale Amministrativo Regionale del Lazio* did not challenge the conclusion of the Antitrust Agency but decided to cancel the fines because they were seen as too severe (Il Sole 24 Ore, 9.08.1995, p. 23). This judgement was upheld by a subsequent decision of the *Consiglio di Stato*. However, Italian consumer associations have managed to get the European Commission to review the decisions taken by the Italian administrative judiciary. In fact, in the justification of their decisions, both courts have violated the principles of European competition law (Il Sole 24 Ore, 11.05.1997, p. 7).

The antitrust case in the insurance sector is interesting because, apart from the relationship with the two tiers of judicial review, it points to another potential source of conflict that could restrict the scope of the Antitrust Agency. Prior to the sentence of the TAR Lazio, which abolished the fines, a controversy over the supervision of the insurance sector ensued between the Antitrust Agency and the older Agency. The debate centred on the evaluation of insurance company practices.[13] The TAR Lazio came to the conclusion that the Antitrust should not have completely ignored the opinion of the sectoral Agency (Il Sole 24 Ore, 9.08.1995: 23). This case demonstrates the more general risk: namely, that the Antitrust Agency may increasingly be challenged by sectoral regulatory agencies because the domains of these agencies' competencies are not well delimited (Cassese, 1995a: 6). The question to be settled is where the power to settle competition issues resides (De Nicola, 1995).

To date, the judicial review and the sectoral regulatory agencies have not been a serious challenge to the Antitrust Authority. This may partially be due to the fact that the Antitrust Authority often tries to obtain a consensual solution with the firm which is violating the competition law (Saja, 1991: 464). In the case of a consensual agreement, no formal decision arises and there is no motive for the culprit to challenge the decision. One reason for the low restrictions that have resulted from sectoral regulatory agencies is that many of them have not been set up yet. One instructive example indicating the relationship between Antitrust Authority and the regulatory agencies is in the banking sector, where the *Banca d'Italia* traditionally enjoys extensive rights. Another example is provided by the newly-founded regulatory agency in the energy sector. Recently, the national electricity monopoly *ENEL* has launched a joint venture with *ENI*, the national gas and petroleum giant, setting up a joint company for the production of electricity (Il Sole 24 Ore, 14.05.1997: 14). This has aroused the interest of the sectoral agency as well as the Antitrust Agency. Both have started an inquiry procedure, albeit with different goals. The sectoral agency has been interested in the consequences for the future privatisation projects in the energy sector, whereas the *Autorità Garante* has been interested in possible negative effects on competition in the sector. To date no serious conflicts seem to have emerged.[14]

The Autorità Garante *in Action*

Decision making was drastically accelerated because the law was institutionalised by a particular body which aimed to implement it. In fact, by mid-1997, after roughly six and a half years of activity, the number of decisions made had swollen from a modest number of cases per year (Pavesio, 1989) to well over 3,000 (when considering solely decisions concerned with competition issues). The number reaches to about 4,600 if the cases regarding the legality of advertising are included (Autorità Garante, 1997: 17). The Antitrust Authority has continually reflected upon its guiding principles as this proliferation has occurred. This reflection has taken place as part of a more general discourse on legal doctrine, which has led to the consolidation of a genuine organisational action programme. More specifically, my contention is that the innovative character of the Italian antitrust law lies in the fact that it has institutionalised an Agency that is fundamentally opposed to current patterns of economic policy in Italy. One of its most important roles, if not the most important one, has become the advocation of regulatory reform by permanently revealing the anti-competitive nature of the regulatory status quo in Italy. For the first time, in Italy an agency that is formally part of the public administration is in fundamental opposition to the standard operating procedures of economic policy making.

This logic of action is a peculiarity of the Italian antitrust body; in fact, it runs completely counter to the origin of this type of economic regulation. In the USA antitrust legislation was adopted because the rapid increase in the size of corporations at the end of the last century was perceived as a threat to democracy. Antitrust law was thus designed as a force aimed at defending democracy against private economic power (Millon, 1991). The very name suggests this role: 'trusts' were the agreements large companies employed to become even larger. To speak of an 'Antitrust Agency' in Italy, where the public promotion of anti-competitive behaviour is the main problem, is misleading. The designation 'Anti-State-Trust Agency' would be preferable.[15]

This anti-state-trust bias may hardly be interpreted as an incremental development. For the first time, economic policy itself is not seen as a major remedy, but as a major source of problems. This is a break with the past, in which state intervention was viewed as a near universal remedy to all kinds of economic problems. The nationalising of monopolies was most emblematic of this belief.

In the first sectoral studies, the conclusion was that private economic power was not the main impediment to competition. The real problem was state intervention (Ministero dell'Industria, 1988, pp. 561-62.).[16] This view is in line with the general analysis of the Italian economy. The most dynamic economic sectors are dominated by small and medium-sized enterprises (e.g. Bagnasco, 1988, chapter one). This is not to deny that important large firms, such as *FIAT, Olivetti,* and *Barilla*, also exist. However, even after a recent wave of mergers and acquisitions, the number of large companies remains small and modest compared to other OECD economies (Bianchi, 1995). Furthermore, it is common knowledge that state intervention has been diagnosed as having a crippling effect (e.g. Padoa-Schioppa, 1993). This has raised the question of the rationale for antitrust law. The (negative) expectation that it would leave the public sector unscathed and would imply further discrimination against the private sector has not been confirmed. Two high-ranking members of staff have concluded that 'the frequency with which public enterprises have been subject to condemnation for violation of competition rules is without doubt relevant and dominant.' This has been due to 'the apparently mundane principle of equality between public and private enterprises' (Gobbo and Salonico, 1995, p. 507). Thus the peculiarity of the Italian situation does not come as a surprise. That the nature of Italian antitrust enforcement and policy is fundamentally 'anti-state-trust' is one of the casual observations of practitioners. However, seldom has it been at the centre academic reflection. The following sections are therefore dedicated to substantiating this hypothesis. It will be shown that the Antitrust Agency has a substantial general competition-policy mandate that it has continually used to promote regulatory reform. Furthermore, it will be shown that even in the core area of competition law enforcement, the activities are concerned with countering the anti-competitive effects of economic intervention by the state. The quantity and quality of decision making, as well as the type of problems addressed, all seem to support the claim about the peculiar character of the Italian Antitrust Agency.

Competition Policy: Studies on Economic Sectors and Opinions The legal definition of the powers of the Antitrust Agency show that its mission goes well beyond the mere enforcement of the antitrust provisions. It also contains powers related to general competition policy. The following competencies are granted to the Agency:

• It may conduct studies on economic sectors whenever there is suspicion that competition is malfunctioning.[17]
• It has the task of identifying (for the Government, Parliament, and the units of the public administration involved) all bills and laws detrimental to competition.[18]

In both cases, the Agency's initiative may be due to a demand from the Government, Parliament or the public administration. These may address specific questions about the state of certain sectors (as has happened with the antitrust law itself, which identified three priority sectors), or they may be a demand for an *ex ante* opinion of the Antitrust Agency on a specific bill. However, the important point is that the Antitrust Agency does not depend on such a demand, but that it has the right of initiative. Furthermore, in this area of consulting and advice, the Agency's range of activity is not limited to the question of whether an action is in line with competition law; it is also able to formulate concrete proposals on how to introduce conformity with the competition policy. And finally, the Agency may make its opinions and activities public in any way that it finds adequate, thus enhancing the probability that its opinions will have an effect (Aquilanti, 1993a, p. 1141). Taken together, on a formal legal level, these aspects suggest that these powers are not just auxiliary or symbolic, but that they considerably enhance the power of the Agency by giving it 'the general means to intervene into the process determining market order' (Aquilanti, 1993a, p. 1143).

In a comparative perspective, the competition-policy mandate of the Italian Antitrust Agency is considerable. It is wider in scope than that of many other European antitrust agencies (Parcu, 1996, p. 23). From the start, the Antitrust Agency has made ample use of its broad competition-policy mandate, examining any regulatory reform that involves a profound change in economic policy making. The most general example of this tendency has been the constant public effort to promote the process of privatisation in order to reduce the role of legal monopolies in general and especially in the service sector. These activities date back to the first President of the Antitrust Agency, Francesco Saja, who saw the promotion of a modern type of capitalism in Italy as one of the major tasks of the Antitrust Agency (Cafagna, 1995). A specific section on the evaluation of the process of privatisation in various sectors of the economy has been part of many of the yearly reports to the Government, formally presented during the presence of representatives of the political elite and widely covered in the media. The criticisms have often been quite explicit. For example, the 1996 report concluded that the privatisation in the service sector was significantly slowed down by the lengthy process of initiating regulatory reform in the various sectors, which was a prerequisite for privatisation (Autorità Garante, 1996a). The same holds true for the 1997 report. The strongest obstacle to competition is seen as state intervention and interventionist policies are removed only very slowly (Il Sole 24 Ore 9.05.1997, p. 3; Il Manifesto, 9.05.1997, pp. 6-7). This explicit criticism of the politics of privatisation and regulatory reform has not been challenged by the political elite. However, it has provoked the accusation that the Antitrust Authority is going far beyond its institutional competencies. According to one of the founding fathers of the antitrust law, Guido Rossi, as an independent administrative body, the Antitrust Agency, does not have a general competition-policy mandate that would permit such far-reaching statements about general political questions. Misusing the antitrust powers to reform the economy is similar to the immodest attempt of the Italian magistrates to reform the political system via the judiciary (Il Sole 24 Ore 10.05.1996, p. 25). This criticism may be seen as another indicator that exposes the general attempt of the Italian Antitrust Agency to promote regulatory reform.

The 'anti-state trust' has not merely criticised the speed of the regulatory reform process in Italy. By making use of investigative powers and the right to issue reasoned opinions the Antitrust Agency has promoted it as well.

Table 4.1   *Autorità Garante*: Policy Making According to Sectors (1991-03.1997)

Sector	Opinions (Art.21)	Consultations (Art.22)	Studies (Art.24)	Total
Agriculture & industry	4	5	-	9
Electricity & gas	1	5	-	6
Commercial distribution	2	1	1	4
Transport, related services	8	10	-	18
Telecommunications	1	18	-	19
Financial services	-	4	-	4
Public works	-	1	1	2
Professional services	4	4	-	8
Other sectors	4	11	1	16
Total	24	59	3	86

Source: Adapted from Autorità Garante (1997, 23).

The number of investigations in these areas seems to suggest that they are of prime importance.[19] One of the first indicators of this is the number of opinions issued to the Government. Table 4.1 indicates a total of 86 policy-making decisions referring to anti-competitive regulation. Furthermore, it shows that the policy-making activities are concentrated in the service sector. This is noteworthy because, within the service sector, the public utilities constitute one of the most important targets, especially transport and telecommunications. Agriculture and industry together are only involved in around 10% of all policy decisions. The service sector is characterised by a high degree of state intervention in Italy. In fact, the regulations were considered detrimental because they were either fixing tariffs, limiting market access, discriminating between enterprises, or introducing, extending or defending legal monopolies (Parcu, 1996, pp. 11-12). Judging from the most representative cases, all of these decisions identify the regulatory *status quo* as the prime reason for a competition deficit (Parcu, 1996, pp. 12-15). In no case is the problem that the regulation has failed to keep up with a new type of anti-competitive behaviour developed by private firms.

The state regulation itself is the problem. This is also confirmed by the three sectoral studies commissioned by Art. 24 of the antitrust law. They all concern the service sector.[20]

Competition Law Enforcement: Decision-making The anti-state-trust character of the Italian Antitrust Agency does not only manifest itself by issuing reasoned opinions but also by hard-core decision-making. Decision-making often involves public enterprises. Where private enterprises are involved, the regulatory regime – and not the economic power of the firm – may be identified as the prime reason for an infringement against competition policy. This is shown by the decision-making statistics of the Antitrust Agency.

Table 4.2   Decision Making of the *Autorità Garante*

	1991-95	1996	-03. 1997	Total
Agreement	136	66	8	210
Violations	30	15	3	48
O.K. after modifications	18	4	-	22
Abuse	96	54	14	164
Violations	24	7	-	31
Merger	1240	357	72	1669
Violations	4	-	-	4
O.K. after modifications	5	3	-	8

Source: Autorità Garante, 1997; figures refer to completed procedures.

The decisions listed are categorised according to the three main ways that the competition law is infringed upon: agreements, abuse of a dominant position and mergers. A first glance at the decision statistics from 1994 to March 1997 does not seem to show that state interference is a major factor. The large majority of decisions regard *mergers*;[21] and mergers normally involve the private sector (Autorità Garante, 1997, chapter 3). The public sector plays a lesser role in the acquisitions of other firms due to the privatisation policy (Autorità Garante, 1997, p. 195). However, a second look reveals that only a minor fraction of these concentration procedures were actually judged to be illegal. Of 1669 decisions, only four concluded that the law had been violated; and eight decisions were conditional promotions. In this way the Antitrust Authority confirms the initial expectation that mergers are not the major threat to competition.[22] The analysis of antitrust decision-making therefore has to concentrate on decisions regarding restrictive agreements and the abuse of a dominant position. Of the 210 decisions made about *restrictive agreements*, it was determined that 48 were violations and 22 were conditional promotions. The number of violations is much higher in absolute terms and constitutes a much higher proportion of the total number of decisions made. At least half of the decisions regard the service sector (Autorità Garante, 1997, table p. 171) and may thus be taken as referring to enterprises which operate as legal monopolies or in an environment of protective regulation. The ratio may even increase if all the decisions involving enterprises in the public sector are included. However, the most extreme type of decision making regarding the public distortions of competition, is concerned with the *abuse of a dominant position*: 'Nearly all the procedures of the *Autorità Garante* regarding the abuse of a dominant position have involved firms linked to the public authorities' (Rangone, 1995, p. 1312). Table 4.2 shows that the ratio of violations is roughly the same as the ratio of restrictive agreements. In conclusion, the decision statistics show that the two decision-making areas with the largest share of *violations* in the antitrust law (in absolute terms and relative to the number of procedures) both concern public regulation ('special or exclusive rights'). This confirms that the Antitrust Agency is essentially 'anti-state-trust' in character.

A second conclusion can be drawn form this decision-making bias. Since no national Antitrust Agency has the powers of the European Commission to abolish norms detrimental to competition, the fact that most distortions to competition arise from legal norms might seem to seriously reduce the Italian Antitrust Authority's powers. Yet, in fact this does not seem to take place. Despite the *de jure* powerlessness with respect to the public sector, the Antitrust Agency has actually managed to erode anti-competitive legislation (Meli, 1997, p. 253). This has been accomplished in two ways: First, antitrust powers have been extended by an ingenious interpretation of the antitrust statute regarding the scope of its competencies. Art. 8.2 of the antitrust statute explicitly excludes legal monopolies from investigation as well as any enterprise that has been entrusted by law with an economic activity in the general interest (Meli, 1997, p. 251). However, according to the interpretation of the Antitrust Authority, the area of exemption has to be interpreted restrictively. Firms operating as legal monopolies are not exempt from Italian competition law *a priori*. Even core public-utility activities, like the fixing of tariffs by ENEL, are not exempt from antitrust scrutiny. According to the decision-making practice of the Antirust Agency, significant distortions to competition are only legal when the behaviour is an inevitable consequence of the task assigned by the law (Meli, 1997, pp. 247-48). Furthermore, exclusive concessions which have not been granted by law are not considered sufficient to define a legal monopoly in the sense of the antitrust statute (Meli, 1997, pp. 248-49).

A second strategy to extend the competencies of the Antitrust Agency has been to contrast norms restricting competition with superior norms. This may seem unconstitutional because of an undue restriction on the freedom of economic initiative, safeguarded by the Italian constitution. Since the Antitrust Agency still lacks the right to bring the case to the Constitutional Court, this strategy remains less effective than the direct application of European regulations. But it has been successfully applied to the telecommunications and the transport sectors (Meli, 1997, pp. 254-56).

These two strategies have left the multitude of Italian legal provisions very vulnerable to the intrusions of the antitrust laws (Meli, 1997, p. 251). According to the antitrust law, the legal provisions obstructing competition are often not comprehensive regulatory regimes that define and justify the limits of excluded sectors (Valdina, 1995), but are an innumerable number of administrative rules that have sedimented over more than a century. These rules have proven to be easy prey for the onslaught of the Antitrust Agency. More often than not, they have proven an inadequate shield for antitrust scrutiny (Meli, 1997, pp. 251-52). Administrative concessions were often granted not by law but rather by ministerial decree. Many laws failed to explicitly specify the mission for which the special right was granted, and if such a justification was provided, it was often obsolete due to technical progress. Finally, many of them contradicted EC regulations.

To conclude, the analysis of the Antitrust Authority has shown the importance of the agency as an agent of regulatory reform. Some even argue that it has become the main agent (Meli, 1997, p. 246):

> (...) because of static legislation, the Antitrust law has taken on new responsibilities, including redefining the boundaries of the public sector. By using courageous and sometimes risky interpretations of legal provisions, a pincer has been created. This pincer movement, formed by Rome and Brussels, is attacking protected sectors, forcing them to open up to competition.

The European Link of the Italian Antitrust Law

The last two sections have presented evidence that the Italian antitrust law is a force to be reckoned with in regulatory reform. This section is designed to substantiate the contention that the Italian antitrust law is part and parcel of international, and especially *European*, reform pressures on Italian economic policy. This claim is likely to encounter disbelief, since the antitrust law is a national law, enforced by a national Agency and rooted in the national political system and a legal system involving judicial review. The problem usually discussed with reference to the antitrust body concerns which branch of government an independent regulatory body belongs to. The fact that it is a national institution seems to remain unquestioned most of the time.

In Europe, antitrust policy has primarily been of international origin. In fact, in the most important European economies of Britain, France and Germany it was introduced after the war because of the US desire to prevent the distortion of international free trade by European cartels. For a few decades, the enforcement of antitrust statutes remained rather ineffective. Transnational pressure was needed to make antitrust law operational; and only with the Single Market Programme of the European Union did antitrust law enforcement become fully effective (Dumez and Jeunemaître, 1996).

In contrast to this general European tendency, Italy adopted an antitrust statute only in 1990, and (as shown above) its implementation was effective soon afterwards. However, as in the major European economies, transnational influence was the prime reason for the rise of antitrust policy. The evidence for this is overwhelming.[23] The Commission and the European Parliament were of the opinion that the future Single Market would require an equal antitrust regime throughout the Community and therefore urged member states without an antitrust statute to adopt one (Amato, 1996, p. 161). The Commission even provided an outline of how the Italian antitrust statute should be designed (Ministero dell'Industria, 1988, pp. 569-71). Consequently, the core provisions that define anti-competitive behaviour, the 'abuse of a dominant position' and 'restrictive agreements', were nearly faithful translations of the corresponding articles of the Treaty of Rome. The rest of the statute is also very close to the European model (Bernini, 1996, p. 10).

The sophisticated attempt to co-ordinate the scope of the national and the European antitrust jurisdictions is another piece of evidence for the very close connection between the European and the national law. The Italian antitrust law may be seen as an innovative contribution to the tricky legal problem of deciding which law applies to a specific antitrust case. Whereas the standard solution in the past was to assign cases on an ad hoc basis according to a rule of predominant relevance, the Italian law introduced a principle of reciprocal exclusivity (Scassellati-Sforzolini and Siragusa, 1992, pp. 99-114).[24] Cases of mere national relevance are treated by the national Agency; cases of international relevance fall under Community jurisdiction (F. Rossi, 1996, p. 1360). This mechanism of co-ordination between the Community and the national antitrust regime has recently been revised (see below).

Finally, another indication of the innovative character of the antitrust law is the fact that the body, founded for the task of enforcement, was established as an independent regulatory agency (Militello, 1995). Until recently, this model was not among the rich organisational varieties of Italian administrative bodies. It has to be considered a copy of the US model (Cassese, 1995a, p. 56). This explains the difficulties in accomodating this new form into the existent institutional structure. It is sometimes treated as part of the administration and sometimes as a part of the judiciary, although it does not correspond to either of the two (Cassese, 1995a, p. 910).

The international origin of the Italian antitrust law is not surprising, not only because it is similar to the general European experience, but also because imitation is a common form of policy innovation. It has been pointed out that this type of innovation does not imply mere copying but usually involves institutional adaptation. The model may be foreign, but the national result is usually quite different (Majone, 1991, p. 80). Therefore, the fact that the antitrust law is of international origin does not imply that there is a *sustained* international influence. In the process of adaptation, the national antitrust policy may depart significantly from the original model by developing its own decision-making principles. It is likely to become a national policy with distinct characteristics, different from the same policy in other countries.

The institutionalisation of an antitrust regime in Italy also involved institutional adaptation. As has been shown above, the peculiarity of the Italian Antitrust Agency is its central importance as an agent of regulatory reform. The development of this specific national trait was not accompanied by increasing national isolation. Quite to the contrary, its deregulatory function depended heavily on external (especially European) legal resources. The paradox of the Italian antitrust experience is that its *national* peculiarity consists in the fact that it is to a large degree *transnational*. The international influence is not confined to legal statutes, it also affects routine decision-making. Antitrust decision making develops its own decision making principles in close connection with European antitrust decision-making. Art. 1.4 of the antitrust statute states that the national antitrust enforcement should be based on the principles of Community antitrust law. This 'substantial co-ordination' goes well beyond the usual mode of co-ordination between individual nations and the Community (Rangone, 1995, p. 1344). An analysis of the decision-making practice reveals several ways in which this has taken place (Rangone, 1995; Amato, 1996, pp. 163-71). First, the Italian Antitrust Agency utilises the international legal terminology even when a national equivalent exits. For example, the concepts of 'enterprise' and 'public enterprise' are defined according to Community antitrust jurisdiction (Rangone, 1995, pp. 1309-12). Second, the Antitrust

Agency justifies national decisions on the basis of Community cases. For example, the decision that *Alitalia* was abusing its dominant position on the most important national routes between Rome and Milan was based on two Community precedents (Amato, 1996, pp. 164-65). Finally, this very close co-ordination between the Community and the national level has not been limited to the initial period, when national jurisdiction had not yet been delineated and a doctrine to guide decisions was still missing. Antitrust enforcement in Italy is closely following the evolution of Community juris-prudence. For example, the development of the concept of the 'abuse of a dominant position', which makes it possible to determine if a powerful market position is illegal or not, has been adapted by the national agency (Rangone, 1995, pp. 1323).

These observations lead to the conclusion that Italian antitrust en-forcement has become Europeanised to its very core. The importance of this external legal resource and the scope of its use from its inception make future contradictions between national and the Community level difficult to imagine (Rangone, 1995, p. 1347). On the contrary, the future is more likely to lead to even closer co-operation between the national level and the Community. Currently a reform of the Community antitrust law enforce-ment is under way. In an effort to reduce the increasing workload for the Community antitrust enforcement organ, DGIV, an effort has been made to decentralise antitrust decision making by involving the national antitrust bodies in the enforcement of Community law (McGowan and Wilks, 1995, pp. 155-56.). In Italy, the Antitrust Agency may now conduct the investi-gations of specific cases on behalf of the Commission; it also assists the Commission's personnel in investigations in Italy. The consequence of this development is that the *Autorità* will be directly involved in the decision-making process of the Commission, thus further favouring common en-forcement principles on the Community and the national level (Di Pietro, 1996, p. 497).[25]

Antitrust and Transport

The argument of the preceding sections has been that the Italian Antitrust Agency is an important centre for the promotion of regulatory reform and that the high degree of internationalisation of its policy and enforcement activities is the precondition for effectively exercising this function. How-ever, the argument has been confined to the general level of the state. The question concerning the way it became relevant for the transport sector remains. Here, the most prominent international precedent also suggests that the influence of antitrust on deregulation in the transport sector is neg-ligible. In the USA deregulation in the airline and the road-haulage sectors was promoted by sectoral regulatory agencies. The fact that the reform started within these sectors instead of being forced by external pressures – such as new Congressional legislation or antitrust cases – has been interpreted as comforting evidence that the U.S. political system is able to promote the general interest and escape regulatory capture (Derthick and Quirk, 1985a).

In contrast to the experience in the US, in Italy the Antitrust Agency promoted regulatory reform in the transport sector. This will be shown in the following by a quantitative and qualitative overview of the antitrust activities in the area of transport. The aim is to find out what ratio of the general activities of the agency is dedicated to transport in comparison to other public utilities. Furthermore, I shall assess whether the activities are directed towards the core of the regulatory *status quo* and could thus be the starting point for a fundamental reform, or whether the aims are less ambitious. The argument advanced here is limited to showing that the agency invests a considerable amount of its resources in this area of decision making. The impact of these activities will not be assessed in this chapter. The actual consequences of the antitrust activities for transport regulation depend heavily on environmental factors (such as the general political institutions and the political situation in the sector) and not exclusively on the actions of the agency. They are thus not a good measure of the antitrust efforts. As a consequence, its impact on the transport sector will be dealt with in sectoral case studies.

The analysis of antitrust policy making presented so far has already shown the prominence of advisory activities in the service sector in general and in transport in particular (see above table 4.1). Table 4.3 shows that this is true even in the area of decision-making proper (e.g. when decisions determine if an actual violation of the antitrust law has taken place).

Table 4.3   Antitrust and Transport: Decision making

		1991	1992	1993	1994	1995	1996	Total	%
Agree-	Total	3	14	16	14	5	24	76	100
ment	Services	2	5	10	7	3	12	39	51
	Transport	-	2	3	1	2	5	13	17
	Total	-	5	7	10	11	10	43	100
Abuse	Services	-	3	5	7	6	8	29	67
	Transport	-	1	3	5	3	5	17	40

Source: Autorità Garante (various years, own calculations). Figures refer to proceedings. Mergers are excluded; they rarely violated the antitrust code.

Table 4.3 gives a complete panorama of the history of decision-making in the Antitrust Agency since its foundation. Slightly over half of the proceedings opened refer to restrictive agreements in the service sector (51%), and transport regulation is involved in 17% of the cases. Two thirds of the proceedings regarding the abuse of a dominant position refer to the service sector (67%), and no less than 40% regard transport regulation. Although the service sector is less predominant and transport is less important than in the policy-making activities, the same tendency can easily be identified in the decision-making activity.

The quantitative overview of the distribution of decision making between different sectors and within the transport sector only gives a superficial indication of the importance of the antitrust activities in the transport sector. By analysing some of the major decisions and opinions regarding transport in the following section, I will substantiate the view that something of importance has happened in this sector. The task at hand is not to assess the performance of the organisational structure of the Antitrust Agency's decision-making. The question is whether the activities of the Antitrust Agency have contributed to reforming the area of transport. Since the outcome of decisions depend on factors well beyond the control of the antitrust agency, the *success* in influencing ongoing reform processes or even starting them up does not seem to be an adequate evaluation standard for determining the significance of decision making. Instead, decision making in a given sector is considered to be important when one or both of the two following conditions are fulfilled:

- The action fundamentally questions the regulation or the behaviour of a legal monopoly, where the case is an important precedent for subsequent antitrust action.
- The preconditions for success are respected. The agency tenaciously pursues a case if success is not immediately obtained. Furthermore, decision making and policy making is combined for a stronger impact. Finally, European directives are used to overcome national regulation.[26]

In the following, some of the decision making shall be briefly presented and evaluated according to these, admittedly, arbitrary criteria. Sea and air transport, which are not at the centre of interest in this study, will be treated more superficially. All the major aspects will be dealt with for the two remaining modes, rail and road. First the problems addressed by one or more decisions will be dealt with. Then the decisions addressing them will be illustrated.

The major infrastructure problem addressed by the Antitrust Agency in the sector of maritime transport was the complete absence of competition between different providers of port services. The sole provider of services, such as loading and unloading, etc., was the *Autorità Portuale*. The absence of competition was seen as one of the prime reasons for the low standard of these services and for the subsequent loss of traffic to northern Europe.[27] The activities of the *Autorità Garante* fulfil both criteria established above. The agency aims to overcome the monopoly of the *Autorità Portuale* by removing entry barriers. This is done by deeming the construction of entry barriers as an 'abuse of a dominant position' (Pezzoli and Venanzetti, 1996, pp. 6-7).[28] Furthermore, this decision has been buttressed by a general study on port management and criticism of a new ministerial decree hampering competition in the sector. All of these activities were facilitated by a European directive liberalising the provision of services in ports and by an ECJ decision declaring the national regulation of ports incompatible with European directives (Pezzoli and Venanzetti, 1996, p. 6).

The market regulation of maritime transport has also been subject to comprehensive antitrust activity. A series of decisions have condemned the behaviour of the state-owned firms that provide transport between the mainland and the islands. The firms had developed a number of strategies to keep out competitors. For example, they offered discounts which were not justified by economic rationale, and the operational losses were compensated for indiscriminately with public subsidies (Pezzoli and Venanzetti, 1996, pp. 9-13). This series of decisions, however, was not supplemented by any other activity. The negative view of the plan to sell the holding *Finmare* which owned all the public commercial maritime activities, was aimed at curbing the FS's ambitions in intermodal expansion. This was seen as extending a dominant position. Despite the absence of integrated activity, a series of no less than four decisions addressing the same problem may be interpreted as demonstrating the tenacious pursuit of the goal of reducing entry barriers. Furthermore, the decision *Marinzulich-Tirrenia* was a decision with subsequent relevance for decision making in other sectors.

The competition problems regarding airports, one of the main components of the air transport infrastructure, were the same as the problems that appeared in sea ports. The activities were not as comprehensive as in the case of sea ports since the actions were restricted to decision-making about competition obstacles in that sector. (Pezzoli and Venanzetti, 1996, p. 8). However, there were still a whole series of decisions pursuing the same objective.

The most important activity in the air-transport sector regarded the national air carrier Alitalia. This is a particularly striking example of the

Antitrust Agency's fight against legal monopolies. Like other transport sectors, air transport has recently been liberalised by European regulations (e.g. Kassim, 1996), opening up the national markets to other national and foreign airlines. The prospect of increasing competition in national markets was not greeted enthusiastically in Italy. The Italian national airline Alitalia developed counterstrategies to stop the advent of competition in the Italian market. First, the company tried to defend its legal monopoly in court, challenging the market access of new national companies. After this strategy failed because the administrative court decided that the national monopoly could not be upheld in the face of contradicting European directives, Alitalia tried to obstruct new competitors (Autorità Garante, 1996b, pp. 5-37). The obstruction relied on using its role in distributing landing rights ('slots'), a power which had been granted to Alitalia as a national carrier. By meticulously revealing the unfair and illegal practice that Alitalia had developed to do this, the Authority dealt a blow to the image of Alitalia as a public company. However, the government was also tarnished. In the opinion of the Antitrust Agency, part of the responsibility for the anti-competitive behaviour lay with the Ministry of Transport. The fact that Alitalia was still in control of slot assignment was due to the faulty implementation of the European directives liberalising air transport (Autorità Garante, 1996b, pp. 10, 24). As in the areas previously mentioned, the activities concerning Alitalia can be considered fundamental for the regulatory structure of air transport. Furthermore, decision making was supplemented by policy making, and both were developed with reference to Community directives.

This brief overview shows that decision making in this area was relevant, according to the criteria established above. Especially in the area of public procurement but also in the restriction of the monopoly powers of the state railways, fundamental practices were called into question. All the available instruments were used to develop a powerful strategy. However, in the area of public procurement, the combination of sectoral studies, decision making and reference to the new Community legislation gave rise to the most elaborate strategy.

The quantitative and qualitative analysis of antitrust decision making presented here leads to the conclusion that the Antitrust Agency has directed a considerable amount of attention towards transport.[29] A large ratio of their activities have regarded transport matters, and in many instances competition problems were addressed with comprehensive strategies. The only other sector subject to such intensive antitrust activity was telecommunications. The expectation that antitrust is an important agent of regulatory reform in transport is well founded.

Conclusion

In this chapter the formal link between Europe and Italy has been analysed. The lead question was: to what extent did Europe influence national policy making? The analysis was focused on a general state level as opposed to a specific sectoral level. On this level, the conclusion is that prospects for a European influence on Italy have improved considerably. The gloomy picture – that prospects for implementation are bad – has to be modified. It is based exclusively on the formal implementation structure, especially on the low efficiency of the Italian administration. Admittedly, there has been no radical reform of the Italian administration. The modest success of administrative reforms does not justify a modification of implementation expectations. However, improvements in the second dimension of European-Italian link have improved the chances of a European influence. The creation of the Italian Antitrust Agency has considerably changed the enforcement situation. With respect to the policy development presented in the previous chapter, the present analysis has one important implication: the lack of convergence between national and European transport policies cannot simply be explained on this general level. There is a need to further explain the national policy dynamics and the form of the European influence on them. This will be done in the subsequent chapters, with an analysis at the sectoral level.

Notes

[1] For some examples of such a national co-ordination mechanism aimed at developing a coherent national policy position regarding Community issues see for France Lesquesne (1993), for the Netherlands van den Bos (1991) and for Italy Franchini (1993).

[2] For the most detailed description of the co-ordination structure see Franchini (1993, chapter one) and Ronzitti (1987).

[3] It is a prerequisite of European reforms and Europeanisation, however, that a convergence of different practices towards one common practice is achieved. Therefore, even the most efficient participation at the Community level could never entirely prevent from having to adapt a member state.

[4] The underlying paradox that governments can translate their weakness in the international arena into domestic strength has been highlighted by Putnam (1988) and applied to the analysis of the European Union by Moravscik (1994) and Grande (1996). A good example is monetary policy. Italy participated in the European Monetary System to be able to adopt a strict monetary policy, forcing the Italian industry on international markets

into competition on the basis of product quality rather than price. The aim was to improve the industrial structure (Padoan, 1994).

5 Another problem in implementation may be that administrative implementation of Community law may lead to the pursuit of a different goal than was intended by the Community. A case study of the implementation of social regulation in road haulage in Italy revealed that the Italian administration used the new social regulation not to improve working conditions but to improve the compliance of firms with their obligations on social taxation (Pocar et al., 1988, p. 506). This type of goal displacement may reduce the effectiveness in spite of formal implementation at the administrative level.

6 To my knowledge, no detailed empirical investigation exists on the process of *administrative* implementation, i.e. transposition by '*circolari*' and application. The fact that it does not work well can only be deduced from the bad implementation record.

7 If one considers an increased involvement of parliament in the implementation process to be positive because it enhances its democratic legitimisation, the reform also had a positive side. It did create more room for parliament to act in this kind of process (Morisi, 1992). This normative criterion is less of a concern for this research.

8 Calculations are based on implementation data from 1978 to 1993.

9 This impression is confirmed by the standard reference textbook on economic regulation, which deals with regulation without any systematic reference to antitrust (Kahn, 1970).

10 From the point of view of efficiency it is suboptimal to use antitrust legislation for regulatory purposes and regulation for antitrust purposes (Spulber, 1989, p. 629).

11 The bill by Senator Rossi opted for an enforcement by the ordinary judiciary and by the interministerial committee for economic planning (CIPE). The Senator maintained that antitrust could not be based solely on the goal of achieving competition, but should aim at achieving a multitude of goals such as consumer protection, etc. (Rossi, 1995). The bill by the Minister of Industry Battaglia, on the other hand, contained the provision of an antitrust agency modelled as an 'independent regulatory agency' right from the beginning. This difference has been one of the main contentions in the legislative process. The first bill was questioned because it seemed to put too much emphasis on state control and thus repeated mistakes of the past. The second bill has been attacked for being technocratic and undemocratic (Donativi, 1990, chapter eight, especially pp. 295-313).

12 This article does not seem to offer the basis for further sectoral studies of this kind. However, it demonstrates quite clearly the importance of state intervention as a focus of activity of the Antitrust Agency. Otherwise, the sectoral studies would have been aimed at private firms, for example studies of the concentration level in a specific sector.

13 The reference is to the *Istituto per la Vigilanza sulle Assicurazioni Private e d'Interesse Collettivo* (ISVAP).

14 The sectoral agency also evaluated the competitive situation, but announced that it will notify the Antitrust Agency if it has any suspicion that the agreement is a significant threat to competition (Il Sole 24 Ore, 31.05.1997: 32). This intention of collaboration

seems to make conflict less likely, but the fact that it did explicitly deal with competition issues and gave detailed recommendations about how to ensure conformity with the principles of competition may give rise to some conflict in the future.

[15] This is not to deny that antitrust was important for 'deregulation' in other countries. In the US energy sector, antitrust law enforcement has played a facilitating role in regulatory reform (Wise, 1996, p. 276). However, it would be a gross exaggeration to conclude from this that antitrust legislation is primarily opposed to public protectionism. To illustrate this point with the same example, in the US the regulatory agency of the energy sector itself has taken the lead in deregulation (Wise, 1996, p. 270).

[16] All reports during the legislation period conclude that the abuse of a dominant position, rather than mergers, will be the major antitrust problem (Munari, 1991, p. 496).

[17] Three of these sectors have already been identified as priorities in the antitrust law and a schedule for reports on them was set. The sectors concerned are public works, commercial distribution, and the legal regime of public utilities (Art 24 of law 287/90). The basis for the general competency of investigating sectoral competition dynamics is Art 12.2 of law 287/90. For a legal commentary see Aquilanti (1993).

[18] See Art 21 of law 287/90. For a legal commentary see Aquilanti (1993a). In the case of regulatory reform of the public utilities, these powers have been expanded. The law introducing regulatory agencies for the public utilities in Italy requires a mandatory hearing for the Antitrust Agency on each sectoral reform (Autorità garante, 1996, p. 13).

[19] There are a several ways to measure the importance of this area of decision making. One would be to assess the resources invested in comparison with the true enforcement activities. A rough indicator could be the amount of manpower/hours involved in these type of activities. This could be supplemented by an institutional comparison. Here, a second best solution is pursued. A description of the scope and the type of work is used to make the argument that this area of activity is of comparable standing to competition law enforcement. The primary source is the overview of Parcu (1996).

[20] The significance of the competition policy activities could be substantiated more fully by an analysis of the sectoral studies and the opinions. It is reasonable to assume that their effectiveness increases with the depth of the problem diagnosis and the type of solutions proposed. Furthermore, coherence amongst the different studies may enhance their effectiveness. I could not find any qualitative analysis of this type of activity that goes beyond the description of single cases. However, the sectoral study on public utilities seems to offer a broad outline for more specific investigations and opinions in this area (Autorità garante, 1994a).

[21] 1669 decisions are about mergers compared to 164 about 'abuse of a dominant position' and 210 about 'restrictive agreements'.

[22] For the analysis concerned with the focus of the Antitrust Authority's attention it is irrelevant if this opinion is based on a correct perception of the economic reality or if it is a result of ingenious lobbying by the private sector.

[23] This may be the reason why in the literature cited only one casual remark seems to refer to national factors in explaining the rise of competition law in Italy: the concern that without antitrust regulation denationalised industries would completely escape state control (Scassellati-Sforzolini and Siragusa, 1992, p. 93). National factors are usually only mentioned to explain the take-off of antitrust enforcement. It is maintained that the corruption scandals that led to the crisis of the political system since 1992 have boosted the effect of antitrust legislation. However, this cannot explain the timing of the start of the legislative process since it dates back to the mid-1980s, a time when no one would have predicted the current crisis of the regime. National factors seem to be negligible.

[24] An interesting aspect of this arrangement is that this principle restricts the scope of the national law even further than would have been required by Community law (Scassellati-Sforzolini and Siragusa, 1992, p. 99). The rationale was as follows: 'sovereignty' was voluntarily sacrificed in order to avoid the risk that Italian administrative courts, which 'may be very strict on jurisdictional issues,' overrule a large number of antitrust decisions (Scassellati-Sforzolini and Siragusa, 1992, p. 114).

[25] The Italian case seems to suggest that the Community antitrust policy is not just a supranational policy, because of its firm institutionalisation at the Community level (McGowan and Wilks, 1995), but that it is rather a transnational regime consisting of a complicated integration of national and Community jurisdictions.

[26] For the last two conditions of success see Parcu (1996).

[27] An indication of the level of inefficiency was that ships often preferred the port of Rotterdam to any Italian port, even when the goods were destined for Italy.

[28] In the case *Nuova Italian Coke/Provveditorato al Porti di Venezia*, the latter, as a provider of unloading services for coal, denied authorisation to the former, a private company that wanted to enter the market, forcing all ships to use Venezia's infrastructure.

[29] For a detailed analysis of the influence of antitrust decision making on road haulage policy and for the influence on railway policy see see chapter five.

5 Europeanisation and the Regulatory Policy Cycle

The development of Italian transport policy is puzzling. The previous chapter showed that the structure linking Italy to Europe has been strengthened considerably over the last decade. So why was there no convergence of Italian and European transport policy? Did the CTP exert no influence at all in Italy? If this turns out to be the case, then what is the explanation for this phenomenon? This chapter is devoted to an explanatory attempt based on an implicit middle-range theory of how the EU influences its member states. The functionalist theory of the 'regulatory policy cycle' outlined in the introduction identifies a series of problems that have to be overcome if European decisions are to make a difference at the national level. This chapter shows that several of these obstacles have not been overcome in Italian transport policy. Therefore, the described lack of convergence does not disconfirm the theory. However, given that the characteristics of this case are not so rare after all, the question is whether breakdowns in the regulatory policy cycle will be more frequent and whether the success of the Single Market Programme has to be attributed to other factors. Following from this, we ask whether the functionalist theory offers an adequate explanation of the national impact of European policies.

How Does the European Policy Cycle Work?

The theory of the European policy cycle was developed to explain what is widely believed to be a success story in the European Community. After a long period of stagnation, the Single Market Programme is thought to have finally been highly consequential for the member states, unlike many other policy programmes before. The theory of the regulatory policy cycle combines many partial theories in an attempt to explain the consequences of EU decision making (Mény et al., 1996, pp. 2-9). A fuller explanation was given in the introduction. We shall therefore summarise the four basic obstacles that have to be overcome if a European decision is going to make a difference at the national level.

1. For the policy programmes to become relevant at the national level, a policy decision has to be made. Because of the divergent national interests, this has proven to be difficult throughout the history of the Community. However, these difficulties were overcome in the Single Market Programme. The institutional reform of the Single European Act replaced unanimity with qualified-majority voting. More importantly, the regulatory approach pursued by the Commission changed. Prior to the Single Market Programme, the introduction of equal rules was seen as a prerequisite for enlarging the Common Market. This preoccupation with harmonisation often caused decision deadlocks at the European level, preventing the inception of European policies. These problems were overcome by a new regulatory approach based on the principle of 'mutual recognition' (Alter and Meunier-Aitsahalia, 1994). This principle implies that different rules in different member states have to be accepted as functionally equivalent if they meet some basic standards. These differences may not be used to curb the free flow of production factors between the member states. This principle substantially limits the number of issues that have to be settled on the European level to complete the Single Market, it thus reduced the required consensus.

2. In spite of the more modest approach of European decision making, the Single Market Programme gave rise to policies which were often contradictory to national traditions. The risk was that member states would fight off European policies by implementing them badly. According to the theory of the regulatory policy cycle, effective implementation is ensured by the threat of judicial review (Weiler, 1991). Private and public actors, if they have a vested interest, try to enforce EU legislation via national courts. In the course of the judicial review the original decision has sometimes been enforced by the European Court of Justice. In this way, enforcement is ensured despite the modest ability of the Community institutions.

3. Traditionally, enforcement by judicial review has been the central mechanism securing the influence of European decision making at the level of the member states. Judicial review is supplemented by a second mechanism. Once harmonisation is replaced by mutual recognition, member states have to adjust their regulation to minimise competitive disadvantages with respect to other member states. A 'competition among rules' (Woolcock, 1996) may ensue, forcing convergence. Private actors with economic stakes may force adaptation by voice or exit. Regulatory competition is a po-

litical mechanism rather than a legal one like the enforcement by law. However, it is important to note that the latter depends on the former. Only the effective implementation of deregulation creates a competitive situation.

4. Finally, the process of adapting to a new legal and economic situation in the member states may in turn create a demand for new regulations such as higher standards in harmonisation or controls on negative externalities. This demand for new regulations closes the regulatory policy cycle, permanently linking the European to the national level in a consequential way.

In the following sections, each of these successive steps will be analysed to see if this theory is able to explain Italian transport policy dynamics. The sectors of road and rail shall be treated separately.

European Decision Making

Within the framework of the regulatory policy cycle the problem of decision-making deadlocks at the European level is overcome by a change in the decision-making rules. One particular change in the regulatory approach of the European Commission is of particular consequence: namely, the introduction of the principle of 'mutual recognition'. Is this the way that decision-making deadlocks have been overcome in the case of transport policy? On a superficial level, this is true. In fact, as was shown in the analysis of European transport policy, in both cases examined here major European decisions have indeed been made. However, it is my contention that this has come about at a cost, a cost which will have important consequences for subsequent stages of the policy cycle. The improved decision-making conditions have not eliminated the necessity for compromises between the diverging national interests. Decisions have either entered into force gradually and/or they have involved compromises on the contents. Softening contents and schedules has important effects on the likelihood that they will make a difference at the national level.[1]

In *road haulage* both elements of the European policy cycle are relevant for the decision reached in 1993. For some period the Commission strategy of complete harmonisation was one of the major reasons for the failure to achieve agreement. Despite several changes, some aspects of the comprehensive policy regime proposed by the Commission remained unacceptable to some member states. This strategy of complete harmonisation was abolished at the beginning of the 1970s and replaced with a strategy which was much less demanding. It was therefore much closer to the principle of 'mutual recognition'. The change in strategy did not lead to immediate success, however. The coalition opposing the proposal of the Commission refused to accept the liberalisation strategy without the creation of a truly level playing field. In other words, the approach of 'mutual recognition' was not politically acceptable. This only changed when it was embraced by the Single Market Programme in the *Cassis de Dijon* ruling. Furthermore, the introduction of qualified-majority voting increased the effort required to resist compromise. Although a decision was finally reached, it is obvious that this was no easy task. First of all, only in 1993, eight years after the Single Market Programme was adopted, was the decision to liberalise road haulage made. Second, the decision did not introduce complete liberalisation, but defined a transition phase of another 5 years until 1998. The cost of the compromise was this considerable time delay. If the decision to adopt the Single Market Programme is taken as a base line, it took 13 years to legally introduce an integrated market for road-haulage services. However, it is important to note that although decision-making did take a long time, the issue as such has not been affected. There has been complete liberalisation of road haulage.[2] The level of harmonisation which was reached in the area of taxation and road pricing was very modest and did not curb liberalisation in any way. With respect to road haulage, the impact of European decision making may be limited by this delay. However, this may not be decisive, since member states often anticipate policy developments at the European level.

A decision has also been made on *railway policy*. However, the explanatory factors proposed in the model seem to be less relevant than in the case of road haulage. In fact, the history of the decision-making process leading to the first true Community railway policy differs a great deal from that of road haulage. Whereas the idea of a Common Market for road-haulage services existed for decades before a decision was made to pursue it, the project of a Common Market for railway services was an invention of the 1980s. In the discussions, the main issue was not whether the idea of 'mutual recognition', with a minimum level of harmonisation, was acceptable. On the contrary, due to the high demands of technical compatibility, the creation of a common railway market inevitably involved more technical harmonisation. Another reason why the approach of mutual recognition was not attractive was the high level of uncertainty expected. No one knew what the effect of multi-operator competition throughout the Community would be. As a consequence, the resulting policy only marked a very tentative move towards liberalisation. In the road-haulage sector, by contrast, liberalisation was created in one leap. Reform was limited to a very narrowly-defined market segment. Legal obligations which were necessary to adjust the former state monopolies to a situation of competition were another reason for its modest scope. Although the new decision rules made the compromise more probable, the main reason that the final decision to move towards a Single Market was made was the very limited scope of the policy.[3] Policies in both sectors have been incremental, albeit to a different extent. Road-haulage policy was introduced slowly but without compromising the goal of liberalisation. Unlike the case in road haulage, in railway policy it was and is still not easy to predict the final form of the CRP, let alone its results. The new European railway policy has little to do with 'mutual recognition'. It is the result of the conventional approach of softening the contents of the policy adopted (e.g. Baier et al., 1988). In both cases, however, the necessity of compromising still has an impact on decision making and potentially narrows the impact of the policies.

Implementation and Enforcement

One of the central aspects of European decision making is its relatively low ambition to create comprehensive rule systems to achieve complete harmonisation. This does not imply that implementation and enforcement have become less relevant. In order for the subsequent mechanism of mutual recognition to be able to work, measures to liberalise markets on a European scale have to be effectively implemented. Ineffective implementation of liberalisation measures will prevent further 'regulatory rapprochement' (Majone, 1994a) by competition. We thus come to the question: have the European directives liberalising market access in road and rail been implemented in Italy? Special attention has to be paid to enforcement, which is important for the effectiveness of European policy making, at least according to the theory of the regulatory policy cycle.

Road Haulage

In road haulage the implementation of the European directive liberalising cabotage did not encounter any problems in any of the member states, including Italy (Commission, 1997: 111). The number of Community licences has been steadily increasing from the first decision to partially liberalise European markets (Confetra, 1996, p. 11). This incidence of rather unlikely compliance may be due to the fact that foreign haulier associations would have immediately complained about shortcomings in Italy (with foreign governments possibly retaliating). Another reason may be that liberalisation did not involve any complex legal changes. Only the administrative acts that restricted licences to nationals had to be abolished. The administrative procedures for issuing licences to non-nationals had been in place for a long time (Interview Ministero dei Trasporti, MCTC, January 1996).

Even though the directive liberalising the Community road-haulage markets has been implemented and applied, Italian road-haulage policy did develop a compliance problem. From 1990 onwards, Italy granted domestic hauliers subsidies to compensate for the high level of taxes on fuels. This is generally believed to be one of the main reasons for the poor economic situation of the sector. These subsidies have been classified as illegal state aid by the Commission. This episode of non compliance is of particular importance with respect to the model of the regulatory policy cycle. Since subsidies have the effect of attenuating the economic effects of market liberalisation, they may call into question the efficacy of regulatory competition. In the following, Italian subsidies in the road-haulage sector will be analysed in more detail to find out if the mechanism of enforcement in this case is as reliable as the functionalist theory would predict.

Italian Road-Haulage Subsidies The illegal subsidies for the road-haulage industry introduced in 1990 were granted as discounts on the general system of taxation for the transport sector. The complete list regarding taxation on all transport modes consists of over 100 different taxes, ranging from minor administrative charges to important sources of state revenue, for example, taxes on petroleum products (Centro Europa Ricerche, 1995, pp. 50-51).[4] The taxes relevant for road hauliers may be classified as follows:

- Registration involves several fees that have to be paid to the *pubblico registro automobilistico* (PRA). These revenues are divided among the central administration, the region and the province of registration.
- Vehicle ownership taxes are mostly paid to regions (regional automobile tax, special regional tax for diesel vehicles, special regional tax), with the exception of a tax on insurance payments.
- Taxation on market entry, apart from some minor charges, consists mainly of fees for the three types of transport licences available: national, a regional and local. Furthermore, two types of general commercial charges arise for transport: the *rilascio partita IVA* and registration fees.
- The most important tax is in the form of taxes on the production and sale (VAT) of petroleum and lubricants. The taxes gathered from this source are about three times the volume of the other categories added together (5,859 thousand million LIT in 1994).

Professional road hauliers do not benefit from any *regular* exemptions to this tax system. All the taxes within the general tax system which are applicable to road transport are applied.[5] The tax credit scheme for professional hauliers, which was introduced in Italy in 1990, was an *irregular* exception. Since its validity was temporary, it did not alter the structure of the tax system as such. From 1990 to 1997, a certain budget was allocated for the purpose of granting compensation to the road hauliers for taxes on the production and sale of fuel. The introduction of tax credits for hauliers in 1990 was designed as compensation for an increase in fuel taxes.

The tax credit scheme will now be presented in more detail. The scheme may be analysed according to its major aspects: the recipients, the taxes on which the tax credit is granted, the yearly budget assigned, the calculation formulae, and the taxes on which the discount may be applied.

- The group which benefited from the tax credit were the professional road hauliers. Own account operators[6] were excluded. Furthermore, in the beginning only national road hauliers were included in the scheme. Later, foreigners also became eligible (see below).
- The credit was applied to the most important aspect of the taxation system, i.e. taxes on fuel and lubricants.[7]
- The yearly budget varied and was assigned in a very complicated process.
- To calculate the tax credit assigned to each road-haulage enterprise the following formula was used. After the budget was allocated, the reimbursement for each vehicle was calculated. To take differing petrol consumption into account, four classes of vehicles were established. A maximum ceiling for each vehicle class was established. This was the maximum an enterprise could get for a vehicle of that specific class. Road-haulage enterprises which wanted to benefit from the scheme had to calculate their real expenditure on fuel and lubricants for each of their vehicles over the course of one year. Their reimbursement was a certain percentage of this expenditure. However, it was impossible to get more than the maximum amount established for each vehicle class. (In 1990 it was not possible for a road-haulage enterprise to get more than LIT 5.676.000 per vehicle.) The tax credit scheme did not involve direct-transfer payments of public money to private enterprises, but consisted of discounts on specific taxes that road hauliers had to pay. In 1994 a minor change in the definition

of the distribution formula limited the maximum number of eligible vehicles to 100.

- Road-haulage enterprises may choose to have a discount on four different types of tax: two forms of income tax (Irpef, Irpeg) municipal tax (Ilor) and VAT.

Table 5.1   Tax Credits for Road Hauliers in Italy

		1990	1991	1992	1993	1994 1st half	1994 2nd half
Budget[a]		422	725	665	570	285	210
% diesel & oil		25%	33%	30%	24,3%	10,%	10%
Max.	< 6t	550	900	810	650	295	280
Per	6-11,5t	1,173	1,850	1,680	1,375	625	580
Vehicle[b]	11,5-24t	3,293	5,310	4,800	3,915	1,790	1,670
	> 24t	5,676	9,030	8,200	6,650	3,045	2,850
Ministerial decree		19.1.90	15.2.91	16.1.93	23.9.93	28.11.94	30.3.95

a) Figures in 1000 million LIT   b) Figures in 1000 LIT

Source: Gazzetta Ufficiale della Repubblica Italiana; Official Journal of the E.C.

This tax credit scheme had significant effects on the sector (Centro Europa Ricerche, 1995, p. 71). In 1991, 44,500 firms received a total reimbursement of 314 thousand million lire, whereas in 1992 47,500 firms received 340 thousand million lire.

In this tax credit scheme, cash flows remain entirely within the administration. The annual budget is used to compensate for the lower revenues generated from road hauliers. This differs from the more common types of public aid in the transport sector, i.e. through direct transfer payments. Railways in all European member states benefit from such practices (Commission, 1995b, p. 35). A tax credit is an indirect benefit with lower visibility and greater uncertainty about the amount of money that will eventually be transferred to the sector.[8]

Community Reaction: the Attempts of the Commission to Put an End to Illegal State Aids The European Commission has repeatedly condemned the tax credit scheme as a form of *state aid* which is not compatible with the Treaty of the European Community. According to the EC Treaty, subsidies are only legitimate in special circumstances. The Italian tax credit is not considered legitimate because it is an 'operating aid', helping firms in financial difficulties without reforming the sector. This judgement cannot be easily dismissed by the Italian authorities. The Commission's power to control subsidies is as exceptional as in the area of competition policy. Whereas the Commission's legislative proposals have to stand the test of the Council and the European Parliament, in matters of state aid control it may issue directly-binding decisions to member states. This power, based on Articles 92 to 94 of the EC Treaty, allows the Commission to intervene anytime there is a distortion of intra-Community competition caused by subsidies from the member states to certain national sectors or firms. This important Commission power basically rests on four pillars (Bellamy and Child, 1993, Chapter 18):

First, the member states are obliged to notify the Commission of any state aid project, even if they do not believe that it might be contrary to Community law. The Commission decides within a period of 2 months if there are substantial doubts about the planned aid that would justify the opening of a contentious proceeding under Article 93 (2). If they fail to meet this obligation, the Commission may suspend the payment immediately after having made an 'interim decision'.

Second, should the aid be non-compatible with the Community law, the Commission may close its contentious procedure with a decision that is directly binding for the member state that granted the aid. This decision usually prohibits further payments within the scheme and requires that those who benefited from the aid repay it.

Third, if the member state does not comply, the Commission has the power to seek a declaration from the Court without having to adhere to the infringement procedure of Article 169, which calls for a preliminary procedure before a formal charge from the Commission.

Fourth, the Commission enjoys a wide margin of discretion in determining what is considered competition-distorting state aid (Interview Commission, DG VII, April 1996; Bellamy and Child, 1993, p. 946). This is mainly due to the fact that hardly any further regulation has been issued by the Council to specify the way the Treaty provisions on state aid should be applied.[9] One of the exceptions, the Council Regulation No. 1107/70 and its modifications, does apply to road haulage. The taming effect of this regulation remains modest, however.

The Commission exercised its competence to force the Italian government to abolish the tax credit scheme for road haulage. The Italian authorities did not notify the Commission about the tax credit scheme, as required by Community law. The staff of DG VII, responsible for transport, learned of the tax credits by chance at the beginning of 1992, two years after they had first been granted (Commission Decision 16.09.1993). Since additional information did not remove the doubts about the compatibility with Community law, a contentious procedure was initiated in October 1992. Italian authorities failed to respond to subsequent requests for further information by mail. The Commission issued its decision in June 1993, judging the aid 'incompatible with the common market' and obliging 'the Italian Republic ...[to] abolish the aid ... and [to] ensure that the aid granted is recovered within two months of the notification of this decision' (Commission Decision 16.09.1993, p. 10).

The Italian authorities remained rather unimpressed, at least judging from their reaction to this decision (Commission Communication 6.1.1996). Current payments were continued and subsidies already granted were not recalled. On the contrary, in the correspondence following this decision the Italian authorities informed the Commission that the aid scheme had been extended to 1993 as well. By the end of 1994, the Commission decided to refer the matter to the Court of Justice. The proceedings were formally opened in August 1995 (European Court of Justice 280/1995). Furthermore, after having been either informed of or having learned of the various extensions of the aid scheme up to 1994, the Commission decided to open a second contentious procedure referring to the aid granted to the hauliers in 1992. However, the initiative did not have any effect in the short run. The Italian government refused to call back the subsidies, claiming that this would be technically impossible. Considering the fact that the credit had been granted on a wide range of different taxes, this is not far-fetched. According to Community law, however, the Italian government is only able to use this excuse if it has made a serious attempt to recover the aid (Bellamy and Child, 1993, pp. 938-39). The only change that the Italian administration introduced to justify the aid scheme strikes any observer as highly peculiar. The aid scheme was formally extended to foreign hauliers operating on Italian territory. This involved complicated changes. The yearly budget had to be split between foreigners and domestic hauliers. Furthermore, a new calculation formula and new procedure had to be invented for foreign hauliers. This part of the scheme actually ceased to be a tax credit because foreign hauliers did not pay the taxes in Italy and the discount on fuel and lubricants had been granted via tax breaks. Its implementation would have involved direct payments to foreign hauliers, similar to the present procedure for the reimbursement of VAT on fuel. A procedure was not worked out, however. The necessary co-operation between the Ministry of Transport and the Ministry of Finance failed (Interview Ministero dei Trasporti, MCTC, January 1996).

At first glance, it seems that the Commission achieved one of its objectives, at least in the medium run. Because of the Commission's objections, the tax credit scheme on fuel was not extended to 1995. By the beginning of 1996, however, subsidies for professional hauliers were introduced in a modified form (Decree-law 20.02.1996). The reduction on fuel taxes was replaced by a discount on vehicle taxes and on motorway tolls. This modified scheme, too, is very likely to be challenged by the Commission, the reason being that it is just another way of alleviating operating costs. There are no parallel restructuring measures (Ferrovie dello Stato, n.d., 3f.). In the case of automobile taxes, such an attempt does not even exist. In the case of motorway tolls, there is an attempt to restructure measures in which firms with a higher turnover are privileged. However, in the case at hand, by the time the scheme had been decided upon, the road haulage associations had worked out a way of establishing a consortium to maximise the discount on motorways tolls without changing their business (e.g. FITA, 1996).

At the end of 1997 the European Court of Justice (ECJ) confirmed the Commission's suspicion that the Italian tax credits granted between 1990 and 1992 were an infringement on Community law. This decision triggered further change. Before a new subsidy scheme was finally adopted, it was co-ordinated with the Directorate General for Transport of the Commission (Il Sole 24 Ore 14.02.1998. 11). The result was that the new subsidies were framed as measures to restructure the sector (law 454/1997). Subsidies may now be claimed by hauliers for improving the firm's management (e.g. by telematic equipment), for purchasing new lorries, for reducing emissions, for professional training, for mergers among small enterprises and finally, for single-lorry enterprises going out of business. The planned budget is 1,800 Million Lire from 1998 to 2001. The average of 600 billion Lire per year is close to the annual average granted under the various tax credit schemes.

Despite the repeated objections of the Commission and the supporting decision of the ECJ, the enforcement of Community law was not very successful. At the end of 1997, none of the subsidies considered to be illegal state aid had been recovered (Il Sole 24 Ore 14.02.1998, p. 11). Furthermore, enforcement did not lead to an end of subsidies to the Italian road haulage sector. What was achieved, however, was that illegal state aid was converted into legal state aid. In three successive steps, first by extending tax credits on fuel to foreign hauliers, then by changing the types of credits granted, and finally by more credibly linking subsidies to sectoral reform, decision makers in Italy learned how to legalise formerly illegal practices. However, it has to be stressed that in this respect, national path dependency has not been interrupted by Community law. Since subsidies reduce the strain road hauliers are exposed to by European-wide competition, one may conclude that in this instance, the expectation of the European policy cycle model was not fulfilled. Although there was no voluntary compliance with Community law and enforcement could have played a part, it certainly did not support the mechanism of regulatory competition.

Challenges to Road Haulage Regulation by Transport Users In the summer of 1993, Confetra (an interest group representing freight forwarders, amongst others) and several associations representing transport users (some of which were part of the Confederation of Italian Industries, *Confindustria*, decided to take legal action against the national tariff system. This decision was a reaction to the fact that the compulsory bracket system had been extended, consequently increasing transport costs for transport users and freight forwarders hiring hauliers. In their opinion, the extension of the types of transport contracts to which the bracket tariffs applied underlined the fact that the Italian system was not compatible with Community law and had to be abolished. They therefore decided to support a company willing to challenge the national tariff system, and they hired lawyers to support their case (Confindustria, n.d.).

The case used by the national associations to challenge the tariff system involved two freight forwarders who disagreed on the question of whether the tariff system applied to a contract between them or not (Dani, 1994, pp. 2-4). *Spedizione Mirittima del Golfo* of Genova, a freight forwarder organising intermodal transport for freight arriving at and leaving harbours, had hired another freight forwarder, *Centro Servizi Spediporto*, to carry out transport operations to various destinations in Italy. The price stipulated in the contract was below the minimum prescribed by the bracket tariff system. According to a common practice, the latter challenged the former in Court claiming the difference between the price stipulated in the contract and the legal price of the tariff system. The former disagreed maintaining that the law did not apply to the delegation of a series of transport operations *en bloc*.

The lawyers hired by the transport associations successfully changed the terms of debate in the case. Instead of building up a line of reasoning to support the sued freight forwarder's claim that his contract did not fall under the compulsory tariff system, they reasoned that the whole tariff system was incompatible with Community law (Dani, 1994, pp. 4-5). The challenge hinged on the fact that the committee making the decisions on tariffs was not acting in the common interest but only took into consideration the road-haulage industry.[10] Their claim was accepted by the Court of Genova and was passed on to the European Court of Justice for a decision. In October 1995 it ruled that the Italian tariff system, including the way national tariffs had been determined, did not constitute an infringement of Community law (European Court of Justice 96/1994). The strategy of the national interest associations of promoting liberalisation via the mechanism of legal enforcement had failed. This was not entirely surprising, since the ECJ had refused to declare national tariff systems incompatible with Community law in two earlier decisions (European Court of Justice 185/1991 and 153/1993). The element of reasoning introduced by the Italian lawyers (that the way the level of the tariffs is determined in Italy is illegal) was not enough for the Court to avert from its past line of reasoning.

Several conclusions can be drawn if this case is evaluated with reference to the theory of the European policy cycle. On the one hand, the Italian interest groups' attempt to challenge national rules by activating the Community's legal enforcement mechanism via a national court is exactly what is predicted by the theory. On the other hand, in this case (as well as in the two German cases about the tariff system) there was no evidence that the ECJ plays a supporting role, as would have been expected by the theory. In many other instances the ECJ had built up a reputation of supporting these claims by giving a wide interpretation of EU law. In the Italian case the fact that the judgement was based on an obsolete analysis, which did not include the recent developments that lent stronger support, is evidence of a very narrow interpretation. This may have been due to specific legal circumstances of the case or to an increasing respect for member-state autonomy. Whatever the reasons, apparently there is no guarantee that the mechanism will work once it is activated. When one considers that activating the mechanism was not straightforward in this case, enforcement by judicial review seems to be contingent on specific circumstance.[11] The successful exercise of judicial enforcement cannot be taken for granted.

Challenges to Road Haulage Regulation by the Antitrust Agency In the previous chapter one of the main arguments was that the Italian Antitrust Authority became an important actor in promoting the enforcement of Community law. The question here is: what role did the antitrust play in the case of road haulage? In general, the road haulage sector does not seem to be a major concern for antitrust agencies, since in comparison with other transport sectors it comes closest to the Community regulatory ideal of a competitive market (OECD, 1990). The technical properties of the sector make anti-competitive behaviour more difficult. The level of co-ordination necessary in road transport between infrastructure (roads) and operation (vehicles) is very low in comparison to rail. Whereas in rail transport rolling stock has to fulfil very specific technical requirements to be compatible with the infrastructure, and movement has to be co-ordinated in advance to ensure safe operation, road transport is a very loosely integrated system. The loose coupling of the systems' components means that dominant positions are difficult to establish. Therefore, two major obstacles to competition that arise in other sectors do not arise in road haulage. Access is easy because there are no dominant positions, and no legal monopoly manages the road network and provides services. In fact, road haulage in all countries – and especially in Italy – is characterised by a very low level of concentration: road haulage firms are very modest in size.

This structure of the transport sector, however, does not imply that the Antitrust Agency is satisfied with the state of competition in this sector. The operation of infrastructure – that is, motorways – has been as anticompetitive as in the other sectors. The legal monopoly regulating the provision of services has been condemned by several decisions of the Antitrust Agency (e.g. Autorità Garante, 1997, pp. 99-105). Since these monopolies are only concerned with auxiliary services such as restaurant and breakdown services, they are less important for the operation of the infrastructure than, for example, harbour handling is for sea transport. The main competition problems in the transport sector result from strict market-access regulation and a bracket tariff system in road haulage. This was the object of an opinion at a very early stage in its operation.[12] However, the opinion was not supplemented by any decisions condemning the anti-competitive practice. This was because the ECJ had declared that the national market-access restrictions and the tariff system were compatible with EC law. There has therefore been no follow-up in this area. This is surprising since there were two occasions when there could have been. First, the permanent extension of the state aid scheme was incompatible with EC law, but it did not elicit a new statement by the Antitrust Agency. Furthermore, the investigation on the anti-competitive self regulation of Italian professions did not include the *Albo Nazionale degli Autotrasportatori*, but was limited to the classical professions (Il Sole 24 Ore, 01.07.1997). The impression is that the decision making of the Antitrust Agency is less forceful than in the other transport sectors. The only sign of importance was that the activities in the area of road transport were not just limited to the road hauliers. A decision demanded that the freight forwarder association abolish the reference tariff it had introduced for all its members (Autorità Garante, 1993). The most forceful intervention regarded the customs freight forwarders (Autorità Garante, 1994). The Agency objected to the introduction of a single compulsory tariff for all the members of their professional association. In doing so it sided with a similar ECJ ruling and opposed the national administration, which had supported the custom freight forwarders in this matter. In this decision, reference was also made to the decision against the tariff of the general freight forwarders and to the opinion about the bracket-tariff-system of the road hauliers. However, the importance of this decision must not be overestimated. The customs hauliers have been decimated by the EC policy to abolish custom controls within the EC. The type of service they provide is becoming less important. The measures to introduce the tariff system may be interpreted as compensation measures. It seems that the most forceful type of intervention in the road-transport sector was aimed at a problem of minor importance.

To date, the Antitrust Authority has not been able to play a major role in promoting a change in the Italian transport policy. The reasons seems to be that Community law did not give the national authority enough leverage. The authority was only successful when it could clearly demonstrate that there was infringement on Community law or that the law had not be implemented (Parcu, 1996). In the case of road haulage regulation, this important prerequisite did not exist after the ECJ decisions. Enforcement was no longer possible; the authority now had to rely on education and agreement.

Railways

It is striking that, throughout the period analysed here, no attempts can be discovered to legally enforce the implementation of the Community obligations concerning the liberalisation of the railway policy. Attempts to do so could have originated where there was a conflict about the Italian railway policy. The main contenders of the Italian railway policy to date have not been Community institutions such as the Commission or the European Parliament; nor have other member states launched complaints about the situation in Italy. The main dissatisfaction with the national policy originated among the trade unions and the users of railway services. Organised either in Confindustria or in the Freight Leaders Club, an association trying to generate expertise and promote policy reform in Italy. Trade unions in Italy, as in other European countries, oppose liberalisation for various reasons. Some argue that liberalisation threatens their organisational base. However, during their opposition to a recent government reform plan, the so called 'Prodi directive', they argued that the reform proposal was actually following the radical British model and stood in contradiction to the proposals of the EU. Since this plan had not been converted into a policy, legal measures were obviously not possible. The same absence of legal action is characteristic of the work of the FLC. Rather than trying to promote liberalisation by challenging national rules, it concentrates on providing policy expertise and on lobbying at the European and national level.

The Italian Antitrust Agency is the exception to this general fact. The rail sector has been the object of comprehensive and continual investigation by the Antitrust Agency. The first problem that was addressed was the absence of competition in the vast rail-supply industry. For most of the postwar period, and not only in Italy, competition in public procurement has not been a concern. On the contrary, large suppliers were seen as offering an efficient way to satisfy the needs of the state. The choice of suppliers was also guided by industrial policy considerations.[13] On the issue of public procurement, the Italian legal framework mirrored this state of affairs. Its sole preoccupation was safeguarding the administration's budget from corruption. There was a complete disinterest in the effects of public procurement on competition (Amorelli, 1993, p. 280). In the European Community this state of affairs was changed by regulations liberalising the sector and allowing intra-Community competition. This is the background for the activities of the Antitrust Agency in the railway sector. The first undertaking consisted of a general study on competition in public procurement.[14] This was the basis for a general study on the sector of public procurement of rolling stock, and two subsequent decisions on two consortia supplying the railways (Ninni, 1995). Other decisions in the area of public procurement followed, all of which seem to have been rather successful in reducing obstacles for foreign competitors and lowering the price of the supplies (Pezzoli, 1995, pp. 239-241).

The second type of problem addressed is more central to the concern here: that problem is that the FS was abusing its monopoly power by hampering access to the railway infrastructure. In Italy, free access to service provision in the national railway networks is impossible, even in the very limited form that has become mandatory by Community legislation. Furthermore, demand for access to the railway network in Italy has been very modest.[15] Consequently, competition problems relating to free market access have not been a major problem to date. Two cases of co-operation between railways and companies providing intermodal services have been interpreted as having restrictive implications for market access. In both instances the agreements regarded companies that had close ties with the state railways. According to the decision of the Authority, treating them with preference would have created an obstacle for other potential competitors (Pezzoli and Venanzetti, 1996, p. 4).

Finally, a third problem originated from the railways strategy of expanding horizontally into other modes of transport: the Antitrust Agency interpreted the railways' strategy as an expansion of its dominant position, in short, as a strategy that would be detrimental to competition in the sector. In an opinion voiced to the government and the Ministry of Transport, it opposed the plan to sell *Finmare*, a public financial holding managing all public maritime transport activities, to the state railways. Another decision concerned the FS's acquisition of a group of bus companies involved in long-distance passenger transport. This merger was only allowed on the condition that control was limited to the one company that served the same lines as the FS (Pezzoli and Venanzetti, 1996, p. 13).

The analysis of the antitrust activities shows that they did not promote the market liberalisation initiatives of the CRP. Those activities were aimed at reducing the risk that the railways become a dominant private monopoly power in the transport market. This mirrors a contradiction between the CRP, on the one hand, which promotes co-operation among railways, and between railways and other modes of transport, and European Competition policy, on the other hand. The Italian antitrust action regarding railways therefore has even been viewed as contradicting European transport policy (Interview Italcontainer March 1997).

If we exclude the activities of the Antitrust Authority, given that they are not directly relevant for the enforcement of the liberalisation of railways, we may conclude that the enforcement mechanism has not been activated in the case of railway policy. This finding is surprising considering the regulatory policy framework, especially since Italy has not yet correctly implemented the European provisions. A rather simple explanation for this is suggested by the development of the CRP analysed above. One of the features of the policy is that the legal obligations regarding railway organisation and market access are very modest and have generous deadlines for implementation. The soft character of European railway law is especially pronounced in the delicate area of market access. Here, the most recent progress – i.e. the creation of the European freight freeways - depends on a voluntary agreement between some member states. Given that most obligations only came into force at the end of the study period and given the modest obligations, it is difficult to gain leverage against a reluctant national implementor by activating the European judicial review mechanism.

Conclusion: the Significance of Legal Enforcement

Within the framework of the regulatory policy cycle, legal enforcement is an important component of the formula explaining the success of the Common Market Programme. In the two cases under examination here their importance differed considerably. In the case of road haulage, legal enforcement procedures have been initiated in both possible ways: bottom up by national actors asking for an ECJ judgement, and top down by the Commission signalling an infringement of Community law. The ECJ turned down the national associations initiative which was directed against the Italian tariff system. But near the end of the period analysed it supported the Commission by deciding against Italy in the matter of state aid. In neither incidence, however, did enforcement proceedings lead to a significant change in the Italian road-haulage policy. In contrast to this, in railway policy enforcement proceedings have not been initiated at all. It is therefore safe to conclude that the present development in Italian transport policy has not been significantly changed by the European supranational law.

Regulatory Competition and the Demand for Reregulation

The second component of the regulatory policy cycle model is 'regulatory competition'. Subsequently it will be shown that this component of the regulatory policy cycle also failed to cause changes in the Italian road-haulage and railway sectors. But how exactly does the mechanism of 'regulatory competition' work? How does it cause changes in national regulation? In what respect can it be distinguished from the mechanism of enforcement analysed in the previous section, and finally, in what way is this mechanism relevant for Europe?

The model of regulatory competition was developed to explain the political effects of increasing economic internationalisation. In a world of free trade and unrestricted capital mobility national economies have to compete with one another. To increase national welfare it is necessary that there be national adaptation to international competition. National economic and social regulation and the redistribution policy of the welfare state are seen to profoundly effect the competitive position of a nation-state. Under these circumstances, a relative economic disadvantage between different countries may give rise to pressures to change national rules. Theories usually distinguish between two different kinds of pressures (following Hirschman, 1970): voice versus exit. 'Voice' implies that by shifting the electorate's votes or by influencing interest groups, national governments will adjust the rules so as to reduce the competitive advantage vis-à-vis other national economies. 'Exit' on the other hand refers to the fact that firms – and especially capital – may relocate to more favourable jurisdictions, which may also cause governments to react. Regulatory competition is widely believed to result both in the lowering of standards in economic and (especially) social regulation and in a reduction in the welfare state. However, in some cases standards have increased. This contradiction has given rise to a research agenda which aims to establish a more general model of regulatory competition that is able to explain these opposing dynamics.

Although research on regulatory competition assumes autonomous states in an increasingly integrated global economy, it is obviously relevant for an analysis of the European Union. Economic integration is the core goal of European policy making. Furthermore, in contrast to the situation in the international setting, there is even a supranational law to back up this policy. The mobility of capital and trade between member states of the EU is usually much higher than between EU members and non-members. Furthermore, EU policy making no longer attempts to establish comprehensive regimes within the EU, and it deliberately relies more on the market mechanism to create compatible regimes. Therefore, the mechanism of regulatory competition may be expected to work especially well within the EU.

A problem that arises when applying the model of regulatory competition to the analysis of the EU is that it may become difficult to distinguish it from the mechanism of enforcement. In fact, legal action taken by a private party may be the result of an increase in competitive pressure. The Italian interest groups representing freight forwarders and transport users might have levied an attack against the Italian tariff system because those interest groups faced stronger competition from other European member states. In this case, this episode would have had to be classified as an incidence of regulatory competition. To prevent such a blurring of categories, it is helpful to go back to the general model of regulatory competition and see how the voice mechanism is conceptualised. As mentioned above, the basic assumption is that it takes place between autonomous member states within an international economy. Since there is no supranational law on the international level, regulatory competition excludes even the very idea of judicial enforcement. In regulatory competition, voice only applies to the political action of interest groups (on the governmental and the administrative levels) and to voting by the electorate: 'for institutional competition among states to arise, the actions of *political agents* of different states must be linked to each other' (Gerken, 1995, p. 10, emphasis added). For the context of the analysis within the EU, regulatory competition is only relevant to differences between national rules which have not been harmonised and therefore cannot be changed by legal action. Political action – either at the national or at the supranational level – is necessary to change these rules. To continue with the above example, for the national actors the ECJ's refusal to declare illegal national tariffs implies that increasing compatibility between national and Community rules will depend on the mechanism of mutual recognition, not on the enforcement of Community law. Thus, national actors will continue to be forced to resort to political voice (or exit) to promote change.

The final question about regulatory competition concerns its preconditions. When does regulatory competition work? The first, more trivial precondition is that there be an imbalance in the 'terms of trade'. Political pressure will only arise in countries which suffer a competitive disadvantage because of their rules. Theoretically, this may seem easy to establish. If there is a negative trade balance or firms and capital move away and if national rules are the reason for this, then political pressure is likely. However, all of this may be difficult to verify. Is there really a competitive disadvantage and how can national rules be changed to enhance competitiveness (S. Vogel, 1997, p. 190)? Furthermore, the question may arise concerning how they will have to be changed in order to create a better competitive situation. A second set of preconditions concerns the workings of voice and exit, the two kind of reactions (Sun and Pelkmans, 1995, pp. 72-78). First of all, price differentials may not give rise to exit. For example, firms may choose not to relocate because they feel competitive despite the regulatory disadvantages. Or there is incomplete information about competitive advantages and disadvantages. Second, voice may not arise because of a lack of political influence, or it may be aimed, not at promoting deregulation, but at finding legal escape-routes to mitigate the competitive pressure. Finally, governments may still decide not to change the rules because exit or voice may not be enough of an incentive to make it possible.

Regulatory Competition in Transport

Regulatory competition arises whenever there is a choice between different jurisdictions. Whenever free trade allows a consumer to chose products produced under different regulatory regimes and whenever firms and capital can relocate in the search for more favourable environments, different rules enter into competition with one another. This may be illustrated by a well-known case of regulatory competition in the United States. In the U.S., most companies choose to register in the state of Delaware because it offers the most favourable regulatory environment business. This is possible because companies have the right to chose the law governing the company regardless of where the actual business activity will be located. This choice among jurisdictions would not exist if they would subsequently have to restrict their business to the state of registration only (Trachtman, 1993, pp. 61-62).

In the case of manufacturing, the question of whether a choice between different jurisdictions exists is easier to settle than in the case of transport. A special characteristic of transport is that it is a service that is not produced in one location and subsequently traded. Transport between two different countries within the EU, for example, involves activities in both national territories. Legally there would be no difference from the conventional case of manufacturing if only the rules of the country of origin of the transport firm applied: for example, if an Italian haulier transporting goods from Milan to Munich was only subject to Italian regulation and taxation. However, this is not the case. The production of transport services is governed by rules that originate in the country of origin and rules originating in the destination country. To continue the example, the

Italian road haulier is subject to Italian market access requirements but in Germany he has to adhere to local traffic rules. These are two different types of rules. Rules which apply due to the country of registration are rules that follow the *principle of nationality*. Rules valid within a jurisdiction irrespective of the country of origin are designed according to the *principle of territoriality* (Rommerskirchen, 1985, pp. 217-18). The relative importance of the two principles for the whole complex of rules governing transport varies across different member states. Furthermore, there may be differences in various aspects of the rules. For example, in Germany motorway financing relies on taxes, thus following the principle of nationality. In Italy motorways are financed by user charges. Since these have to be paid by all users irrespective of their nationality, the principle of territoriality applies. Now, why does the fact that rules governing transport are designed according to the principle of territoriality as well as nationality have an effect on regulatory competition? First of all, with respect to all rules following the principle of territoriality, neither firms nor transport users have a choice about jurisdiction. If the Italian road haulier were to register as a German haulier, he would still have to pay Italian motorway tolls. In this respect he would have no competitive advantage compared to his former situation as an Italian haulier. Choice of jurisdiction only applies to rules designed according to the principle of nationality. The Italian road haulier moving to Germany might find out that corporate taxes are lower, and would thus improve his competitiveness. However, it is difficult to compare the costs of different governance structures (Rommerskirchen, 1985). It is notoriously difficult to determine when a level playing field is achieved within the EU, i.e. when no jurisdiction has a competitive advantage over an other.[16]

In the following, the influence of regulatory competition on the policy dynamics in Italy will be analysed. First of all, we shall determine whether a change in the competitive situation was due to market liberalisation, and second, how national actors reacted to this change. It shall be shown that these cases confirm that 'actual processes of regulatory competition in the EC are very difficult to observe. The iterative process fuelled by business-government interaction can be very time-consuming and fraught with many potential obstacles.' (Sun and Pelkmans, 1995, p. 83).

Regulatory Competition in the Road-Haulage Sector

For regulatory competition to arise, a difference in productivity between the different national road-haulage industries is not enough. The competitive disadvantage is only likely to exert force if it has positive consequences on the market, or in other words, if transport users, such as industry or national freight forwarders, increasingly prefer the services of foreign hauliers. The European deregulation of the transport markets has introduced free choice among hauliers. Due to the liberalisation of cabotage, foreign hauliers can provide transport services without any restriction within the Community. The question is, however, to what extent this possibility gives rise to shifts in the market share of each national road-haulage industry. Do national transport users actually change their preferences because of these new possibilities? Which industries are the winners, and by contrast, who loses market shares to foreigners? This question is of special interest to member states which would like to avoid disadvantages to their domestic industries. They have therefore retained the right to temporarily suspend liberalisation in cases when competition would too abruptly disrupt the former market equilibria. The Commission therefore monitors the effect of liberalisation on national markets by statistics on cabotage transport, i.e. on hauliers operating outside their country of registration.

Since licences for cabotage transport were issued, this type of transport has increased throughout the Community, and it now represents a significant share of the market. Transport users have taken advantage of the new opportunities offered by liberalisation (Commission, 1997, p. 41). As anticipated, the negative and positive effects of liberalisation are distributed unequally across member states. Table 5.2 shows how successful national road-haulage industries have been in exporting their services to other member states.

Table 5.2   *Cabotage* **by Nationality of Haulier** *

	1990[a]	1991	1992	1993	1994
Germany	20	74	70	44	56
France	26	110	98	125	172
Netherlands	38	128	202	226	350
Belgium	42	139	142	233	237
Luxembourg	15	48	66	80	78
U.K.	3	33	34	41	41
Ireland	6	13	8	5	11
Denmark	15	58	69	59	n.d.
Spain	2	5	13	19	38
Portugal	0	3	3	3	6
Total	167	611	705	835	989

*Figures in million tonnes-kilometres.   a. Figures refer to second half only.

Source: Commission (1997, p. 41); data for Italy unfortunately omitted without comment.

Table 5.3 shows, the size of the national market for cabotage transport:

Table 5.3   *Cabotage* **in EU-Member States**∗

	1991	1992	1993
Germany	370	431	534
France	54	61	106
Italy	99	103	89
Netherlands	13	12	5
Belgium	17	23	11
U.K.	36	35	28
Ireland	5	5	3
Denmark	3	2	4
Greece	0.08	0.3	3
Spain	15	22	34
Portugal	1	10	14

∗ Figures in million tonnes-kilometers.

Source: Commission (1997, p. 42).

The relevant trends emerging from the data may be summarised as follows:

1. The 'balance of trade' for transport services differs significantly across countries. Dutch and Belgian firms are by far the most successful exporters of transport services, but their markets are not attractive for foreigners. Such road-haulage sectors with a positive balance of trade may be classified as 'winners'. Germany is at the other extreme. It is a very attractive market for cabotage (because of its size and geographical location), but it is less successful in exporting services to other European countries. Industries such as the German road hauliers have to be classified as 'losers'. Finally, there are countries only marginally affected by cabotage operations – for whom they are neither a threat nor an opportunity – such as Ireland or Portugal. These may be classified as 'spectators'.

2. Italy, like Germany and France, has been put under competitive pressure by the liberalisation of cabotage. It has developed the third largest market for cabotage operations in the Community. However, for Italy it is not possible to establish the balance of trade because no figures exist on the number of cabotage opera-

tions carried out by Italian hauliers. Given that the competitiveness of Italian hauliers in international markets has been declining for more than a decade, they are not likely to be successful in cabotage markets either.[17] The Italian road-haulage sector must be classified as a losing industry.

3.   These economic trends justify the expectation that the mechanism of regulatory competition will start working in Germany and Italy. One would expect the national road-haulage industries in these countries to either relocate or exert political pressure to improve their conditions. At first glance, this expectation seems to be confirmed in Italy. During the period under investigation here, political voice has been a decisive factor in the development of the transport policy. The alliance of the interest groups representing the small hauliers had a formidable impact on the development of national policy (see chapter 6). The political pressure on the numerous governments and the administration was aimed at increasing the protectionist market regulation (raising the barriers for new entrants and fix high tariffs). Secondly, as clear from the analysis above, it tried to increase tax subsidies on petroleum. There is no doubt that political voice was a highly salient feature of transport policy making during the last decade. Political voice did not result in the more prominent dynamics of competitive deregulation, but in competition for subsidies.[18] Nevertheless, this seems to be a case of regulatory competition. A closer examination of the history and the contents of political voice, however, shows that it is very hard to link it to European deregulation and the subsequent rise of cabotage. It is much more plausible to think of political voice in road haulage as being entirely nationally framed. This is true for both of the political goals of the small hauliers. The demand for subsidies first arose in 1990, after the Italian government increased fuel taxation. There is no evidence that the subsidies were designed to be compatible with Community law. Still, occasionally the demand for subsidies was justified by refering to competitive disadvantages the companies had in comparison with other European hauliers. However, this type of justification is weak because it ignores that foreigners also have to pay more for fuel in Italy. Since this is a tax that is levied according to the principle of territoriality, it does not create competitive distortions. The administration so much as admitted this by giving foreigners the possibility of profiting from the tax subsidies as well. The second aspect of political voice, the demand for increasing protectionism, cannot be considered a part of the mecha-

nism of regulatory competition induced by European deregulation. In fact, in the context of European deregulation, the hauliers' strategy of increasing their revenues by raising protectionist barriers is actually self-defeating. Market access restrictions are illegal, because they contradict the Single market policies in road haulage, and the tariff system, which is difficult to enforce among nationals, would be even more difficult to apply to foreign hauliers. Therefore, all market restrictions would *de facto* only apply to national hauliers. In the context of a protectionist market in Italy, any foreign haulier would have an advantage over nationals. A protectionist policy only increases the benefits if it applies to all hauliers, as was the case before cabotage was liberalised.[19] As in the case of fuel taxation, historical circumstances also run counter to the hypothesis that Europe exerted influence in this area, since the struggle of the haulier interest groups for more protectionism goes back to the 1960s, well before the advent of the CTP. To conclude, although political voice by economic actors was a very prominent feature of the period under study here, it is hard to attribute it to European liberalisation. Neither timing nor policy content lead to such a conclusion. On the contrary, they correspond to the general inward-looking character of economic policy making in Italy, an 'introvert state' (Bianchi, 1995).

If the previous analysis is correct in primarily attributing the pressure on the Italian hauliers to national factors, then it follows that political voice was not triggered by the mechanism of regulatory competition, as had been predicted by the model of the regulatory policy cycle. There are two major reasons that regulatory competition failed in the case of road haulage, despite considerable pressure from cabotage transport. As was noted before, European liberalisation creates pressure only in the areas where the principle of nationality applies. In Italy this is especially true for market regulation, i.e. the regulation of market access and conduct. In this area of national regulation, no pressure for deregulation was exerted by the national hauliers. This is due to the fact that for decades they had been fighting to enforce this type of market regulation in order to improve their lot. Demanding deregulation would have required an about-turn by the hauliers. Furthermore, it is important to note that most of the costs that hauliers have to bear, and which therefore have a detrimental effect on their competitive position within Europe, are levied according to the principle of territoriality. In contrast to Germany, for example, where roads are mostly paid for by national taxes and no road user charges exist, in Italy a system of motorway tolls is in place. Therefore, Italian hauliers do not suffer from the costs of the former regulation, but rather from their former benefits. For this reason, it is more unlikely that they respond in the way predicted by the model. Still, the hauliers may have reacted differently if the external pressure of cabotage had greatly deteriorated the economic position of the national hauliers. However, the increase in cabotage in Italy was unlikely to produce such an external shock. The Italian road haulage sector has been experiencing difficulties for decades (Ministero dei Trasporti, 1977, n.d.a). Road haulage enterprises are very small and inefficient. The sector has severe structural problems. The low efficiency of the Italian, as compared to other European road-haulage sectors, may be traced back a long time. Ever since 1970, the Italian hauliers have been losing market shares to their European competitors in the international market. In spite of the fact that no new ordinary licences were issued from 1985 to 1997, the domestic market was characterised by ruinous competition. In this dismal state of affairs the significant rise of cabotage was not enough to provoke regulatory competition. The political struggle of the national haulier associations remained firmly focused on the national context.

Regulatory Competition in the Railway Sector

The mechanism of regulatory competition only works if there is competition for goods or services that have been produced in different jurisdictions. In the case of road haulage, such competition has indeed been created by the CTP. In some member states of the EU, the liberalisation of cabotage has given rise to a considerable amount of competition between foreign and national hauliers. Developments in the railway sector, in contrast, are much more modest. The CRP has not liberalised the market for railway services to the same extent. As is clear from this analysis, the CRP has extended access rights to allow other firms to offer railway services on the national networks, which were formerly exclusively used by the national railway monopolies (see chapter 3). However, this extension of access rights has been very modest: it is restricted to 'international groupings of railway enterprises' providing freight services. A further restriction of regulatory competition arises from the fact that at least one of them has to be registered in the country where the service is provided. In Italy the impact of the CRP's modest steps has been hampered by the slow and ineffective implementation of European liberalisation measures.[20] The technical and procedural prerequisites which would allow other operators free network access still need to be created. Given these circumstances, it is no surprise that there is no equivalent to road-haulage cabotage in the case of railways. No foreign enterprises have yet provided regular freight transport service from the port of Genova to Milan, for example. Instead of compiling and interpreting statistics about cabotage as Italian road haulage interest groups do (e.g. Confetra, 1996, pp. 11-14), the division of the Italian railways in charge of studying market trends observes foreign investment and joint ventures between different national railway enterprises in Europe (Spirito, 1996, pp. 2-5). These developments are being watched closely since they are perceived as a competitive threat (Interview Ferrovie dello Stato, February 1997). However, these observations are about possible future competition that has not yet materialised. Therefore, considerable uncertainties are involved in estimating the quantity and quality of competitive pressure that may arise. This may be changed in the future by the introduction of the first 'Trans European Rail Freight Freeway'. These are important corridors on which freight transport on a European scale takes place and which are planned to be opened up to competition between different railway enterprises. A first pilot project of such a freight freeway was started at the beginning of 1998 by a voluntary agreement between Austria, Germany, Denmark, the Netherlands, Sweden and Italy. The corridor basically runs from North to South, from the port of Rotterdam in the Netherlands, through Germany, and all the way down to the South of Italy (Zefelippo, 1997). Although one cannot deny that this could be a decisive step towards creating true competitive pressure between the Italian railways and other European railway companies, it remains to be seen how competitive pressure will develop and which type of political pressure will arise. This question can only be answered in a future analysis.

The observation that the competitive threat to Italian railway enterprises was merely hypothetical until the end of 1997 gives rise to the question regarding whether it was able to trigger any significant form of political voice. As predicted by the regulatory policy cycle model, it shall be shown that – as in the case of road haulage – political voice was indeed a common feature but that it was predominantly linked to national factors.

The Italian railway reform has been characterised by strong political pressure from the railway management and the trade unions. The reform centred on one of the crucial questions for nationalised railways in Europe: the optimal relationship between the state and the railways. The two steps of privatisation focused on redefining this relationship by increasing the railways' autonomy. The first reform was primarily promoted by political pressure from the trade unions. It is mainly due to their initiative that the legal status of the railways was converted from *azienda autonoma* to *ente pubblico economico*. The second major change in the legal status of the Italian railways turned it into a joint stock company. This reform was not due to a change in policy by the government, but to political pressure by the railway management, who had managed to overcome the resistance of the trade unions to the project. As the subsequent conflict between the railways and the Ministry of Transport, the Transport Committee of the Italian Parliament and the Antitrust Authority showed, this step, too, involved increasing the autonomy of the railways. In neither case can political voice be attributed even to hypothetical competitive pressure from other railway companies. This is obvious in reference to the first railway reform of 1985. Although it did take into consideration some aspects of the earlier European-railway policy to justify the increase in autonomy (Coletti, 1985, pp. 339-73), the main reason for the pressure of the trade unions was that the new legal status allowed them to formalise the informal system of industrial relations that had been developed over the years, and thus gave them increased bargaining strength (Interview Federazione Italiana Trasporti, February 1997). The European railway policy had not yet created any legal obligations in this respect. In the second privatisation of the Italian railways it is more difficult to argue that this measure was not linked to projections about future European competitive pressure. The decision took place after the major directive re-launching the CRP had been decided upon. In this case, too, reference was made to the European policy in order to justify the reform. However, there is reason to believe that linking the Italian railway reform with Europe was only a political manoeuvre. This is borne out by the fact that the railway management was actually opposed to the introduction of intramodal competition in rail (Necci, 1994). This attitude is mirrored in the slow implementation of European provisions regarding market access. It contradicts the justification of increasing autonomy with reference to the CRP. Another, more convincing reason for this instance of political voice is the fact that the new entrepreneurial possibilities were essential for managing the big modernisation projects of the Italian railways. The High Speed Railways were especially believed to be important for the economic recovery of the railways. It is therefore safe to conclude that the most important factors triggering political voice were national. Reference was made to the CRP to muster up additional support, but at no point was the political voice a direct consequence of the fact that a Common Market for railway services might be created.

Conclusion

To conclude, during the period studied here shifts in the competitive situation in both sectors did not result in regulatory change. The mechanism of regulatory competition was not set in motion. This is less surprising in the railway sector than in the road-haulage sector, since in the former competitive pressure remained a hypothetical risk, whereas in the latter it became reality. Apparently, the competitive pressure has to be rather drastic for the mechanism of regulatory competition to work. In both cases, potential competitive pressure was mitigated due to political reasons. *European decision making* was a compromise on liberalisation, especially in rail; it thus severely limited the possible increase in competition. Furthermore - especially in the road-haulage sector - unsuccessful *enforcement* of faulty implementation also reduced the competitive pressure on the industry. The dynamics of regulatory competition are strongly dependent on the prior history of the regulatory policy cycle. This weaknesses has had detrimental effects on the working of the mechanism. This conclusion has to be limited to the period of analysis, though. Some protagonists, of course, hope that with liberalisation, advancing regulatory competition may cause convergence in the future.

The Explanatory Power of the Regulatory Policy Cycle

The analysis of the influence of European decision making on Italian transport policy based on the model of the regulatory-policy cycle has shown that each mechanism within the model has performed poorly. Decision making has been based on a compromise (a long transition period in the case of road, weak legal obligations in the case of rail). The legal enforcement of poor implementation was not successful, or it did not work because the legal obligations did not allow for it. Finally, the competitive pressure in both sectors was not enough to trigger regulatory competition and the accompanying regulatory convergence.

What are the implications of these results for the model of regulatory competition? First, it is important to note that the above analysis does not contradict the regulatory-policy-cycle model. The regulatory-policy-cycle model predicts that if the identified obstacles are overcome, there will be national policy adaptation. Since they have not been overcome, the theory explains why the national policy has not adapted to the European policy. Doubt about the model may arise with respect to the claim that in most cases it does explain the success of the policies set out in the Single Market Programme. The transport case is a good starting point for questioning the generalisability of the functionalist model because other factors promoting convergence besides Europeanisation – especially international competition and technological innovation – do not play a role. This point will be further pursued in the general conclusions (see page 181). Second, although the model of the regulatory policy cycle is successful in explaining the absence of policy convergence, it may lead to the conclusion that Europe did not influence Italian policy at all. This is wrong. Europe did influence Italian policy making in various ways. However, the consequences of the European influence have depended on the domestic institutional structure. This is the question that we shall turn to in the following chapter: namely, how has European policy influenced Italian transport reforms?

Notes

[1]   Since the decision-making processes have been analysed already, only the relevant points are summarised here. For a more detailed analysis the reader is referred to the corresponding sections.

[2]   One potential limit could be the 'crisis mechanism' enshrined in the regulation (Gronemeyer, 1994: 270) This allows any member state to suspend liberalisation if the market equilibrium is upset. To my knowledge, no member state has asked to suspend liberalisation on these grounds. The reason could be that no such development has taken place or that the burden of proof is too high to allow such a step.

[3]   Hints that the some aspects were weakened to overcome French opposition seem to support this.

[4]   An exhaustive description of taxes relevant for transport, including tables of revenues to show their relative importance, is offered by the report of the Centro Europa Ricerche (1995).

[5]   The lower taxes on diesel as compared to normal petrol may be considered an implicit regular tax alleviation (Centro Europa Ricerche, 1995: 70).

[6]   In Italy, firms are classified as own account operators if transport is not their primary activity, e.g. a chain supermarket handling its own distribution (see Volta, 1993: 80).

[7]   See *Decreto* Ministry of Transport 30.04.1990 and Commission Decision of 9 June 1993. According to the Commission decision, a tax credit on automobile taxes had been granted as well. This is not mentioned in a later communication (Commission 6.1.96). I will neglect this aspect since it was irrelevant for the ensuing conflict about the scheme, at both national and Community level.

[8]   Besides political convenience there are other advantages. Private petroleum distribution is an obstacle to lowering the price of petroleum and lubricants at the petrol station. Reembursing every petrol station would involve enormous administrative costs. Another alternative to a complicated tax credit scheme would be the lowering of diesel taxes. But although hauliers consume a considerable share they are by no means the only consumers of diesel. So lowering taxes would be a benefit for the road hauliers at the price of a considerable decrease in tax revenue. Tax credits allow an increase in petroleum taxes without harming road hauliers.

[9]   The state aid policy pursued by the Community is specified mostly by the Commission itself through directives and communications to the member states (Commission, 1995).

[10] For an analysis of the work of the Committee in determining the tariffs, see chapter six.

[11] Finding a plaintiff was not an easy task for the associations. Any freight forwarder involved in such a lawsuit risks losing his past and future haulier contractors, because hauliers see the tariff system as a guarantee of an appropriate income (Interview Confindustria May 1996). Furthermore, such a law suit involves considerable economic risk.

[12] See Autorità Garante (1993) and Munari (1994). For details on the regulation of the road-haulage sector see chapter two.

[13] A wide variety of goals were used to justify the absence of competition in the public procurement sector (Pontarollo, 1989)

[14] This study was one of the three general investigations called for by Art. 24 of the antitrust law.

[15] For more details, see chapter three.

[16] Often, competition among different jurisdictions will work even with ambiguous data about respective competitive advantages and disadvantages. It has been observed that 'globalisation' has been invoked to justify policies even in the absence of sound underlying data. The discourse on 'globalisation' has a dynamics of its own (Cerny, 1997: 256). However, this 'constructivist' twist is not included in the conventional 'realist' model of regulatory competition. The model assumes that real differences exist. Deviation from a rational reaction to these objective differences is due to imperfect information (e.g. Sun and Pelkmans, 1995: 84). The examination of the workings of this mechanism is therefore restricted to the effect of 'real' differences in the competitive situation.

[17] The share of Italian hauliers in the international transport market declined from about 50% in 1978 to 32% in 1987 (Strati, 1996: 81f.).

[18] For an analogous distinction between 'locational competition' and 'competition in protectionism', see Gerken (1995: 13-18). The latter is less likely within the EU, since most forms of competitive subsidies are ruled out by the Treaty of Rome.

[19] The purely national frame of reasoning is also emphasised by the German case, where the reaction to liberalisation resulted in the demand for a level playing field on a European scale, not an increase in national protectionism (Teutsch, forthcoming).

[20] For details on the CRP, see chapter two.

6 Europeanisation and Institutional Mediation

The regulatory policy cycle approach to Europeanisation focuses on explaining the influence of European policy on national decision making. It identifies the prerequisites for successfully influencing and changing the mechanisms for the enforcement of EU law and regulatory competition. This approach explicitly does not exclude an institutional dimension. On the contrary, it is hypothesised that once the regulatory policy cycle is operating, it will have consequences in two respects: The structure of interest intermediation will put exclusive national state-interest group relationships under pressure, opening up new and increasingly important access points on the European level. On the cultural level, it is presumed that national policy paradigms will be replaced by European policy paradigms. It is easy to note, however, that the underlying concept of the 'institution' has a functional bias to it: institutions adapt to external influences. The institutional status quo itself does not influence outcomes. Furthermore, because national decision making may be changed easily by European forces, it is not seen as embedded in a national institutional setting. The advantage of this theoretical strategy is parsimony: the national institutional setting does not have to be analysed in order to explain Europeanisation.

In the previous chapter, I concluded that this approach does indeed explain a significant aspect of the dynamics of Italian transport policy. The first question was, why was there no *second-order convergence*, that is, *why did Italian decision-makers not break with their protectionist past and anticipate full liberalisation*? According to the approach, the mechanisms that may overcome the contradictory policy developments did not start working and were thus ineffective in overcoming national policy inertia. Two questions remain unanswered by the theory of the regulatory policy cycle: Why was there *first order divergence* in the case of road haulage – that is, a policy of increasing protectionism in the face of European liberalisation? Furthermore, why did a development of *first order convergence* – that is, incorporation of some European policy elements without a break with the tradition – ensue in the case of rail? Answering this question is required in order to answer another important open question: namely, what is the European influence on national decision making? The 'functionalist bias' of the regulatory policy cycle theory rules out the possibility that a European influence on national decision making is possible when European constraints are weak. The underlying assumption seems to be: if external European forces fail, Europe does not influence national policy making at all. Contrary to this view, however, an analysis of the national institutional context shows that European decisions have been influential; and what is more surprising, they have contributed to divergence as well as to convergence. To show this, first an institutionalist framework for the analysis of Europeanisation shall be presented. This consists of a particular view of institutions, a specification of the institutional variables taken into consideration, and finally, the change mechanism that is included. The two cases – of road and rail – will then be analysed to explain the national policy dynamics and the patterns of Europeanisation. Finally, in the conclusion, the institutionalist development will be evaluated, taking into consideration more recent developments in the road-haulage sector.

How is Europeanisation Mediated by National Institutions?

There is no need to repeat the general discussion of new institutionalism in the analysis of politics. Here, the task is to briefly summarise the main aspects of the model that will be used to guide the institutionalist analysis of Italian policy development.[1]

The central assumption shared by all institutionalist approaches analysing political life is *path dependency*. This is because political action is institutionalised in the form of rules, which can be conceptualised as formal, legal rules or as organisational routines. The consequence of institutionalisation is a political order which adapts to changes on the premises of existing rules. This type of first-order change is the rule; rapid change which involves a break with the past is the exception. In the perspective of the institutionalist model, the impact of European policy making therefore depends on the national context in which decision making occurs. It is here where the mode of translation from the European to the national context is determined.

The institutionalist paradigm seems to be geared more to explain inertia than change. Institutionalists have had difficulties rooting mechanisms of change in the theory itself.[2] 'Learning' is considered one possible mechanism for change. Contrary to the common sense perspective, which links learning to human beings, in an institutionalist perspective learning is applied to the level of organisation. Organisational learning takes place when an organisation changes its routines in reaction to past experiences. Above we argued that this does not exclude learning or action on the individual level. In fact, it has to be acknowledged that individuals have often been very important agents of change. Important actors of this kind figure as policy entrepreneurs in the literature. However, in an institutional perspective, they only make a difference if they contribute to changing processes on the organisational level. Action that does not change organisational routines will remain inconsequential. Successful policy entrepreneurship will have to detect and respect the given set of institutional constraints and opportunities. Including the level of individual action as well as the institutional level does not imply that this level always has to be analysed. Rather, it implies that the decision as to whether change processes have to be included in the analysis depends on the empirical case.

The final step in applying an institutionalist approach to the analysis of the impact of European policies on national policy dynamics is selecting the institutions that matter. The political world potentially consists of an endless number of structures that could be identified as 'institutions'. Furthermore, these may be classified and linked in different ways. Therefore it is essential to choose among different types of institutional structures in order to keep from being overwhelmed by the complexity of a national polity. This choice cannot be justified in a strictly deductive manner from a well established body of undisputed theory, but analytical frameworks commonly used in policy research offer some guidance. For the analysis of Italian transport policy, it is important to chose an approach which is not limited to the analysis of the government and administration, but which also includes sectoral interest groups. In fact, it is widely acknowledged today that Western capitalist economies are governed by a compound of central administration and sectoral interest groups which combine to form sectoral governance structures. This governance structure (also called a policy network) manages the affairs of a sector in a routine way. The relationship between the state and the sectoral interest group, i.e. the structure of the interest intermediation, is crucial in determining the policy outcome. Usually, the relationship can be more suitably characterised by exchange than by a power relationship. It is rare that the administration has a hierarchical mode of policy making. In complex industrial societies the central government needs the co-operation of the interest groups to get the relevant information and prevent the representatives of the sector from building up obstacles to implementation. Under exceptional circumstances, however, the administration may escape the logic of sectoral governance and act against the interests of the sector. This is important for fundamental reform. EU policies have the potential to allow national administration to escape the influence of national interest groups.

The following variables and relations are included in the analysis in order to explain policy development in Italian transport.

- The analysis of the *state capacity* will show how much power the central administration has to influence the course of policy in an extraordinary case.
- The analysis of the *structure of interest intermediation* involves an analysis of all the relevant *sectoral interest groups*, and focuses on the *possibility of influencing* policy according to their own strategies.
- Finally, the *patterns of European influence* on national policy making will be established to find out what influence these have on the dynamics of national policy making. This influence may be exerted on decision-making as well as on the underlying structural variables of the state capacity and interest intermediation. It may even change the preferences of the actors.

The sections analysing these variables will be introduced with the respective hypotheses concerning Italy.

Road Haulage Sector

In the last decade, road haulage policy in Italy has been characterised by little or no reform. Neither the force of EU law nor the market pressure caused by the CTP have been enough to disrupt Italian policy-making routines. In the last chapter, reasons were presented for why the European policy cycle failed to bring about the expected change. This was sufficient to explain why no second-order convergence took place. The reasons are still lacking for the actual development that can be observed, a development called first-order divergence. In the following the national institutional variables responsible for the specific and peculiar development of Italian transport policy development shall be shown. The institutionalist explanation does not primarily aim at supplementing the explanation of the regulatory policy cycle. Rather, the argument is that the European influence can only be observed and analysed within an institutionalist framework. The effect of the European influence on the national policy dynamics, the 'Europeanisation pattern', can only be understood as a product of the interaction between European policy making and the national institutional variables. The result of this analytical perspective is that although the CTP failed to promote policy convergence between Europe and Italy, it did exert an influence at the national level. The surprising result of the institutionalist perspective is that, in the case of road haulage, European influence actually contributed to strengthening the path of first-order divergence.

State Capacity

The structure of the Italian state is the first explanatory factor for the inertia of the governance of road haulage. The probability of comprehensive administrative reform increases with the state's capacity to formulate *autonomous policy goals* and *implementing* them, even if they be against societal interests (Skocpol, 1985, pp. 9-20).[3] According to these factors, Italy has a *'low state capacity'* in the transport sector. First, autonomy from private interests is low. Parliament has largely fallen prey to the onslaught of the lobbyists of the road-haulage sector. Second, the influence of the small haulier association has increased with the ever more prominent role of the Central Committee of the National Register of Professional Road Hauliers.[4] Finally, the possibility of implementing reforms is jeopardised by the high degree of horizontal fragmentation within the central bureaucracy.

In the decade since the beginning of the CTP, Parliament has not been enhancing state autonomy. No proposals have been advanced which would have involved a fundamental reform of the sector. The latest initiative by a member of the Transport Commission of the Chamber of Deputies, Paolo Oberti of FORZA ITALIA, would not lead to a new structuring of the road haulage regulation (Oberti et al., 1995). In fact, neither the traditional restriction on market access nor the mandatory tariffs are questioned. Furthermore, the various recent provisions such as the tax credits and the reinforcement of the protectionist market regulation were criticised but were finally approved (Il Sole 24 Ore, 5.12.1997). Parliament did not offer any significant resistance to the old transport-policy routines (Interview Camera dei Deputati, April 1996).

The National Register of Professional Hauliers has been largely responsible for the low degree of state autonomy. This body has increasingly offered a means for transferring decision making from the public administration to the small-haulier interest groups. This was meticulously demonstrated in the case of mandatory tariffs in the European Court of Justice (Case 96/1994). The advocates' strategy was to challenge the legality of the mandatory tariff system on the grounds that setting tariffs was no longer controlled by the public authority. The Presidents and General Secretaries of road-haulage associations who are members of the Central Committee. are not independent experts on tariffs. On the contrary, the minutes of the negotiations show that they openly speak on behalf of their associations, and that the civil servants have no choice but to agree to decisions made by the hauliers. Economic reasoning is usually ignored in this process. Finally, they reveal that the Minister of Transport actually delegated the power to control tariffs to the Central Committee by agreeing to a new procedure for setting tariffs. Instead of making an autonomous decision, the Minister of Transport issues the agreement reached amongst the hauliers as a ministerial decree. The sole purpose is to convert these agreements into laws. These decrees even contain an explicit reference to its basis, i.e. the agreement reached by the Central Committee. In 1993 the power of the Central Committee was further biased when a majority of the seats were given to the representatives of the hauliers (Decree-law 82/1993). The conclusion that the advocates draw from this evidence is that the public interest is no longer taken into consideration (Dani, 1994, p. 19). The colonisation of the state by the interest groups via the central committee is the most extreme example of low state capacity. This is an obvious obstacle to restructuring the road haulage sector.

The problem of policy co-ordination is another challenge for the action capacity of the state. The administration dealing with transport-related issues is highly fragmented. Contrary to federal systems, the Italian transport administration is highly centralised at the national level. Consequently, the co-ordination problems of federal systems (Scharpf, 1988) are not relevant for Italy. But the high degree of horizontal fragmentation leads to co-ordination problems which are no less severe. The competencies of the administration are divided among several ministries, the most important of which are, besides the Ministry of Transport, the Ministry of Public Works and the Ministry of Merchant Shipping (Russo Frattasi, 1984). The list has to be expanded if further tasks are to be included: the Ministry of Finance is in charge of customs, the Ministry of the Interior is concerned with traffic safety, the Ministry of Health exists for the establishment of safety standards, the Ministry of Labour for the regulation of the professions, and last but not least, the Ministry of the Environment is for transport-related environmental regulation (Strati, 1996, p. 98).

Numerous administrative reforms have aimed to reduce horizontal fragmentation. In 1965 the Directorate General for Planning, Organisation and Co-ordination was founded to improve intermodal co-ordination within the Ministry of Transport.[5] However, at no stage during its 30 years of existence did it effectively fulfil its task (Sanviti, 1992, p. 58, Interview Ministero dei Trasporti, May 1995). Since it was at the same hierarchical level as the other Directorate Generals, it could not contribute to co-ordination without closely collaborating with the Minister's Cabinet. The Cabinet, however, rarely consulted the Directorate General (Interview Ministero dei Trasporti, May 1995). Intermodal co-ordination is not easily achieved at the Cabinet level either, because the contact offices to the various ministries are themselves organised into different transport modes (Sanviti, 1992, p. 57).

From the beginning of the 1990s, several measures were adopted to reduce horizontal fragmentation across different Ministries. In 1993 the Ministry of Merchant Shipping was incorporated into the Ministry of Transport (Costa, 1994). This was designed as a first step in concentrating transport competencies.[6] Formal integration has not yet enhanced actual co-operation (Interview Ministero dei Trasporti, May 1996). The incorporation of the Ministry of Merchant Shipping into the Ministry of Transport marked the end of another reform attempt, started in 1991. The Interministerial Commission for Economic Planning of Transport (CIPET) was abolished after less then two years of existence. In the brief period of its operation, the Committee never managed to influence the Ministries since it failed to gain control over the transport budget (Fontanella 1993). The proposal to create an independent regulatory agency for the transport sector, to safeguard competition in the sector after privatisation and liberalisation was debated for some time without a decision being reached (Il Sole 24 Ore, 12.05.1995; Il Sole 24 Ore, 15.05.1996). Even today, the overwhelming impression is that administrative reforms did not significantly improve the co-ordination capacities. It is therefore still impossible to foresee a major increase in state capacity. The low capacity of the state in the transport sector, which has been analysed in this section, is closely related to the structure of the relationship between the state and interest groups. This is another factor which impedes fundamental reform.

Administrative Interest Intermediation

In the period from the beginning of the 1980s to the present the formerly unified haulier interest groups (Crespi, 1986) went through a period of secession and developed into two opposing coalitions. The different road-haulage organisations that were united before 1985 split up into two opposing blocks with a rather homogeneous membership and a clear cut interest profile. The COORDINAMENTO, a joint venture of *Unione Imprese Trasporti Automobilistici Italiana* (UNITAI)[7] and ANITA, represent the bigger enterprises. This group is determined to face the challenge of the Common Market and is therefore opposed to the protectionist market. U-NATRAS, on the other hand, now represents the small road haulage enterprises, i.e. the *Federazione Autotrasportatori Italiani* (FAI), the *Federazione Italiana Trasportatori Professionali* (FIAP) for industrial enterprises, *Federazione Italiana Trasportatori Artigiani* (FITA), *CONFARTIGIANATO TRASPORTI*, and *Sindacato Nazionale Autotrasportatori Confederazione di Artigianato (*SNA/CASA) for the artisan enterprises. The small road hauliers feel ill-prepared for a Common Market and therefore believe that liberalising the market should be preceded by measures to improve their own competitiveness. Until then, the protectionist regime should be kept in place. UNATRAS boasts a higher number of associates than CO-ORDINAMENTO. From the general political proclamations as well as in the strategies employed, there can be no doubt that there has been an increase in the polarisation of interests between small and big hauliers.[8]

The Interaction Between Interest Groups and the State

The two blocks represented by UNATRAS and COORDINAMENTO do not only differ in their membership structure or their basic interests. They also have developed different strategies to pursue their goals, leading to two distinct types of interaction with the administration. For the purpose of distinguishing between the two, it is useful to draw a distinction between two different forms used to influence public institutions. *Lobbying* mainly aims at influencing policy formulation, and lobbyists address Parliament and the government. Lobbying is thus concerned with more important legislative proposals. *Administrative interest intermediation*, on the other hand, is mainly concerned with collaboration with the administration in implementing new laws (Lehmbruch, 1987).[9]

UNATRAS represents the interests of its clientele predominantly by lobbying and rarely resorts to long-term co-operation with the public administration. However, in characterising the activities of UNATRAS, 'pressurising' is a more suitable term than 'lobbying', since it pursues its various objectives mainly by calling strikes. These strikes are a very powerful instrument since they threaten to paralyse the entire economy. They are primarily addressed to the government. Neither parties, the transport commissions of Parliament nor the administration play a role: 'we always negotiate with the government' (Interview UNATRAS, February 1996).[10] The pattern by now is familiar: first the demands such as tax credits or legislative changes are listed. The presentation of the list is followed by the announcement that a strike will be called if these proposals are not met. Whether there is going to be strike depends on the outcome of the negotiations with the government. With or without a strike, in the end an agreement is inevitable. The government then issues a decree which is usually a copy of the agreement reached with the association. By now this strategy has become self-enforcing since it is the prime source of the new occasions to strike. The wide range of demands is more than the frequently-changing governments can cope with. The unfulfilled promises offer ample reason to announce a new strike in order to remind the government of its obligations and to add some new demands (Interview ANITA, March 1996). In contrast to the activities in lobbying, collaboration with the administration is rare, leading to complaints from the association about the lack of information (e.g. Scazzocchio, 1995, p. 4).

The interest groups within the COORDINAMENTO interact with the public institutions differently. On the one hand, they collaborate closely with the various ministries on technical questions. A few examples are provided by the activities of CONFETRA (Interview CONFETRA, December 1995). The association participated in the reform of the Road Traffic Act, which was dealt with in the Ministry of Public Works. Another example is the reform of special-load-transport regulation. CONFETRA also participated in a working group of the Ministry of the Interior which sought to solve the problem of lorry theft in the South of Italy. This type of collaboration is based on close personal contacts between civil servants and the functionaries of the association. CONFETRA was the only association from the transport sector that was consulted for the first financial law of the Dini Government. The *'canale preferenziale'* (Interview CONFETRA, December 1995) to the administration, however, does not exist as far as the government is concerned.

The COORDINAMENTO does not have the means to counter the power of UNATRAS. Therefore governments are obliged to yield to the demands of UNATRAS, without being able to rely on COORDINAMENTO. In conflicts, COORDINAMENTO does not resort to strike action. It tries to negotiate with the public administration and usually tries to pursue its goals by legal procedures.[11]

So far this section has been dedicated to the analysis of the structure of interest intermediation.[12] The important question still to be resolved is how these developments relate to the lack of regulatory reform in Italy and to the increasing divergence from the model of the CTP. The double structure of interest intermediation has detrimental effects on the capacity of the state to reform the regulatory regime of the sector. First of all, there is an imbalance between lobbying and administrative interest intermediation. Many issues that have to be dealt with at the highest level, such as the determination of tariffs etc., could be treated as technical issues at lower administrative levels. Given limited time and resources, there is less room to attempt to bring about general reforms. Furthermore, the lobbying component is dominated by interest groups which aim only to represent the interests of the (small) road hauliers, not the entire transport sector. They thus do not pursue a more generalised interest, but merely to protect the status quo of a rather homogenous clientele. Interests groups thus mainly influence decision making with particularistic demands. The impact of this type of demand is amplified by the strategic use of blackmailing power, which is not only invoked to influence the government but also to marginalise the representatives of the more general interests of the sector.

A second question arises concerning the influence exerted by the structure of interest intermediation. How does the new polarised structure - with the COORDINAMENTO, on the one hand, and UNATRAS, on the other - compare with the former more unified structure of the *Comitato Permanente d'Intesa*, which represented all of the hauliers? Did the possibility of achieving reforms improve, deteriorate, or has there been no change? The prospects of convergence seem to have improved, when one considers that the establishment of the COORDINAMENTO created a clearly delimited group which is in favour of the CTP, whereas formerly there were merely factions within the single interest groups (Interview ANITA, March 1996). But this advantage has to be weighed against some serious disadvantages. The proponents of liberalisation are much less influential than the proponents of protectionism. Furthermore, because the interests are split into two different coalitions, there is less possibility of conflict mediation. Finally, the administration has lost routine contact with a large part of the sector. It has become more difficult for CONFINDUSTRIA to promote the liberalisation of the sector (Interview CONFINDUSTRIA, May 1996):

> The conflict of interest has become more radical. Whereas in the past artisan hauliers had been members of ANITA, and the first mediation of interests took place within the association, now this group has become external, and they have radicalised their opposition to their former association. This has made things more difficult. In the past, we managed to negotiate the tariffs amongst ourselves, that is Confindustria and all the transport associations. The Minister just formalised the agreement reached. This does not work anymore.

This opinion is in line with all of the recent regulatory developments in the sector, which provide numerous benefits for the small hauliers, such as advantages in legal litigation concerning transport contracts. No signs of regulatory reforms are yet able to be detected.

The Pattern of European Influence: Deviation Amplification

The low state capacity, on the one hand, and the structure of interest intermediation, on the other, are the reasons why the association representing small hauliers is able to exert such a strong influence on policy development. Thus far, increasing protectionism has been their prime goal. The analysis has been restricted to the national level. But what about Europe? How did the CTP influence these national developments? Contrary to the impression conveyed by the analysis employing the theory of the regulatory policy cycle, European policy making did indeed influence the national institutional setting. Surprisingly, the CTP did not promote the convergence between national and European policies. A detailed analysis reveals that the European influence on national policy dynamics supported the trend towards divergence. In the case of Italian road haulage, Europeanisation has amplified deviation. This shall be demonstrated in reference to the European influence both on decision-making dynamics and the structures in which decision making is embedded. The following will present the instances where Europe exerted an influence on national decision making and contributed to increasing divergence.

The European influence is most important in the area of policy making. European transport policy started to influence Italian road haulage regulation long before the Single Market Programme was adopted in 1985. In fact, European transport policy had considerably influenced the major and only post-war road-haulage reform in Italy. By the end of the 1960s, there was considerable debate in Italy on how to reform the national sector in order to overcome what was perceived to be a very unsatisfactory sector, characterised by poor service standards and ruinous competition. The answer was not to decrease the control of the market, but to increase it. In 1974 market access regulation was supplemented by mandatory tariffs. One of the major reasons for this was the European transport policy of the period. Designed as a first step towards a European-wide regulatory regime, the Community introduced a mandatory tariff system for cross-border transport within the Community. In Italy the experience of the Community tariff system favoured the introduction of a national tariff system (Santoro, 1974, pp. 174-75; Interview Ministero dei Trasporti, May 1995). Admittedly, since increasing market regulation on the national level can be seen as a move towards convergence, the fact that Italy emulated Community policy in the early 1970s did not constitute an act of 'deviation amplification' at the time. Only later, after the Single Market Programme had substantially changed the CTP, did this former impetus to the European influence, ironically, make convergence more difficult to achieve.

As was pointed out in the previous chapter, one of the major attempts to influence national policy making was the effort of the Commission to abolish Italian road-haulage subsidies. It was shown that supra-national European law did not have sufficient power to achieve its aim. Italian hauliers have continued to profit from the subsidies. This is not to say that EU law did not make its effects felt on the national level. The ways that subsidies are granted has changed because of the Commission's challenge. According to the perspective of EU-law, one problem with the subsidies was that only Italian hauliers could profit. This constitutes a violation of the Common Market principle of non-discrimination with respect to nationality. As a reaction to this, Italian policy makers did not abandon the scheme but (unsuccessfully) tried to include foreign hauliers as well. A second problem of the Italian road-haulage subsidies related to European law is that subsidies have been granted unconditionally. According to European Union law, subsidies are only acceptable if they are tied to credible restructuring policies. To achieve this, there was an attempt to redirect the funding to industrial-policy programmes. This was done by changing the legal basis of the funds from *ad hoc* laws to industrial policy law for the sector, without, however, tying them to serious re-structuring measures. For example, incentives for mergers between very small enterprises may well lead to formal legal arrangements which satisfy the subsidy criteria. But the economic viability of the enterprises is unlikely to improve (for an example see FITA 1996). In both instances, Italian policy makers reacted to Community decisions by trying to find ways to legally continue former practices. The effect of Europeanisation may be viewed as amplifying deviation, because it increased the legal institutionalisation of the subsidies. The *ad hoc* nature of the legal basis on which funds were granted was overcome and replaced with a more comprehensive system based on industrial policy.

Another case in which the direct European influence on Italian road-haulage regulation can be seen relates to national market access. Part of the liberalisation policy of the CTP aimed to abolish the quantitative access criteria to markets and replace them with qualitative criteria (e.g. financial soundness and professionalism of an enterprise). This goal once again stood in contradiction to the national regulation. In Italy market access has been controlled very strictly indeed. In fact, since 1985 no new licences have been issued on a regular basis. The administration has attempted to keep the transport capacity at the same level for more than a decade. In spite of this, the new European qualitative access criteria were adopted rather swiftly. This even happened with the support of the small interest groups, which are usually opposed to the Community liberalisation policy. They defended the strict implementation of Community provisions on market access, whereas the Ministry of Transport pursued a softer strategy (Tuttotrasporti, September 1988). The reason for this is simple: the qualitative market access criteria were added to the quantitative restrictions. The qualitative access criteria resulted in even higher entry barriers. Arguably, this is the strongest instance indicating how Europeanisation has caused an amplification of deviation. It is not only that protectionism was reinforced, but more fundamentally, that this reinforcement regarded the most important aspect of any protectionist market regulation.

Besides these European influences on decision making, the CTP had other more structural effects on the Italian institutional setting. First, the prime CTP goal of liberalising road haulage policy was one factor that contributed to the polarisation of the Italian interest groups in the second half of the 1980s (Interview Confindustria, May 1996). Second, the decision of the ECJ that the Italian mandatory tariffs are compatible with European Union law has strengthened the Italian opponents of liberalisation, especially the fact that the ECJ does not even consider the determination of tariffs in Italy to contradict European Union competition law even though they are dominated by haulier interest groups (Dani, 1994). This decision enhanced the legitimacy of the opponents of liberalisation, who now use the ECJ decisions as an argument against deregulation and to counter the antitrust criticism of the sector (Interview Ministero dei Trasporti, January 1996, No 1; Interview UNATRAS, February 1996).

To sum up, this analysis has shown that the European influence on national decision making and institutional structures in Italy has lead to an increasingly protectionist trend in the Italian road haulage sector. Nevertheless, the fact that a pattern of deviation amplification has been found has to be put into perspective. With the exception of the issue of market access, Europeanisation has not led to an immediate increase in the protectionism. It has led to a strengthening of pre-existing trends. National factors – namely, the dominant interest groups representing small hauliers – have been primarily responsible for establishing this trend. Identifying a Europeanisation pattern of deviation amplification certainly does not imply that a policy dynamics of divergence would not have evolved at the national level had there been no European influence.

Railway Sector

The development of Italian railway policy has followed a trend more compatible with the European framework than the development of road-haulage policy. Nevertheless, this more favourable development has not lead to a radical break with the original railway reform of the 1980s. It was pointed out above that Italian railway reform was primarily an organisational reform. Since market building was never a high-priority project in the period analysed here, path dependency was not interrupted.[13] The trend has been classified as *first-order convergence* in order to capture the two major aspects of Italian railway policy: that is, a higher compatibility with Europe than road-haulage policy, on the one hand, and reform that does not move beyond the traditional way of framing problems, on the other.

As in the previous section, railway policy development is explained in reference to national institutional variables. The application of an institutionalist approach is plausible, especially when it is compared to the development of road-haulage policy. Whereas EU railway policy has not thus far produced nearly as many legal obligations as road-haulage policy, Italian railway policy has been more compatible with the EU than road haulage. Since the development of Italian railway policy cannot be attributed to the comparative strength of the European policies, it seems obvious that national institutional factors are the explanation. The subsequent question is again: which patterns of Europeanisation resulted from the European pressures on national policy making and structure? Did the European influence promote convergence or did it have little effect?

State Capacity

In contrast to the U.K., in Italy the government and the administration did not develop any clear preference for abolishing the national railway monopoly.[14] Their very first attempt to achieve policy convergence with Europe began as late as 1997. In most sections, the so called *Prodi directive*[15] reads like a catalogue of past Community decisions and proposals: it discusses the organisational separation between infrastructure and operation, and financial restructuring to increase managerial responsibility and reduce state transfer payments. Even a reform of the tariff system has been planned (Il Sole 24 Ore, 01.02.1997). However, it is still not clear if this plan will lead to a new railway policy in the future. Although it contains fundamental changes, no consultation process with either the railway management or the trade unions preceded the directive. Furthermore, the author of the directive, the Minister of Finance, launched the directive without consulting the Minister of Transport (Il Sole 24 Ore, 05.02.1997). The directive has to be regarded as an *ad hoc* answer to the problem of the Italian budget deficit. It was probably triggered by the announcement of new and heavy losses by the railways in 1996. The *ad hoc* nature of the plan stands in stark contrast with its ambitions. Not surprisingly, the intentions of the Government met strong opposition from all of the trade unions. In fact, the only immediate consequence of the Government proposal was that the railway trade unions unified in common opposition to the '*spezzatino ferroviario*', the 'railway ragout'. The major point to which the trade unions objected was the plan to abolish the unity of the railway organisation, creating one company for the railroads and many others for the operation. After only two weeks, the negotiations led to a neutralisation of the directive. Organisational separation ceased to be a short-term policy objective; it was agreed that the financial re-structuration of the railways would not be carried out at the expense of the workers; and the autonomy of collective bargaining was reconfirmed. Subsequently the *direttiva Prodi* remained a force, but only as a long term policy plan (Il Sole 24 Ore, 13.02.1997). Its major aspects later resurfaced in a new policy outline designed to promote market liberalisation (Ministero dei Trasporti 2000).

The episode of the *Prodi directive* is typical of the entire decade of railway reforms. The government never managed to play a crucial role in the railway-reform process of this period. The major promoters of the first reform of 1985 were the trade unions, the protagonist of the legal privatisation of 1992 was the railway management. The Government was mainly preoccupied with mediating between the trade unions and the railway management. The perspective has been short term indeed: how can the next strike be avoided? Considering the magnitude of the financial problems, this finding is a surprise. The low strategic capacity of the Government has to be explained by institutional factors. The instability of governments is one of the most important institutional factors that have weakened the power of the state in Italy. In the period from 1986 to 1996, on average the Transport Minister changed once a year (Ministero dei Trasporti 1996, p. 425). This considerably reduces the relevant time available for action. Furthermore, conflict within the cabinet is rather frequent, as is shown by the recent conflict over pension schemes (Il Sole 24 Ore, 05.12.1997). Under these circumstances, any successful reform in the future will probably add to the reputation of the successor government. Policy is restricted to crisis management.

A second institutional factor is the condition of the Ministry of Transport. It has to rely exclusively on the FS for information about the FS. There is no independent source of information on the railways (Ponti 1996). In fact, the Court of Auditors has criticised the Ministry of Transport for not establishing an adequate supervisory structure for the complicated task of surveillance (Corte dei Conti, 1996). Although the railways were formally privatised in 1985, even by 1997 there was no department contributing to the development of a railway policy within the Ministry.[16] No such structure existed within the Minister's Cabinet (Interview, Ministry of Transport, November 1996). Single advisers external to the Ministry seem to be the only source of independent expertise.[17] This is a weak base for challenging the policy views of the railways.

Yet the institutional weakness of the Government and its administration is not the only reason a comprehensive reform has not yet been drawn up. Neither are there strong institutions that could criticise the present concept of public service. In spite of the resistance of the target industry, in the USA the powerful criticism that certain economic theorists exercised on the protectionist regulatory regime was one of the elements that led to the success of the deregulation policy (Derthick and Quirk, 1985, pp. 246-52). All the requirements necessary for such a mechanism to work seem to be absent in Italy. First, the economic analysis of transport has never produced a coherent and convincing set of arguments against public ownership in that sector. The major research effort in Italy, by the Italian national science foundation, the *Progetto finalizzato trasporti*, focuses on new technical solutions for vehicles and traffic control systems (Bianco, 1996). It does not include economic analysis. Economic transport research seems limited to academia and is ineffective in its criticism of public ownership.[18] This may be because a second important prerequisite for the unfolding of economic ideas is missing in Italy. The mechanisms that transformed economic ideas into policies in the USA are less well developed in Italy. Recruitment patterns in the public administration in Italy are not conducive to the hiring of innovative economists (Bilotta, 1983). Furthermore, no specialised advisory organisations exist to specifically advise policy makers. There is little transfer of scientific knowledge into policies (Regonini and Giuliani, 1994, pp. 138-39).

The lack of institutional prerequisites for reform explains an interesting detail of the *Prodi directive*: although it closely follows the major aspects of the CRP, Europe has not been refereed to in order to overcome national resistance. Since its beginnings, the Italian railway reform process has been well served by invoking the Community when it has sought to introduce unpopular measures. Its provisions came very close to the CRP, and opposition from the trade unions was stiff. Taking these circumstances into consideration, it is surprising that Community obligations were never refereed to in justifying this directive. On the contrary, Community obligations were camouflaged as national decisions. In fact, in the ensuing debate the *Prodi directive* was treated as a national decision, and the trade unions complained that the government did not try to follow the CRP, but the problematic U.K. model (e.g. Interview CISL, February 1997; Interview FISAFS/CISAL, March 1997). The decision makers' poor political management may partially explain this. But it may also be due to the fact that in the case of railway policy, 'cutting-slack' may be as dependent on a high strategic capacity as it is on the national reform itself. The CRP is ambiguous and leaves ample room for interpretation concerning what constitutes compliance. Therefore, it is more difficult to use references to Europe as a substitute for the low strategic capacity of Government.

To conclude, the Government and administration have not become effective promoters of the reform of the railways. Part of the reason why there has been no sustained reform effort on the part of the Government, in spite of the severe financial problems of the railways, is that the Government's weakness is fundamentally due to several institutional factors. This analysis of these institutional factors will be supplemented by an analysis of the role of the other major actors, railway management and the trade unions.

Administrative Interest Intermediation

The structure of the administrative-interest intermediation is more complex in the case of railways than in the case of road haulage. In road haulage this is a bipolar structure, with the administration, on the one hand, and the interest associations, on the other. However, an analysis of the railway policy has to acknowledge a triangular structure of interest intermediation between the Government and administration (especially the Ministry of Transport), the railway management and the trade unions. In the following, the analysis will first deal with the railway management and subsequently with the trade unions.

Management of the State Railways During the last decade, the railway management has reformed the railway organisational structure in various ways. Still, most of the time, management has not univocally pushed for policy convergence with Europe. A closer look at the various management strategies of this period shows that intramodal competition was not seen as a good remedy for the economic difficulties. Since 1986 the railways have had four different managers and corresponding management periods: Ligato (1986-1988), Schimberni (1988-1989), Necci (1989-1996) and Cimoli (since 1996). Two different approaches to the economic difficulties of the railways correspond to these management periods (Ponti, 1992, pp. 130-36; La Repubblica, 23.09.1996). The first type, pursued by Schimberni and Cimoli, consists of a strategy of saving and reducing personnel to reduce the railway budget deficit. Schimberni, for example, decided to abandon plans for building a high-speed railway network in Italy until the FS had brought its deficit under control. Similarly, Cimoli wanted to improve the railways by cutting costs (La Repubblica Affari & Finanza, 18.09.1996). Necci's problem-solving approach contrasts with this, and his is the most ambitious management period in the decade analysed.[19] He attempted to improve the economic performance of the railway by expanding their activities and by conquering new markets. Unlike Schimberni, Necci decided to go ahead with the High-Speed Train, and he planned huge investments in new infrastructure and rolling stock, despite the existing budget deficits (Mondo Economico, 15.07.1996, pp. 10-15). Unlike Cimoli, he decided not to concentrate on providing transport services, which has been the traditional task of the railways; instead, he attempted to diversify the activity of the railways. In attempting to do this he pursued what is known as the strategy of *societarizzazione*. This involved founding over 100 sub-enterprises, and it allowed the FS to involve private partners and to expand its activities into other modes of transport (Ministero dei Trasporti, 1996, p. 88).

Both of the major managerial strategies of the railways welcomed increases in organisational autonomy. During the period of Schimberni the railways tried to enhance their autonomy with generous interpretations of the newly-acquired power to abolish former Ministerial Decrees that were in contradiction with the new legal situation. This gave rise to continual conflicts with the Ministry of Transport (Correale, 1989, p. 5; Colacito, 1989, p. 7). During the period of Necci there was an increased defence of autonomy. First, legal privatisation and contractualisation were actively promoted by the railway management (Il Sole 24 Ore, 1.05.1992, p. 22). This was again opposed by the Minister of Transport (e.g. Il Sole 24 Ore, 17.05 1992, p. 15). It was successful as part of the general privatisation programme that the Amato Government launched in order to overcome the severe economic and political crisis (Claudiani, 1996, p. 7). Furthermore, during the negotiations over the third programme contract for 1994-2000, the railways stubbornly refused any measures meant to enhance the public control over the ever-increasing public investments in the railways (Ponti, 1996a).

As in the Italian railway policy, neither management strategy promoted the market-building intentions of the CRP. This is more visible with the first type of strategy. The organisational reform did not consider the transformation of the monopoly. In fact, this approach is more likely to view the introduction of intramodal competition as a threat to a basically non-competitive organisation (Di Miceli, 1990, p. 358). The second type of strategy, pursued by Necci, did include a vision of a competitive environment. However, unlike the European model, the second strategy emphasised competition between different intermodal alliances in the European market. Intramodal competition between different railways seems only to weaken the railway mode, especially in the face of a transport policy that distorts intermodal competition by favouring road transport. In his capacity as head of the UIC, Necci clearly expressed his doubts about the CRP (1994, 4):

> Presently, a tendency is emerging to introduce competition between infrastructures and between the rail-transport enterprises. If an orientation of this nature prevailed, the outcome would be a further strategic weakening of the railways with respect to the other modes of transport. European railways would be increasingly marginalised, especially in comparison with road transport.

During the management period of Necci the strategic capacity of the railways, and thus their possibility for determining the direction of the railway reform, easily exceeded that of the Government or the administration.

As mentioned above, this is shown by the fact that the frequent attempts to regain control over railway financing failed. This was not only due to the fact that Necci remained in power for a much longer period than the Transport Ministers. It was also because he had developed a vision of how to reform the railways which was shared by a large coalition of interests (La Repubblica, 23.09,1996). His idea of re-launching the railways by investing and by conquering new markets was much more attractive to the interests involved than the strategy of down-sizing, pursued by his predecessor Schimberni. The High-Speed Train promised to be profitable for the various private investors and numerous firms that would have been involved in constructing the infrastructure and the new trains. For the trade unions, the reform was acceptable because growth promised job security. For the Government, the promise of severely reducing debts was also attractive. Even though the Necci era came to an end due to a corruption scandal in 1996, his leadership is still acknowledged to have been based on a coherent vision of how to reform the state railways, a vision that seems to have been unrivalled during the last decade (e.g. Interview FISAFS/CISAL; March 1997). This is also mirrored by the fact that he managed to motivate his collaborators and the staff of the railways beyond the usual level (e.g. Ponti, 1996a, p. 18).

To conclude, during the last decade intramodal competition was not a goal of the railway management's reform efforts.[20] It would have been especially difficult for any of the governments to change this during the Necci era since it would have meant overcoming a coherent reform strategy supported by a large coalition of interests. In the next section, the role of the trade unions will be analysed in more detail, because – in a certain phase - they can present another major obstacle to institutional reform.

Railway Trade Unions In the search for explanatory factors for the development of the railway reform in Italy, the overwhelming impression is that the railway trade unions were and still are one of the major obstacles to the convergence of national and European policies. The fierce trade-union resistance to the Government declaration about the future of railway policy at the beginning of 1997 certainly gives one this impression. It was widely held that the outcome of the subsequent negotiations was a victory for the trade unions (Interview Freight Leaders Club, March 1997).[21]

However, the trade unions can hardly be viewed as merely having blocked the management's reform initiatives. In fact, the trade unions were among the active promoters of the first legal privatisation in 1985. They tenaciously pushed the reform process ahead when a deadlock formed at the beginning of the 1980s (Coletti, 1985, p. 339). They viewed the final reform law – passed in 1985 – as an adequate outcome after years of mobilisation and protest (Coletti, 1985, pp. 371f.). The CISL views the trade unions as having played a fundamental role in promoting the reform at a time when privatisation had not yet become prominent in Europe (Claudiani, 1996, p. 4). One of the major reasons for trade-union support was that privatisation would lead to a more favourable system of industrial relations. In fact, the hope was that abolishing the legal status of *azienda autonoma* would allow the past achievements in contractual bargaining to be legally formalised.[22] Furthermore, it was in the trade unions' interests that the railway economic crisis be overcome, in order to stop further increases in unemployment.

Yet after the first reform law of 1985 passed, the trade unions played a less constructive role. They started to resist the efforts of the management to restructure the railways. So even amongst trade unions themselves the impression was that they were just attempting to slow down the reform process (Interview FISAFS/CISAL, March 1997). This fundamental shift in interest needs to be explained, because it is linked to factors that are important for the future prospects of the railway reform. With the railway reform the management acquired financial responsibility. As a consequence, the high costs of the excess manpower in comparison to other European railways became one of the major problems of railway reform. This problem was a legacy of the past, when the railways were still a part of the public administration and shared its fate of being used to reduce unemployment (Interview CISL, February 1997). Another problem was to simplify the system used for classifying professions and wage levels. Due to the wide range of activities pursued by the former state railways, this was a very complex system (Bordogna, 1992, pp. 80-86). The successful resolution of these problems was thus dependent on the constructive collaboration of the trade unions.

The negotiations for the collective contract under the new regime of autonomous industrial relations constituted the first test that the trade unions faced after adopting a pro-reform strategy. This was part of the railway reform of 1985. The major trade unions agreed to both of the fundamental parts of the reform that concerned them. They negotiated over a new professional classification system. Furthermore, they did not hold out for absolute employment levels, but gave into a decrease in manpower for an increase in salary (Interview CISL, February 1997). However, the proposals advanced by the major trade unions led to widespread dissatisfaction amongst their members. The train drivers were especially dissatisfied with the negotiation proposals. They felt that their specific status within the system of the railways had been neglected. In 1987 they founded a new trade union, the *Coordinamento macchinisti uniti* (COMU), which changed the character of the industrial relations within the railways.[23] At the beginning of the reform, representation was spread amongst the transport sections of the four national confederate trade unions, the FILT/CIGL, FIT/CISL, UILTRASPORTI and the FISAFS/CISAL. They collaborated closely in the negotiations on the National Labour Contract (CCNL) (Bordogna, 1992, pp. 86-88). These trade unions were not organised according to professions; instead each had shares of each professional group within the railway industry. It was difficult to integrate COMU into this traditional system of industrial relations for several reasons. COMU did not view itself as offering general representation to all workers; it spoke only for a specific professional group. Furthermore, COMU did not want to be integrated into the system, instead it accused the trade unions of collaboration with the management and of antidemocratic behaviour (Bordogna, 1991, p. 157). These seem to be the preconditions for a rapid marginalisation rather than for becoming one of the most notorious groups of the COBAS, a social movement which challenged the established trade unions in Italy in the 1980s. The protest of COMU was effective because several factors combined to give them considerable bargaining power. Among the most important was the fact that the train drivers could easily paralyse the circulation of trains. Train-driver strikes are effective because they do not only harm the organisation itself, but the whole universe of potential users.[24] In the past COMU has frequently managed to mobilise its members for strikes.

Both the rise of the COMU and the end of the unity of the railway trade unions had a detrimental effect on the railway reform. First of all, the frequent strikes inflicted considerable economic damage on the railways. Second, there was a great deal of conflict between the confederate trade unions and the COMU. This was caused by COMU's fierce attacks and the fact that the established trade unions had different views about admitting the COMU as a bargaining partner for the national contracts. This made any agreement between the several parties involved very difficult.

In the first half of the 1990s several factors combined to solve the problems generated by excessive trade union activity. After COMU was admitted to the bargaining table and after most of its other demands had been fulfilled, its strikes became less frequent. Furthermore, Necci was successful in winning over the trade unions to his plans by adopting a new financial restructuring strategy. His strategy of re-launching the railways, especially in light of the High-Speed Train project, promised the substantial development that would be needed to secure higher salaries and prevent further job losses. In this period the trade unions returned to their former, more constructive role. It was with their consent that the number of employees was reduced by over 40%, thus putting the Italian railways on a European level of productivity per labour unit. However, Necci's undisputed success in this case came at a high price. Whereas the number of employees dropped, the cost per unit of labour rose sharply, so that in the short- and medium-term the reduction of the work force did not result in a significant improvement in railway finances (Il Sole 24 Ore, 19.12.1997, p. 11).[25] But the established trade unions still feel that they had done their part and they blamed the management for not achieving the growth rates that would have countered this unfavourable development (Claudiani, 1996).

In addition to resisting the reduction in railway employment, trade unions slowed down the reform process in other ways. Their opposition to any form of privatisation prevented gains in efficiency and the possibility of increasing revenue that could be gained through outsourcing. The resistance to the privatisation of the data-processing segment of the railways, TSF (Il Sole 24 Ore, 11.06.1996), not only prevented the railways from making a possible profit and hindered customer service, it also had negative repercussions on the reform of rail freight. Because the telematic infrastructure needed to modernise, combined transport could not be provided (Interview Italcontainer, March 1997). The trade unions' opposition was due to the fact that the workers do not fall under the railway contract if they are no longer integrated into the organisation of the railways. The reason for this is that the National Labour Contracts (CCNL) are classified according to the type of product or service provided (Interview FISAFS/CISAL, March 1997).

It seems fair to conclude that although the national railway reform process was started by the trade unions, the same unions later slowed down the reform process and increased the costs. They were opposed to the organisational division of the FS up to the time of this writing (Il Sole 24 Ore, 3.12.1997) because this would severely reduce their bargaining power. It is important to note that with the rise of the small trade unions representing the train drivers, such as COMU, the structural condition for including the trade unions in the reform processes seems to have become more difficult. A settlement reached with the major trade unions is worth less than before the reform process started because the small autonomous unions can effectively strike whenever they disagree.

European Influence on National Policy Dynamics: Random Enforcement

National institutional factors explain the national policy dynamics and why the influence of the European policy did not lead to convergence between the national and the European policy development. Analysing the national institutional setting provides an opportunity to explain national policy dynamics and the pattern of Europeanisation that prevailed in this sector in the period analysed. In the following it will be demonstrated that, in contrast to the case of road haulage, in rail no coherent pattern of Europeanisation emerged. Over the last decade, European influence has sometimes promoted, at other times delayed, national policy reform. In contrast to the case in road haulage, European influence has never actually promoted divergence, but has enforced the national trend of first-order convergence. A Europeanisation pattern of random enforcement has consequently prevailed. The reason for this is that, in the case of railways, no hegemonic policy project dominated throughout the whole period of analysis. For this reason, at different times different actors have used only parts of the European policy to promote their reform projects. This has resulted in a number of different outcomes. In the road-haulage sector the main actors tried to promote their interests invoking Europe. But when they did so the small hauliers managed to exert a continuous, dominant influence, preventing other national actors from forging a closer link with European actors. This can be shown by briefly recalling how the main actors used references to European policy to influence national decision making. An examination of these episodes also reveals that the references to European decision making has been highly selective.

Railway trade unions were among the main promoters of the 1985 railway reform. This reform preceded all the other European railway reforms by at least a few years. Reference to the European railway policy of the day was used to enhance the legitimacy of the project. In this phase, European railway policy advocated organisational reform in order to overcome the notorious deficits of the European state railways. At the beginning of the Italian railway reform, the trade unions thus created a dynamic of Europeanisation which promoted convergence. After the change in the legal status was achieved, however, trade unions often resisted further liberalisation because they perceived it as a threat to their existence. In the case of the *Prodi directive*, they successfully opposed further reforms with reference to the CRP. When the trade unions put up such stiff opposition with an unchallenged reference to the CRP, they created dynamics that obstructed further reform.

Like the trade unions, the activities of the railway management also resulted in Europeanisation having mixed effects. On the one hand, the CRP was referred to in order to legitimise the formal privatisation of the state railways; the European policy was evoked for this purpose, even though it does not contain obligations regarding the ownership of state railways within the EU. In the same way, Necci's expansionist management strategy was justified by referring to Europe: he claimed that this was part of a modernisation process which had become necessary in the face of imminent European competition. On the other hand, the legal obligations that did result and were designed to lead towards a liberalised market for railway services were not implemented for a long time. The essential measures are still being adopted; that is, the infrastructure and the operation of the railways are still being separated, and the rules for market access criteria are still being developed. With respect to organisational autonomy, an enforcement pattern of Europeanisation can be observed. With respect to market making, the European influence has been mitigated.

The successive Governments exerted no major influence on railway policy. In fact, the central administration was at times desperately fighting to retain a minimum of control over the railways. If the major governmental initiative, the *Prodi directive*, had succeeded, this would have contributed to the pattern of random enforcement. However, since this directive was not part of a coherent policy, but rather a measure adopted to alleviate the national budget and meet the Maastricht convergence criteria, it did not make a difference.

The overall impression conveyed by the random pattern of Europeanisation is that it was not very consequential for Italian policy development. The influence was limited to reinforcing trends that had already been established on the national level. Increasing organisational autonomy has been an issue in Italy since 1985. However, this is not conceived of as part of a bigger project of market building, but rather as an end in itself. Therefore, it may be concluded that the impact of Europeanisation was limited to promoting decisions that would have been made anyway. The above analysis of road haulage resulted in a similar conclusion. Given the former course of decision-making patterns, deviation was not amplified in the rail sector.

Europeanisation and National Entrepreneurial Politics

A comparison between the two transport sectors, road and rail, offers us an opportunity to refine the explanation of the policy development presented so far. From a comparative perspective, the explanation is not yet satisfactory. The choice of state capacity and the structure of the administrative interest intermediation are plausible explanatory variables in each case. However, when rail and road are compared, it is striking that the national policy dynamics as well as the patterns of Europeanisation differ. In the case of road haulage, a national pattern of first-order divergence has been identified, with a Europeanisation pattern that amplifies deviation contributing to this trend. In the railway sector, by contrast, a trend of first-order convergence has been dominant, with Europeanisation randomly enforcing it. Yet, the explanatory variables in both cases have had the same characteristics: in both cases state capacity vis-à-vis the transport sectors has been low. In the period under analysis here, the government and the central administration were paying but not supervising. In spite of not issuing large amounts of money (to road hauliers in the form of subsidies and to railways for their deficits and for investments), the administration was struggling to gain control. Furthermore, in both sectors the structures of the interest intermediation resemble each other in a striking way. Road-haulage interest groups are polarised into two camps, one co-operating with the administration on a routine basis, the other refusing any routine contacts. This split between UNATRAS and Coordinamento is similar to the split between the traditional railway trade unions of CGIL, CISL and UIL, on the one hand, and the autonomous railway trade unions, the *Cobas* and – most notoriously – the train drivers' union, COMU, on the other. In both sectors the camp opposing liberalisation has considerable blackmailing power. Given these close similarities, how is it possible to explain the significant difference in policy dynamics?

The decisive factor determining the national policy development and the pattern of Europeanisation is the type of entrepreneurial politics dominating the sector. Entrepreneurial politics was defined above as the activity of promoting a policy by moulding coalitions, and even more importantly, by shaping a dominant vision of the characteristics of the sector it refers to, i.e. its boundaries, actors, problems and solutions. In both sectors, policy leadership was decisive in this sense. In the railway sector such leadership was exerted vigorously during Necci's exceptional management period. His vision that the Italian state railways was a company that could be modernised by expanding into new areas of business, especially into high-speed passenger transport, mustered up considerable support and even enthusiastic support among the younger staff of the Italian railways.[26] Contrary to his predecessor's project of restructuring the Italian railways by reducing its size and activities, Necci's vision entailed the promise of a positive-sum game for all the parties involved: the end of a burden for the public budget; the promise of a socially acceptable reduction of unemployment for the trade unions; the promise of lucrative orders for construction firms and the supply industries of the Italian railways. Under these conditions, it was difficult for the trade unions to remain in fundamental opposition. In fact, during this period the opposition of the trade unions to the modernisation of the railways reduced significantly, even though the number of employees was cut by nearly fifty percent. Nor did the *Cobas* resort to their blackmailing strategy nearly as frequently as before (Gallori, 1996, pp. 95-104). Part of the explanation for this may be the fact that the privileges of the *Cobas'* clientele were not touched, and generous compensation was granted for premature retirement. The fact that the trade unions would have been resisting a hegemonic reform project that seemed promising for the Italian railways was also important for the acquiescence. In sum, in the case of railway policy, first-order convergence may be attributed to the type of domi-

nant entrepreneurial politics practised. The 1998 road-haulage reform episode (see chapter 3) also confirms the hypothesis that the type of dominant
political leadership in existence determined the national policy dynamics
and the pattern of Europeanisation. This has been neglected in the analysis
so far because this reform attempt failed to overcome the past policy trajec-
tory. However, it shows that the possibility of convergence with Europe
also depends on the entrepreneural politics at the national level.

In 1998 the Italian government advanced proposals that called into
question all the major parameters of the administration of the sector. Once
implemented, the reform would entail substantial sacrifices for the Italian
road hauliers (Interview IVECO, March 1998). If the subsidies are adapted
to European rules, it could become more difficult to obtain them in the
future. They will probably not just be an additional guaranteed income, as
they were in the past. Abolishing the tariff system would put an end to the
possibility that the hauliers now have of charging below the legal minimum
and reclaiming the difference later (often just before abandoning the market). A complete liberalisation of market access would be most painful for
all, not just the small enterprises. Most enterprises operating today have
acquired their licences on the black market. For an average vehicle these
have cost as much as 40 million Lira. Even for a large road haulage enterprise this was a considerable investment. So a common practice among
single independent hauliers was to sell the licences at the end of their working life, this often being their only 'pension scheme'. Thus the most immediate effect of the liberalisation of the domestic market would not be to
increase competition (although this threat has been invoked to muster up
opposition against the reform); instead, the immediate effect would be a
sudden and complete devaluation of the licences that hauliers have had to
pay for and which they regard as an investment and as a property value.
Given the sacrifices required, one would have expected the small hauliers
to resort to the strategies that proved so effective in the past. Why is it
thought that this resistance has not effectively prevented this tentative departure from the previous policy trend?

The obvious answer seems to be that European pressure has finally
overcome the resistance of national policy inertia. The fact that the transition period for the liberalisation of cabotage ended in July 1998 and it is
now valid without any restrictions (Commission, 1997, p. 13) is one piece
of evidence supporting this view. Furthermore, European pressure regarding subsidies has increased. The ECJ supported the Commission's opinion
that the subsidies are not compatible with the EC-Treaty and that it is justified to ask the beneficiaries to pay them back (Il Sole 24 Ore 14.02.1998).
However, it is doubtful that these formal aspects can explain the reform
episode. The liberalisation of cabotage in 1998 had been anticipated for at

least five years, and the decision by the ECJ did not come as a surprise.[27] The rise in European pressure has been modest at best. It cannot explain how the government managed to adopt a new strategy on subsidies and – even more importantly – liberalise market access (see also Interview ANITA, March 1998).

The changes in the coalitions of the road-haulage interest groups are a great deal more important than the European pressure. The former opposition of UNATRAS and COORDINAMENTO broke down. In the middle of 1997, the dominant haulier association, FAI, led by the charismatic, Paolo Uggè, was expelled from the Union of the small haulier associations (Il Sole 24 Ore 10.07.1997, p. 10), mainly because the FAI had acquired too much power and because the artisan hauliers, especially FITA, felt too close to the reform Government to continue the disruptive methods of the past. The FAI has been isolated ever since, and it has been the only force left opposing reform. The former natural representative of the sector, Uggè, has increasingly been seen as an irresponsible politician who was harmful to the sector (Interview ANITA, March 1998; Il Sole 24 Ore 14.02.1998, p. 11). Under these circumstances, a small group of reformers around the Secretary General of ANITA intensified their secret diplomacy to win over the remaining associations. The result of this was the legislative proposal that was subsequently adopted by the Government.

Not only did the hauliers accept liberalisation, they themselves shaped the reform – and in close co-operation with the Government. This reform, which is in outright contradiction with the short-term economic interests of the hauliers, was only possible after the haulier association and their members underwent a slow and painful learning process. The account of one of the major protagonists is revealing in this respect (Interview ANITA, March 1998). He describes the movement towards the reform as a process of convincing the haulier associations that the old political goals were no longer viable (Interview ANITA, March 1998):

> The interests of the hauliers had to be changed. For example, an enterprise with 500 licences demanded half of their present market value as compensation for their devaluation. We have convinced them not to move in this direction; the government would have to refuse. I also argued against suggesting an exchange: liberalisation in exchange for compensation for the present market value of licences. We convinced them that this would imply a vicious circle for the government: hauliers could ask for ever more money for their licences. It is wrong to think of licences as a personal property. We even persuaded enterprises which had hundreds of licences, and therefore were about to lose billions of Lire, that they have to accept this loss. It took us a long time to convince our members to accept this. At one point, after an agreement on liberalisation had been reached within the association, some member at-

tempted to question this decision again. But the Executive Council of ANITA refused to reconsider the issue. It was a long and laborious process to convince our members of this stance.

The same process of deliberation and education has taken place with respect to the subsidies (Interview ANITA, March 1998):

> Hauliers have to learn that the national subsidies have been limited by Brussels to only certain types of investment. There has to be an investment plan: funding may not be used to go on holidays. This is slowly entering into the conscience of the enterprises. You have to explain this a thousand times, on the phone, in letters to our members, in reunions of the members. Members nowadays don't call me anymore to tell me: we have to ask for this from the government and if you do not get it for us you are not worth your money. Nowadays, the question is if it is possible to ask for something like that. I even had the chance to talk to members of other interest groups to convince them of viable strategies and that the era of short-term interest maximisation is over. This is a big change in the mentality of the hauliers. FITA and Confartigianato Trasporti did a tremendous job changing the beliefs of their members. They had to achieve this in one year only, and they managed to do it, in spite of stiff opposition.

The testimony of one of the main protagonists shows that the most important prerequisite for a constructive role in the liberalisation effort was that the strategies and the underlying interests of the road hauliers be remoulded. Given the formidable power of the haulier interest groups, this was an essential step towards the fundamental reform presently in progress. Thus, the reform episode was based on a social learning process initiated by entrepreneural politics. Admittedly, political exchange also played a role. Single haulier enterprises leaving the sector are to be granted benefits which implicitly compensate them for the devaluation of their licence. However, large firms do not get an equivalent compensation. Furthermore, these benefits will only be granted for a limited period of time. Compensation does not imply that there is no sacrifice, only that there is some alleviation. Given the past political behaviour of the hauliers, it may be assumed that a change in preferences was the decisive factor, not the subsequent bargaining process.

It is important to acknowledge that sectoral entrepreneural politics alone did not bring about this change. Another important prerequisite was the change in the public forms of intervention. Instead of ignoring the sector as long as no strike was imminent and then having to react to haulier claims with emergency measures, a long-term strategy was announced. The government rebuilt its lost credibility by providing subsidies without having to be blackmailed into doing so and tying these subsidies into a more comprehensive framework of sectoral reform. Furthermore, it initiated a discussion process among representatives of the sector about sectoral reform. This strategy of 'concertation' also helped to build up trust (Interview ANITA, March 1998). A further important prerequisite for this change was surely the Prodi government's successful launching of many other reforms. What is more, besides being merely successful, the Prodi government appeared to be rather stable. So a fundamental condition for a long-term reform strategy existed. Finally, all the reform efforts converged in the attempt to prepare Italy for the European Monetary Union. The Government thus strengthened the road-haulage reform project by linking it to the general Italian effort for 'entering Europe'.

Several conclusions may be drawn from the institutional analysis presented in this chapter. The first conclusion regards the explanatory value of this approach compared to the approach based on the regulatory policy cycle. Whereas the regulatory policy cycle has convincingly demonstrated why there is no second-order convergence of national and European policies, it has not captured the reason for the resistance of the national policy. This is captured by the institutionalist approach. Furthermore, the institutionalist approach shows how Europe exerted an influence on the national policy dynamics. In the case of rail, this influence resulted in a pattern of random enforcement. In road haulage, the European CTP caused deviation to increase.

To conclude, the comparison between road haulage and the railways shows that in Italian transport regulation the dynamics of Europeanisation depend on national entrepreneural politics. This comparison also allows one to assess the usefulness of two different approaches to the concept of the policy entrepreneur. Presently, various institutionalist approaches are distinguished. A rational-choice-institutionalist framework is adequate whenever preferences remain constant, whereas a fundamental change of actors, strategies, preferences and conflicts is more appropriately analysed in the language of sociological institutionalism. In order to arrive at an action-oriented explanation of change, the concept of the policy entrepreneur as a 'mediator' (Jobert and Muller, 1987; Muller, 1995) is useful. This is most obvious in cases of second-order change, as has been shown by the attempted road-haulage reform. However, the Necci era of railway management shows that mediators can also play an important role in first-order change.

Finally, the explanatory value of the institutionalist approach in comparison to the approach based on the regulatory policy cycle now seems beyond question. Whereas the latter convincingly demonstrated why no second-order convergence of national and European policies occurred, it was not able to give reasons for the resistance of the national policy. This is captured by the institutionalist approach. Furthermore, the institutionalist approach shows how Europe exerted an influence on the national-policy dynamics. In the case of rail, this influence resulted in a pattern of random enforcement. In road haulage, the European CTP caused deviation amplification. In the subsequent general conclusions, the comparison between different approaches to Europeanisation is extended in order to draw some theoretical lessons.

Notes

[1]   See chapter one for the extended presentation and for references.

[2]   See for example Krasner's 'punctuated equilibrium model' (1988).

[3]   Autonomy in this context does not imply perfect independence, but should rather be understood as the ability of the state to manage its dependencies on the environment *according to its own criteria* (Luhmann, 1991: 156). Defined in this way, the concept does not contradict a model of policy making and implementation based on networks of public and private actors (Manytz, 1993).

[4]   The official name of the institution is *albo nazionale degli autotrasportatori di cose per conto di terzi* (see law 298/1974: Title I).

[5]   Intermodal co-ordination is a widespread problem, for the case of Germany see Lehmbruch (1992).

[6]   An ambitious reform in this respect has been proposed by an important governmental advisory body, the Consiglio Nazionale di Economia e del Lavoro (1994). It essentially includes the transfer of competency in the area of infrastructure and the breaking up of the organisation according to different modes of transport.

[7]   UNITAI has replaced FAI as the haulier association belonging to CONFETRA. FAI left the *comitato permanente d'intesa* as well as CONFETRA by 1986.

[8]   Polarisation has not yet put an end to all forms of co-operation. An example for collaboration of UNATRAS and COORDINAMENTO is the foundation of the consortium 'Unione Autotrasportatori Toscani Alta Velocità' (UNATAV). This consortium regulates the work on the High Speed railway line between Florence and Bologna (La Nazione, 25.04.1996).

9   This is only an analytical distinction since the two phases of the policy cycle are closely interrelated.

10 That influencing government decision making is the exclusive aim is shown by the fact that strikes are not called in crisis periods when there is no government in charge (Interview UNATRAS, February 1996).

11 A good example is the decision by the Ministry of Finance to abolish a number of customs offices, creating inconveniences for transport operations. CONFETRA responded to this decision with a letter to the Ministry and was considering legal action. A strike was not considered (Il Sole 24 Ore 24.08.1995 and 31.08.1995).

12 In the case of road haulage the structure of interest intermediation does not correspond to either of the ideal types that LaPalombara proposed for the analysis of Italy (LaPalombara, 1964; 1994). The absence of a *parentela* relationship (LaPalombara, 1964: 306) between haulier associations and a dominant party which offers to specifically promote the haulier interests is obvious. But even a *clientelistic* relationship, where the administration treats an interest group in a sector as its exclusive representative (LaPalombara, 1964: 262), does not fit the situation well since the candidates for such a relationship, CONFETRA or the COORDINAMENTO, did not effectively monopolise their influence on the administration.

13 This may have changed recently with the introduction of the Freight Freeways, which may play a fundamental role in introducing the market issue.

14 For analysis of the British railway reform, see Zahariadis (1996).

15 This directive is not a government decree, thus it has no immediate binding effects. It has to be converted into a law by Parliament. It only has binding effects for the responsible Ministers (Merlini, 1994: 456). It may also be considered a proposal that may be turned into law sometime in future (Interview Camera dei Deputati, February 1997).

16 The unit where one would expect to find such a section on railway policy is called 'Programmazione, Organizzazione e Coordinamento'. The organisation chart does not specify a section that deals specifically with railways.

17 Here the experience of Marco Ponti, a professor of transport economics who has been an advisor to the FS as well as the government, seems to be very illustrative of the limited power of this type expertise (see e.g. Ponti, 1996a).

18 In Germany a liberal approach to transport economics has never been interrupted and has become increasingly influential (Willeke, 1995). This contrasts sharply with the Italian situation. This is not to deny that state ownership has occasionally been identified as a problem for economic efficiency (e.g. Loraschi, 1984).

19 The management period of Ligato is excluded from the analysis here. In the short time before he was swept away by a corruption scandal, he did not leave a mark (see Ponti, 1992: 132).

[20] Admittedly, since 1998 the railway management has become much more open to the possibility of increasing competition in the railway sector (see e.g. Ferrovie dello Stato, 2000). Competitive pressure is now seen as facilitating modernisation rather than threating it (L'Espresso 30.03.2000). Since implementation is still lacking (Il Sole 24 Ore, 24.06.2000), it is still too early to decide whether Italian railway reform has entered a phase of second-order convergence.

[21] It is interesting to note that the protest of the trade unions did not in any way involve a protest against the CRP (see e.g. Interview FIT/CISL, February 1997; Interview FIS-AFS/CISAL March 1997). According to most of the unions, the Government was proposing the U.K. model of reform and not the European model. Since this is only partly correct (the Commission proposal includes the mandatory separation into two independent companies), the question is why this was not highlighted by the trade union protest. They seem to take the introduction of intramodal competition for granted but think that reorganising according to the U.K. model is not the route to take.

[22] This view is supported by the observation that industrial relations existed before the reform of 1985, but only informally, as negotiationed agreements between workers and management. The reform changed the formal status of the system of industrial relations by introducing a system of collective bargaining (Stocchi and De Angelis, 1992).

[23] For the history of the Italian railway trade union movement in general and the rise of COMU, see the account given by one of its main protagonists, Ezio Gallori (1996).

[24] All public sector strikes have high leverage due to their effect on the general public (Ferner and Hyman, 1992: 578).

[25] The train drivers managed to be much less affected than the other professional groups. For example, they managed to defend the need for two drivers on every train. One is sufficient for many European countries.

[26] The transport policy community has baptised this group of loyal supporters 'Necci boys' (Interview FIAT, March 1997).

[27] The decision of the ECJ may only have been a surprise in another respect. In the professional press and in interviews, the Commission's objections to road-haulage subsidies were often equated with an EU decision against them. If any, the surprise might have been that the last word on the matter had not yet been spoken.

7 Conclusions

The analysis of the Italian transport reform presented in the chapters above has been dedicated to the question of how the process of European integration affects the participating member states. The investigation was motivated by two related assumptions. The first expectation was that it would be fruitful to analyse this case within the broader Community context. It was implicitly assumed that a European influence on national policy developments could be expected, but that the nature of this influence and the factors shaping it have to be explained. The chapters above have demonstrated that this approach was justified. The results of the case study shall be summarised in the first section of the conclusion. It was less certain that the second expectation regarding this investigation would be fulfilled. In the introduction I claimed that a study of Italian transport reform has wider implications, since it may contribute to the more general question of how the process of European integration affects the participating nation-states. It is time to see if the case yields some more general lessons regarding the process of Europeanisation. Two interrelated questions were raised at the beginning of this study concerning possible generalisations. First, which approach is suitable for studying Europeanisation processes, and second, more theoretically, how can the factors determining these Europeanisation processes be specified? Finally, the results will be compared with the claims of the Europeanisation literature. The present case study suggests more optimism about the possibilities and effects of the European influence on the national administration and the structure of interest intermediation.

Images of Europeanisation in Comparison With Italian Transport Reform

In order to draw conclusions about the case study presented above, it is convenient to recall the course of the analysis with a brief summary of the main findings of the chapters.

In the introduction different approaches to studying Europeanisation were presented in an attempt to explain the mechanisms through which European policy making can influence the organisational aspects and decision-making patterns of national political systems. Furthermore, reasons were given for why it would be an interesting example to study Europeanisation. Most importantly, the newly consolidated European transport policy stands in stark contradiction to the Italian tradition. This should make any influence clearly visible.

In chapter two the European Common Transport Policy (CTP) was discussed, along with the type of pressure that it may create for member states. Liberalisation in both areas of surface transport, road and rail, has created two forms of pressure: specific legal obligations give rise to implementation pressure; and transport liberalisation also creates pressures to adapt legislation.

As could be expected of Italian policy making in general, chapter three shows that the Italian transport policy in 1985 stood in contradiction to the CTP. It was therefore reasonable to expect the Italian policy to adapt. In the light of European transport policy, however, the developments in Italy are surprising. Although it is not characterised by complete paralysis, for more than a decade, Italian decision making remained on a path contradictory to European policy. Another puzzling aspect of the national policy development is that reforms in the railway sector have been more compatible with Europe than in the road-haulage sector, even though the pressure in the first sector has been lower than in the second.

Given these difficulties of matching the Italian with the European development, and given the traditionally poor Italian record of adapting to Europe, the suspicion arises that European policy has not exerted any influence on Italy. In chapter four the more recent changes which have improved the link between Europe and Italy are presented. Whereas changes in the administration have been modest, the establishment of the Italian Antitrust Agency marks an important step towards improving the likelihood that European policy will influence national policy sectors.

In an attempt to explain why there has been no fundamental move towards adaptation, the first explanatory approach is presented in chapter five. According to what may be viewed as the regulatory-policy-cycle approach, European influence on national policy development has increased because of specific mechanisms which keep the policy cycle running in Europe. It has been shown that these mechanisms did not work in the Italian context. The high level of consensus required in European decision making resulted in compromises which weakened the impact on the national level. Furthermore, implementation was not aided by a multi-level enforcement game. In neither sector were private actors successful in getting European actors to enforce national compliance with European law. Finally, the expected competitive pressure on national regulation has not been found. For these reasons, no second-order convergence occurred in either road or rail.

In chapter six the second explanatory approach is presented. Instead of explaining the absence of a counterfactual development, this approach explains the path-dependent development at the national level to be a product of the state capacity and the structure of the interest intermediation. Using this approach one can see that Europe did exert an influence on the national level. In the case of rail, there has been a random enforcement of convergence, but only within the limits of the national path dependence. In the case of road haulage, the European policies have even encouraged divergence by promoting incremental changes within a protectionist framework.

In the introduction the frameworks used to study Europeanisation were grouped into three mechanisms, the first focusing on legal problems, the second focusing on the economically-driven process of regulatory competition and the third being the adaptation of organisational routines. The first two images have been combined to form the regulatory policy cycle. This may be called the functionalist approach, since the external pressure generated is expected to translate into internal changes without much delay and modification. The functionalist approach may be contrasted with the institutionalist approach, in which the external pressure is modified by a translation process depending on the internal institutional structure. One of my expectations was that it would be possible to see that the institutionalist approach is superior to the functionalist approach. As a result of the analysis, this view can now be substantiated and specified. The functionalist approach is not disproved by the case of Italian transport policy, since this case cannot be considered a crucial test. We have seen that the necessary prerequisites for a crucial case are not given. The expected second-order convergence does not take place because European policy obligations are weak. Therefore the enforcement game cannot get started and the competitive pressure on national regulation is not strong enough. The conclusion is that in the Italian case the functionalist account is *irrelevant* for conceptualising and explaining Europeanisation. The functionalist approach cannot capture how and why Italian policy making was influenced by Europe. This, however, is revealed by the institutionalist approach. The institutionalist approach explains the two different first-order developments that are observed. It also highlights how the European influence has contributed to them. The strength of the institutionalist analysis is that it shows how the European influence has been transformed by the national institutional structure. Yet the disadvantage is that any institutional analysis involves a much larger collection of data. Identifying the relevant structures and actors of the sector and of the general administration for a longer period of time is no straightforward task. It is difficult to specify the institutional variable in advance. In this respect, the functionalist approach has the important advantage of being more parsimonious. The mechanisms exerting external pressure are easily identified and checked in an empirical investigation. Unfortunately, in this case study the more parsimonious approach does not yield satisfactory results. It thus warns students of Europeanisation not to use exceedingly simple frameworks.

A second conclusion is related to the institutionalist approach. Because of the widely different policy paradigms at the European and at the national levels, one may have expected a version of sociological institutionalism to be better suited to explain the Italian policy dynamics - and especially its resistance to Europe - than an approach based on rational choice. The empirical evidence suggests that both approaches are valid for the present case study. Whereas an approach employing the rational-choice perspective focuses on coalition building by reconciling diverse interests, a sociological approach assumes that a precondition for such coalition building involves shaping these preferences. Accordingly, the first approach sees policy-entrepreneurs as coalition builders (e.g. Wilson, 1980), whereas the second approach sees them as promoting social learning processes (e.g. Muller, 1995; Dobbin, 1993; Majone, 1989). Both views are relevant simultaneously for explaining policy change. A first example may be taken from the Italian railway reform. It was shown that the leadership of the head of the Italian railways has been vital for the course of the reform. This leadership has been practised in two ways, both shaping interests and reconciling them. Without having elaborated his grand vision of the railways as an intermodal transport enterprise, Necci may not have been able to motivate his staff or to convince outsiders. But to pursue his vision, he had to overcome the resistance of the trade unions to reducing the number of employees. His success in this respect was based not so much on the power of his ideas as on a political exchange which was agreed upon by the trade unions. In return for their agreement to reduce the workforce by almost fifty percent, they were offered higher wages for the remaining staff and a generous pension fund for early retirement. A second example in which a sociological institutionalist view on policy change is important in explaining change is presented by the latest reform in the road-haulage sector. Preliminary evidence shows a social learning process in which preferences have been effectively changed. This was an important prerequisite for the fundamental reform. In fact, the hauliers agreed to the reforms in spite of substantial and immediate economic losses. But even in this more clear cut case, policy leadership could not rely entirely on the force of the better argument. Some compensation was offered in this case as well. The subsidy scheme for the sector was continued at previous levels. The disadvantage of the stricter conditions for eligibility were offset by the advantage of a long-term, three-year commitment on the part of the Government. As in the railways, funding was provided for the early closure of small haulier firms, thus offering compensation for the cases where the devaluation of the licences is likely to cause social hardship. In this example, compensation is clearly second to changing preferences. This would suggest that second-order changes are more likely to depend on social learning processes.

A third important result of this case study has been a certain disenchantment with the power of Europeanisation. This finding is not a surprise in the light of much of the history of the European Community. Progress in European integration has often been slow or elusive. This is still true for some policy areas. The European Union is weak in redistribution policies, and it is argued that one should never expect the EU to replace national welfare states (Majone, 1996a). However, the Single Market Programme is widely perceived to be a success story. The CTP is designed for the same purpose. In the Italian case, the CTP has not been able to overcome a contradictory regulatory tradition at the national level. On the contrary, it shows that European influence depends on national institutional intermediation. The case of Italian transport policy is interesting because a national *status quo* is being challenged by an opposing European policy and there are no other external influences. The main empirical finding of the case study is that a Europeanisation process leading to convergence is highly contingent on factors beyond its immediate influence. This aspect of the case leads to the next point, the question of whether any general conclusions can be drawn.

Possible generalisations

The advantage of a case study, such as the one presented here, is that it allows an in-depth investigation of the phenomena of interest. Methodologists frequently point out that a big disadvantage is tied to this advantage: the results of a case study have no validity beyond the phenomena examined. One way to escape these limits to generalisation is to conduct a crucial case study (Eckstein, 1975) in which a theory is confronted with a case that validly tests the theory and may lead to modifications. This seems to be one possible way to arrive at more generalisable results from the case study of Italian transport policy. With respect to the theory of the regulatory policy cycle, it may not be too risky to argue that Italian transport reform constitutes such a crucial case. It has already been argued that the advent of Italian antitrust policy has shown that the main doubt is no longer justified: there is not complete absence of linkage between Italy and Europe. Neither is it justified to doubt whether the Italian experience may be in any way meaningful for other cases. An examination of transport policy has indicated that Italy is not well-described as a *partitocrazia* in which parties dominate policy making. Rather, as in all other advanced capitalist economies, in Italy sectoral governance structures are well-established. Italy may be different in some respects, but it is no general exception beyond any possible comparison (see Regini, 1995). However, even if it is justified to treat Italy as a crucial case in which Europeanisation may be expected, the Italian policy development does not invalidate the theory of the regulatory policy cycle, since not all the mechanisms it proposes work. The European-proposed solutions to the problems of effective decision making - i.e. implementation and regulatory competition - did not work well. Therefore, the theory of the regulatory policy cycle has not been disconfirmed by the Italian policy development.

A more fruitful starting point for generalisation is the observation that Italian transport reform is an interesting case in that it may be regarded as a laboratory setting for studying Europeanisation. Unlike in many other policy areas in which liberalisation is an issue, two major competing factors that influence national development are absent. In contrast to the telecommunication or finance sectors, the transport sector is not subject to fundamental technological change. This is not to say that no new technologies have been developed in transport. That is blatantly not true: telematics is playing an increasing role in many areas of transport, for example. However, it takes political intervention to introduce these new technologies to modernise transport.[1] There is no technological push originating from the sector that challenges the former regulation as there was telecommunications and finance. Another difference from other policy areas is that surface transport (road and rail) is much less exposed to international competition. Again, telecommunications and financial services provide a good example of an entirely different situation. In these areas, technological change has influenced market structures and made competition possible on an unprecedented scale. Surface transport has not remained completely isolated from increased economic internationalisation. In fact, it has been claimed that the competitive advantage of a national economy also depends on a working transport infrastructure. Still, in surface transport there are no sectoral developments which call for a regulatory reform to introduce liberalisation. Hence, in contrast to many other policy areas, in the case of Italian transport reform, many external influences which usually influence policy development are absent. Furthermore, domestic factors also are favourable for methodological reasons. In the beginning of the period studied, there was no government programme aimed at liberalisation,[2] and the regulatory tradition in the transport sector was different. In short, the effect of European policy making may be observed in isolation. It has been shown that the CTP did not have a very strong impact on the national policy development for most of the time and that the type of influence that could be seen depended on the national institutional structure. Given this fact, the question arises concerning whether European decision making really makes a difference. A consequential process of Europeanisation may be contingent on many other factors. The suspicion arises that cases of successful liberalisation may have been attributed to Europe without sufficiently checking for other variables. Therefore, studies which attribute change to the impact of Europe will have to be questioned in this respect. The European impact, as such, seems to have little momentum.

The scepticism about the possibility of a dramatically significant European influence leads to a theoretical conclusion. The empirical observations in the case of Italian transport policy suggest that a functionalist view is not useful as a rule, and that the processes of Europeanisation may be better explained by the institutionalist approach.

Yet, this seems too radical a conclusion. Admittedly, it cannot be denied that there are cases where the impact of Europeanisation is strong. The Italian transport sector itself offers such an example. Air transport regulation changed radically due to European intervention. The state air carrier Alitalia was forced to abandon anti-competitive practices and the Italian government to stop issuing subsidies that distorted intra-Community competition.[3] There was also a strong European influence in the telecommunications sector. Here national governments were forced to abandon their monopolies as a consequence of the vigorous action of the European Commission, based on the rarely-used Article 90 of the EC-Treaty (Taylor, 1994). A detailed description of these cases cannot be presented here. But the regulatory policy cycle model seems to provide a satisfactory explanation. In both cases, deregulation created pressures and opportunities for economic stake holders. The ensuing legal and political action helped to sustain the reform effort. For example, in both cases the new competitors fought for competition on equal terms with the old monopolies, both by lobbying the European Commission and by legal challenges. However, there is reason to believe that these cases are not just examples of Europeanisation. The search for explanatory factors cannot be limited to Europe. Air transport and telecommunications are subject to intense competition on a global scale. Furthermore, the liberalisation of these sectors in the USA was widely perceived to have been successful. The magnitude of this external pressure was essential for the direct impact of EU reforms. The reforms in these industries should be seen as resulting from a process of globalisation and not of Europeanisation. Thus these cases show that the regulatory policy cycle model depends on external factors such as intense global competition and fast technological change. There is a further argument against the functionalist approach. Even strong external pressure does not force a single response across different national institutional settings. As was also shown for telecommunications and financial markets, different countries adopt different coping strategies (Vogel, 1997).

Our conclusion that the functionalist approach to Europeanisation does not offer a satisfactory explanation for national adaptation processes leads to a further question. In the beginning of this study we introduced the concept of the 'state' to denominate general patterns of legitimate policy making. We identified two different forms of the state, the Keynesian welfare state and the regulatory or competition state. If Italian transport policy adapted in accordance with its own institutionalist legacy (and we expect that this is true for other nation states as well), does it still make sense to use such a general concept of the state? In my view this case study does not indicate that it is superfluous to use this abstract concept. The development of a new form of the state does not necessarily imply the homogenisation of national practices. It is more useful to understand the 'state' as a basic form, institutionalised in diverse ways in different nation-states. Furthermore a transforming the state does not imply that every aspect of the state is redefined according to a new pattern. But it does imply that exceptions to the rule have to be justified; they are not taken for granted (Willke, 1997). According to this definition, the patterns of Europeanisation found in Italian transport policy may be understood as a specific Italian reaction to the transformation of the state which is promoted by the Single Market Programme of the European Union. This perspective shows the strength of this transformation. Italian transport policy had to take counter-measures to defend the *status quo*. It also reveals the nature of the Italian adaptation process. It is largely *post hoc* and often managed badly. No viable *alternative* solutions emerged in the process. The result is that the trend in Italy is ambiguous. Europeanisation jeopardises the old form of the state but does not lead to a new form of the state.

Finally, this case study could suggest a conclusion about EU policy making. The European Commission has identified the failure to fully implement Community law as a prime problem in EU policy making (e.g. Commission, 1996a). It has devoted considerable effort to closing the presumed implementation gap. According to an institutionalist perspective this political goal may be problematic. First, given different institutional contexts, different implementation solutions may in fact be functionally equivalent. Thus it could be difficult to establish the satisfactory level of implementation. Second, this goal entails a political risk. Pointing to large gaps in implementation without having the power to close them can amount to identifying insoluble problems. This does not seem to be a good way to increase the legitimacy of the EU. An alternative approach which avoids these problems could be based on models of 'correct implementation' that evolve over time in the different member states. The task would then be to foster the search for the best practice. Promoting discourse about these matters among the member states could lead to more effective policy making than identifying cases of implementation failure does.

Lessons for Europeanisation Research

There is reason to believe that the concern with the impact of European integration on national structures has been firmly established on the research agenda. An increasing number of edited volumes, books, and articles focus explicitly on this issue.[4] The research area is also becoming increasingly reflexive. A literature review is dedicated to mapping the development of the field (Radaelli 2000), and a methodological debate seems to be starting (see below). The present study of the effects of Europeanisation on regulation in Italy also contributes to this agenda.

Research on the impact of the EU on the national level has already yielded a few rather robust hypothesis. One of them is that there is a great deal of resistance from national administrations, even if change is required by European policies (Börzel, 1999; Knill, 1999). Inertia is only likely to be overcome when the national administrative tradition allows it to be done and when reforms are initiated at the national level. The general hypothesis of bureaucratic immunity is confirmed by the Italian case. The implementation of surface-transport reforms would have required administrative adaptation. The analysis has shown that the lack of ability for the national administration to act autonomously was a considerable obstacle to change. In road haulage, continually changing transport ministers did not allow for a commitment to a long-term policy plan. The reform of the Italian railways was hampered by the fact that there was no unit in the administration which was charged with developing a railway policy independent of the plans of the railway managers. But neither government stability nor administrative reorganisation ensued. Thus, the Italian case seems to confirm that there is high degree of national administrative inertia with respect to the European influence. However, it also points to one way in which the European influence can overcome national bureaucratic inertia. The Italian Antitrust Agency is an example of one institution in which national administrative traditions have clearly been overcome. It has established itself as a new centre of authority for the regulation of markets, and its pro-competitive stance stands in stark contrast to the former interventionist approach to governing the economy. Admittedly, the Italian Antitrust seems to confirm rather than disprove the hypothesis of administrative immunity, since it was founded only in 1990, thus did not have a long independent administrative tradition. However, according to an institutionalist perspective, one should not expect that such an innovation escape the former administrative traditions. Therefore, even in this instance, it is surprising to see a European influence. What is more, the Italian Antitrust case points to the possibility that there is an influence on national administrations which may be neglected when the focus is on the implementing bureaucracy. As has been shown above, the Italian antitrust has also continually challenged what it sees as unjustified public interference into markets. In this way, the Italian antitrust has become an important agent of change in the national administration as well. It seems that procedural or organisational innovations due to a European influence can have far-reaching long-term repercussions on established administrative traditions. Thus, the Italian case also warns against overly-pessimistic conclusions about the innovative potential of the European Union.

The second major dimension in which the effects of Europeanisation have been examined regards the structure of interest intermediation. In this dimension change is expected to be more pronounced. It is assumed that the increasing importance of European policies opens up closed national co-operative networks of public and private actors. Increasing economic integration leads to a loss of control of the economic processes at the national level. As a consequence, corporatist bargaining at the national level is devalued. Furthermore, the capacity for collective action required for corporatism is unlikely to be reconstructed at the European level. National corparatisms are replaced by 'transnational pluralism' (Streeck and Schmitter, 1991; see also Majone, 1997). The present case study is not an example of a general decay of co-operative public-private partnerships in decision making. In Italian surface transport, the interest intermediation in both sectors have been clientelistic in structure, and sectoral interests have been able to regularly extract advantages. Interestingly enough, European transport policy reforms did not make this exclusive arrangement more permeable. Although transport users represented by Confindustria have been advocating reform for a long time, they have not had a strong influence. As has been shown, this has largely been due to the breakdown of the mechanism of judicial review. It turned out to be impossible for transport users to promote national deregulation via European law enforcement. The same was true for the railways. Here, European and national antitrust law were too weak to block the expansion of the railway monopoly. At first, the European influence exacerbated clientelistic policy making. The small hauliers united in UNATRAS as well as the train driver's union, COMU, managed to benefit considerably by frequently going on strike. Thus, the effect of Europe tended more to enforce closure than to transform clientelism to open pluralism at the national level. Whenever the European impact resulted in a more radical change, the result was not pluralism either. Rather, the effect was a shift from clientelism to corporatism. The 1998 reform episode in road haulage was also an episode of sectoral corporatism. The haulier associations involved in drafting the reform laws represented a very large majority of hauliers, and they were capable of making the agreements binding for their members as well. Similarly, railway reforms that sometimes even resulted in a large number of lay-offs were inevitably linked to agreements with the railway trade unions that guaranteed a high level of income and social protection for the remaining staff. Thus the European influence on national interest intermediation seems to involve a transition from 'national clientelism to national corporatism'. Apparently, the entrenched interests in clientelistic interest intermediation can only be overcome by intensifying cooperation. The present case study thus confirms the more recent hypothesis that the European influence is not eroding corporatist cooperation at the national level, but is actually fostering it. The reason for this is that national governments try to strike bargains with interest groups in order to promote reforms aimed at enhancing European competitiveness (Schmitter and Grote, 1997).[5]

Another issue of research on Europeanisation has been the link between the European and the national level (for an overview see Radaelli 2000). So far I have argued that the functioning of the legal mechanism of judicial review and the economic mechanism of regulatory competition is contingent on the national institutional status quo. This view questions the robustness of a rather popular mechanism for explaining European influence, i.e. the 'two level game'. In its original version, the 'two level game' was a model for conceptualising the link between the international and the domestic political arena (Putnam, 1988). The intriguing idea was that if governments had little leeway on an issue in one of the arenas, this could be used to increase its leeway on the other. Thus, political pressure 'at home' could justify uncompromising behaviour in international bargaining and vice versa. This model has become rather popular in European integration studies, because it allows the reconciliation of the intergovernmentalist view that 'member states are ultimately in control' of all policy developments in the EU with the empirical fact that member states sometimes agree to policies that are obviously not in their self-interest. Member states agree to such decisions whenever their governments want to use the European constraint to promote their national reform capacity (Moravscik, 1994; Grande, 1996). To be sure, it sometimes makes sense to explain national decision-making in this way. However, the results presented above point to some of its important functioning requirements. Legal obligations and economic pressure have to be strong in order to establish credible external constraints. In surface transport, EU policy has not established such strong constraints. In road haulage, obligations were only concerned with removing barriers to cross-border operations within the territory of the European Union. National reforms could not be based on these constraints. The same holds true for economic pressure resulting from cabotage, i.e. from foreign firms operating within a national territory. The competitive threat resulting from this was not so strong as to enforce national laws. The railways are even more extreme in this respect. Legal obligations are modest and competition among different service suppliers is still largely elusive. Thus, a wide range of different national reform models can be referred to in order to justify reform initiatives. Demands for liberalisation which point to the British model can easily be countered by pointing to the very modest French reforms, which are also legal according to EU law. Probably because of this, the Italian government refrained from playing a 'two-level game' in railway policy. The Prodi directive has not been justified with reference to the CRP, although its policies and structures very nearly met all of CRP's provisions. Since many EU policies share these characteristics, the windows of opportunity for playing two-level-games could be small indeed. But this does not necessarily imply that Europe does not exert any influence at all. This would neglect the working of the cognitive mechanism of influence (Radaelli, 1997). In the analysis presented above, there is some evidence that Europe did indeed exert a strong influence on the political discourse at the national level. The logic of Italian antitrust action was heavily influenced by the European antitrust doctrine. Furthermore, Italian railway reform has been developed from the outset with reference to Europe, which was employed in justifying the expansion of private monopolies during the Necci era and the promotion of intramodal competition in the subsequent period. European policy discourse was probably least influential in the case of road haulage. Being mainly deregulatory in nature, it was not embedded in an elaborate programme. Still, the reform episode of 1998 was possibly also due to the pro-European reforms introduced by the Prodi government to qualify Italy for European Monetary Union.

Finally, the study of Europeanisation in reference to regulation in Italy suggests a methodological lesson.[6] The incipient methodological debate regarding Europeanisation research could be characterised as follows. On the one hand, there is the position that Europeanisation research needs to develop middle-range theories by specifying causal mechanisms by which European developments exert an influence on the national level (Knill and Lehmkuhl, 1999). On the other hand, it is denied that such general mechanisms are useful in analysing Europeanisation because they cannot do justice to the complex institutional adaptation processes found at the national level. According to this latter position, Europeanisation research should employ comparative research to identify the mediation of national institutional factors (Risse, 1999). European transport policies confirm that it is impossible to explain the EU influence (and certainly not the national policy development) by a single Europeanisation mechanism. For road haulage, regulatory competition is the main mechanism. Still, other influences resulted from both the European competition law which challenged road haulage subsidies, and the European Monetary Union, which also promoted sectoral reform. Although the impact of Europe on national transport policies could not be reduced to a single Europeanisation mechanism, middle-range theories of this type are still useful for Europeanisation research.[7] Specifying a dominant Europeanisation mechanism highlights the fact that the same European cause had different effects at the national level and that Europe was influential in other ways as well.

Notes

[1] Guerci (1996) is an excellent source documenting the beginning of an effort to introduce computer technology in the Italian transport sector.

[2] National governments often use European constraints to overcome national resistance in a two-level-game (e.g. Grande, 1996). However, unless this strategy is also induced by European decision making, the outcome of such a two-level game may not be attributed solely to the European influence on the national level.

[3] For an excellent overview of the Alitalia case, see Autorità Garante (1996b).

[4] Besides the literature cited in the introduction and below, see for example Haverland (1999), Lavdas (1997); Lawton (1999); Lehmkuhl (1999); Cole and Drake (2000); Green-Cowles et al. (forthcoming); Héritier et al. (forthcoming).

[5] I want to thank Dirk Lehmkuhl for bringing this alternative hypothesis on national interest intermediation in the EU to my attention.

[6] This paragraph relies heavily on Kerwer and Teutsch (forthcoming).

[7] See Scharpf (1997, chapter one) for the importance of middle-range theories in policy research.

Bibliography

Books and Journal Articles

Alter, K. (1998), 'Who Are the "Masters of the Treaty"?: European Governments and the European Court of Justice', *International Organization*, vol. 20, pp. 121-47.

Alter, K. and Meunier-Aitsahalia, S. (1994), 'Judicial Politics in the European Community. European Integration and the Pathbreaking "Cassis de Dijon" Decision', *Comparative Political Studies*, vol. 26, pp. 535-61.

Amati, A. (1991), 'Ente FS e Stato: il Contratto di Programma', *Ingeneria Ferroviaria*, vol. 46, pp. 231-41.

Amato, G. (1996), 'The impact of Europe on national policies. Italian antitrust policy', in Y. Mény, P. Muller, and J.-L. Quermonne (eds), *Adjusting to Europe. The impact of the European Union on national institutions and policies*, Routledge, London, pp. 158-74.

Amorelli, G. (1993), 'Appalti pubblici e concorrenza: un rapporto difficile', *Concorrenza e mercato. Rassegna degli orientamenti dell'Autorità Garante*, vol. 1, pp. 280-85.

Anselmi, L. (1994), *Le partecipazioni statali oggi. Analisi delle condizioni di equilibrio aziendale*, Giappicchelli, Torino.

Aquilanti, P. (1993a), 'Poteri dell'autorità in materia di intese restrittive della libertà di concorrenza e di abuso di posizione dominante', in A. Frignani, R. Pardolesi, A. Patroni Griffi, and L.C. Ubertazzi (eds), *Diritto antitrust italiano. Commento alla legge 10 ottobre 1990, n 287*, Vol. 2, Zanichelli, Bologna, pp. 877-92.

Aquilanti, P. (1993b), 'Poteri conoscitivi e consultivi dell' autorità', in A. Frignani, R. Pardolesi, A. Patroni Griffi, and L.C. Ubertazzi (eds), *Diritto antitrust italiano. Commento alla legge 10 ottobre 1990, n 287*, Vol. 2, Zanichelli, Bologna, pp. 1139-47.

Atkinson, M. and Coleman, W. D. (1989), 'Strong states and weak states: Sectoral policy networks in advanced capitalist economies', *British Journal of Political Science*, vol. 19, pp. 47-67.

Autorità Garante della Concorrenza e del Mercato (1993), 'Autotrasporto in conto terzi', *Bolletino dell'Autorità Garante della Concorrenza e del Mercato*, vol. 3, 10.

Autorità Garante della Concorrenza e del Mercato (1994), 'Nuovi compiti per gli spedizionieri doganali', *Bolletino dell'Autorità Garante della Concorrenza e del Mercato*, vol. 4, 48.

Autorità Garante della Concorrenza e del Mercato (1994a), *Concorrenza e regolamentazione nei servizi di pubblica utilità. Relazione al presidente del consiglio dei ministri*, Istituto Poligrafico e Zecca dello Stato, Roma.

Autorità Garante della Concorrenza e del Mercato (1996), *Antitrust. Istruzioni per l'uso*, Istituto Poligrafico e Zecca dello Stato, Roma.

Autorità Garante della Concorrenza e del Mercato (1996a), *Relazione annuale sull'attività svolta. Presentata al presidente del consiglio dei ministri il 30 aprile 1996*, Istituto Poligrafico e Zecca dello Stato, Roma.

Autorità Garante della Concorrenza e del Mercato (1996b), 'Associazione consumatori utenti/Alitalia', *Bolletino dell'Autorità Garante della Concorrenza e del Mercato*, vol. 6, 45.

Autorità Garante della Concorrenza e del Mercato (1997), *Relazione annuale sull'attività svolta. 30 Aprile 1997*, Istituto Poligrafico e Zecca dello Stato, Roma.

Bach, M. (1992), 'Eine leise Revolution durch Verwaltungsverfahren. Bürokratische Integrationsprozesse in der Europäischen Gemeinschaft', *Zeitschrift für Soziologie*, vol. 21, pp. 16-30.

Bagnasco, A. (1988), *La Costruzione Sociale del Mercato. Studi sullo sviluppo della piccola impresa in Italia*, Il Mulino, Bologna.

Baier, V.E., March, J.G. and Saetren, H. (1988), 'Implementation and Ambiguitiy', in J.G. March (ed), *Decisions and Organizations*, Blackwell, Oxford, pp. 150-64.

Banister, D. and Button, K. J. (1991), 'Introduction', in D. Banister and K. Button (eds), *Transport in a Free Market Economy*, Macmillan, London, 1-16.

Barbati, S. (1992), 'Pianeta Società Sinport: Pubblico e privato in consorzio. Un accordo originale', *FER-MERCI*, vol. 13, pp. 21-23.

Baum, H. (1993), 'Government and Transport Markets', in J. Polak and A. Heertje (eds), *European Transport Economics*, Blackwell, Oxford, pp. 152-88.

Baumgartner, J.P. (1993), 'Switzerland', in European Conference of Ministers of Transport (ed), *Privatisation of Railways*, OECD, Paris, pp. 25-50.

Befahy, F. (1995), 'Thoughts on privatisation and access to networks', in European Conference of Ministers of Transport (ed), *Why do we need railways?*, OECD, Paris, 11-34.

Bellamy, Ch. and Child, G. D. (1993), *Common Market Law of Competition*, Sweet & Maxwell, London.

Bellini, N. (1996), *Stato e industria nelle economie contemporanee*, Donzelli, Roma.

Beltrami, G. (1995), 'Come ristrutturare le ferrovie: vale la logica di mercato', *FER-MERCI*, vol. 16, pp. 9-11.

Bentivoglio, Ch. and Trento, S. (1995), *Economia e politica della concorrenza. Intervento antitrust e regolamentazione*, Nuova Italia Scientifica, Roma.

Bernini, G. (1996), 'La legge antitrust italiana: esperienze pregresse e prospettive future', *Il diritto dell'economia*, vol. 1, pp. 7-25.

Bianchi, P. (1995), 'Italy: The Crisis of an Introvert State', in J. Hayward (ed), *Industrial Enterprise and European Integration. From National to International Champions in Western Europe*, Oxford University Press, Oxford, pp. 97-121.

Bianco, L. (1996), 'La ricerca nei trasporti', in Ministero dei Trasporti (ed), *30 anni di trasporti in Italia*, Istituto Poligrafico e Zecca dello Stato, Roma.

Bilancia, F. (1992), 'La struttura divisionale', *L' Amministrazione Ferroviaria*, vol. 19, pp. 4-5.

Bilotta, B. (1983), 'La burocrazia italiana tra tre culture: un' ipotesi sullo sviluppo della 'meridionalizzazione' della pubblica amministrazione', *Rivista Trimestrale di Scienza della Amministrazione*, vol. 3, pp. 85-101.

Bishop, M., Kay, J. and Mayer, C. (eds), (1994), *Privatization and Economic Performance*, Oxford University Press, Oxford.

Bordogna, L. (1991) 'Relazioni sindacali e frammentazione della rappresentanza nelle Ferrovie: dalla nascita del Coordinamento macchinisti al suo riconoscimento come soggetto contrattuale', in CESOS (ed), *Le relazioni sindacali in Italia, 1989-1990*, Edizione Lavoro, Roma, pp. 141-163.

Bordogna, L. (1992) 'Ristrutturazione e relazioni sindacali nelle ferrovie. Le difficoltà di un processo di risanamento aziendale nel settore pubblico', in C. Dell'Aringa and T. Treu, (eds), *Nuove relazioni industriali per l'Italia in Europa. Quinto Rapporto CER-IRS sull'industria e la politica industriale in Italia*, Mulino, Bologna, pp. 75-115.

Breyer, S. (1990), 'Regulation and Deregulation in the United States: Airlines, Telecommunications and Antitrust', in G. Majone (ed), *Deregulation or Reregulation. Regulatory Reform in Europe and the United States*, Pinter, London, pp. 7-58.

Brunsson, N. and Olsen, J.P. (1993), *The Reforming Organization*, Routledge, London.

Bull, M.J. (1996), *Contemporary Italy. A Research Guide*, Greenwood, Westport, London.

Bull, M.J. and Rhodes, M. (eds) (1997), *Crisis and Transition in Italian Politics*, Special Issue of West European Politics, vol. 20.

Button, K.J. (1992), *Europäische Verkehrspolitik - Wege in die Zukunft*, Bertelsmann, Gütersloh.

Button, K.J. (1993), *Transport Economics*, Elgar, Aldershot.

Caciagli, M., Cazzola, F., Morlino, L. and Passigli, S. (eds) (1994), *L'Italia fra crisi e transizione*, Laterza, Roma.

Cafagna, L. (1995), 'Saja, pioniere delle battaglie anti-monopoli', *Il Sole 24 Ore* 30.07.1995, pp. 1-2.

Caporaso, J.A. (1998), 'Regional integration theory: understanding our past and anticipating our future', *Journal of European Public Policy*, vol. 5, pp. 1-16.

Carlsson, L. (1996), 'Nonhierarchical Implementation Analysis. An Alternative to the Methodological Mismatch in Policy-Analysis', *Journal of Theoretical Politics*, vol. 8, pp. 527-46.

Cassese, S. (1983), *Il sistema amministrativo italiano*, Il Mulino, Bologna.

Cassese, S. (1985), 'L'amministrazione pubblica in Italia', *Rivista Trimestrale di Scienza della Amministrazione*, vol. 2, pp. 3-29.

Cassese, S. (1993), 'Hypothesis on the Italian Administrative System', *West European Politics*, vol. 16, pp. 316-28.

Cassese, S. (1995), 'La nuova costituzione economica', Laterza, Bari.

Cassese, S. (1995a), 'Il ruolo e la collocazione dei poteri indipendenti nell'ordinamento', in Autorità garante della concorrenza e del mercato (ed), *La tutela della concorrenza: regole, istituzioni e rapporti internazionali*, mimeo Roma.

Cavazzuti, F. (1996), *Privatizzazioni, imprenditori e mercati*, Il Mulino, Bologna.

Centro Europa Ricerche (1995), *Rapporto 6: Il fisco e i trasporti*, Veutro, Roma.

Cerny, Ph.G. (1997), 'Paradoxes of the Competition State: The Dynamics of Political Globalization', *Government and Opposition*, vol. 32, pp. 251-74.

Claudiani, C. (1996), *Ferrovie. La riforma e fallita?* Convegno Nazionale Roma, Hotel Parco dei Principi, 6 dicembre 1996, CISL, Roma.

Colacito, M. (1989), 'Ferrovieri', in Enciclopedia Giuridica Treccani, Istituto Poligrafico e Zecca dello Stato, Roma, pp. 1-9.

Cole, A. and Drake, H. (2000), 'The Europeanization of the French polity: continuity, change and adaptation', *Journal of European Public Policy*, vol. 7, pp. 26-34.

Coletti, G. (1985), *Storia di una riforma. L' Ente 'Ferrovie dello Stato*, Collegio Amministrativo Ferroviario Italiano, Roma.

Collegio Amministrativo Ferroviario Italiano (1996), *La nuova struttura ferroviaria. Organizzazione, missione e responsabilità della FS Spa*, CAFI, Roma.

Commission (1995), *Droit de la concurrence dans les Communautés européennes*, Vol. IIA, Règles applicables aux aides d'États. Situation au 31 décembre 1994, Office des publications officielles des Communautées européennes, Luxembourg.

Commission (1995a), *Communication from the Commission on the Development of the Community's Railways*, COM (95) 337 final, Office for Official Publications of the European Communities, Luxembourg.

Commission (1995b), *Fourth Survey On State Aid In the European Union In the Manufacturing and Certain Other Sectors*, Office for Official Publications of the European Communities, Luxembourg.

Commission (1995c): *Towards Fair and Efficient Pricing in Transport. Policy Options for Internalizing the External Costs of Transport in the European Union*, Brussels, COM (95) 691 final, Office for Official Publications of the European Communities, Luxembourg.

Commission (1996), *A Strategy for Revitalizing the Community's Railways*, Com (96) 421 final, Office for the Official Publications of the European Communities, Luxembourg.

Commission (1996a), *Thirteenth Annual Report on Monitoring the Application of Community Law (1995)*, Office for Official Publications of the European Communities, Luxembourg.

Commission (1997), *The Single Market Review, Road freight transport*, Office for Official Publications of the European Communities, Luxembourg.

Commission (1997a), *Amended proposal for a Council Directive amending Directive 91/440/EEC on the development of the Community's railways*, COM(97) 34 final, Office for Official Publications of the European Communities, Luxembourg.

Commission (1997b), *Trans European Rail Freight Freeways*. COM(97) 242 final, Office for the Official Publications of the European Communities, Luxembourg.

Commission (2000), *Press Release, The Commission has approved the Italian measures for restructuring of road haulage and the development of intermodality*, Brussels, 6 May 1999.

Communauté des Chemins de Fer Européens (1995), *Manuel à l'usage des entreprises ferroviaires à propos de leur accès aux infrastructures ferroviares dans l'Union Européenne, en Novège et en Suisse. Récapitulatif des règles et principes en vigueur*, Bruxelles.

Community of European Railways (1996), *Response to the European Commission's White Paper 'A Strategy For Revitalising the Community's Railways'*, Brussels.

Confetra (1996), *Il libro bianco dei servizi logistici e di trasporto merci*, Roma.

Confindustria (1999), *Il rilancio della competitività in Italia*, Roma.

Confindustria, n.d., *Nota, Causa presso la Corte di Giustizia CE*, Roma.

Consiglio nazionale dell' economia e del lavoro (CNEL) (1994), *La riforma del ministero dei trasporti*, Roma.

Cook, T. D. and Campbell, D.T. (1979), *Quasi-Experimentation. Design & Analysis Issues in Field Settings*, Rand, Chicago.

Correale, G. (1989), *Ferrovie dello Stato*, in, Enciclopedia giuridica Treccani, Volume XIV, Istituto Poligrafico e Zecca dello Stato, Roma, pp. 1-8.

Corte dei Conti (1996), *Relazione sul risultato del controllo eseguito sulla gestione finanziaria delle Ferrovie dello Stato - Società di trasporti e servizi per azioni per gli esercizi dal 1991 al 1994*, Corte dei Conti, Roma.

Costa, R. (1994), *Una politica del trasporto nel quadro comunitario. Linee di azione del Governo in materia di Trasporti e navigazione*, Presidenza del consiglio dei ministri, Roma.

Cozzi, T. and Govoni, C. (1989), *Le tariffe e gli accordi collettivi nazionali per il trasporto delle merci su strada*, Maggioli, Rimini.

Crespi, G. (1986), *Camionisti. La ristrutturazione del trasporto merci in Italia*, Franco Angeli, Milano.

Crouch, C. and Streeck, W. (eds) (1997), *Political Economy of Modern Capitalism. Mapping Convergence & Diversity*, Sage, London.

Dani, A., Conte, G. and Giacomini, G. (1994), *Memoria a sensi dell'art 20 del protocollo sullo statuto della Corte di Giustizia CEE presentata da 'La Spedizione Marittima del Golfo S.r.l.' nella causa n. C-96/94*, Genova, Luxemburg.

De Nicola, A. (1995), 'L'Antitrust non si deve frammentare', *Il Sole 24 Ore* 20.08.1995, p. 13.

degli Abbati, C. (1987), *Transport and European integration*, Office for the Official Publications of the European Communities, Luxembourg.

Del Viscovo, M. (1990), *Economia dei trasporti*, Utet, Torino.

Dente, B. (1990), 'Introduzione, Le politiche pubbliche in Italia', in B. Dente (ed), *Le politiche pubbliche in Italia*, Il Mulino, Bologna, pp. 9-47.

Dente, B. and Regonini, G. (1989), 'Politics and policies in Italy', in P. Lange and M. Regini, (eds), *State, market and social regulation, new perspectives on Italy*, Cambridge University Press, Cambridge, pp. 51-79.

Derthick, M. and Quirk, P.J. (1985), *The Politics of Deregulation*, Brookings, Washington D.C.

Derthick, M. and Quirk, P.J. (1985a), 'Why the Regulators Chose to Deregulate', in R.G. Noll (ed), *Regulatory Policy in the Social Sciences*, University of California Press, Berkeley, pp. 200-31.

Di Miceli, G. B. (1985), 'Considerazioni sulla tariffazione da parte del nuovo ente Ferrovie dello Stato', *Economia Pubblica*, vol. 15, pp. 357-62.

Di Miceli, G. B. (1990), 'I nodi delle ferrovie alla vigilia dell' instaurazione del Mercato interno', *Economia Pubblica*, vol. 20, pp. 353-59.

Di Pietro, A. (1996), 'Prime considerazioni sulle nuove competenze dell'antitrust nazionale attribuite dalla legge comunitaria per il 1994', in *Rivista italiana di diritto pubblico comunitario*, vol. 6, pp. 496-500.

Dobbin, F. (1993), 'What Do Markets Have in Common? Toward a Fast Train Policy for the EC', in S.S. Andersen and K.A. Eliassen (eds), *Making Policy in Europe. Europeification of National Policymaking*, Sage, London, pp. 71-91.

Dobbin, F. (1994), *Forging Industrial Policy. The United States, Britain, and France in the railway age*, Cambridge University Press, Cambridge.

Dodgson, J. (1994), 'Railway Privatization', in M. Bishop, J. Kay and C. Mayer (eds), *Privatization and Economic Performance*, Oxford University Press, Oxford, pp. 232-50.

Dolowitz, D. and Marsh, D. (1996), 'Who Learns What from Whom, a Review of the Policy Transfer Literature', *Political Studies* 44, pp. 343-57.

Donativi, V. (1990), *Introduzione della disciplina 'antitrust' nel sistema legislativo italiano. Le premesse*, Giuffrè, Milano.

Douillet, A.-C. and Lehmkuhl, D. (forthcoming), 'Strengthening the Opposition and Pushing Change, The Paradoxical Impact of Europe on the Reform of French Transport', in A. Héritier et al., *Differential Europe. New Opportunities and Restrictions for Policy making in the member states*, Lanham, Rowman & Littlefield.

Dumez, H. and Jeunemaître, A. (1996), 'The Convergence of Competition Policies in Europe, Internal Dynamics and External Imposition', in, S. Berger and R. Dore (eds), *National Diversity and Global Capitalism*, Cornell, Ithaca, pp. 216-38.

Dye, Th.R. (1990), *American Federalism. Competition Among Governments*, Lexington Books, Lexington.

Dyson, K. (ed) (1992), *The Politics of German Regulation*, Dartmouth, Aldershot.

Dyson, K. and Featherstone, K. (1996), 'Italy and EMU as a *'Vincolo Esterno'*, Empowering the Technocrats, Transforming the State', *South European Society & Politics*, vol. 1, pp. 272-99.

Ebbinghaus, B. (1996), 'Spiegelwelten, Vergleich und Mehrebenenanalyse in der Europaforschung', in Th. König, E. Rieger and H. Schmitt (eds), *Das europäische Mehrebenensystem*, Campus, Frankfurt a.M., pp. 405-28.

Eckstein, H., 1975, 'Case Study and Theory in Political Science', in F.I. Greenstein and N.W. Polsby (eds), *Handbook of Political Science*, vol. 7, Addison-Wesley, Reading, Mass, pp. 111-37.

European Conference of Ministers of Transport 1985, *Improvements in international railway transport services*, OECD, Paris.

Eichener, V. and Voelzkow, H. (eds) (1994), *Europäische Integration und verbandliche Interessenvermittlung*, Metropolis, Marburg.

Erdmenger, J. (1981), *EG unterwegs - Wege zur Gemeinsamen Verkehrspolitik*, Nomos, Baden-Baden.

Erdmenger, J. (1983), *The European Community Transport Policy*, Gower, Aldershot.

Erdmenger, J. (1996), 'Verkehr', in H.v.d. Groeben, J. Thiesing and C.-D. Ehlermann (eds), *Handbuch des Europäischen Rechts*, Nomos, Baden-Baden, pp. I A 30.

Eurolog, SPA (1996), *Relazione del V. Presidente all' assemblea Eurolog*, Roma.

Ferner, A. and Hyman, R. (1992), 'Italy, Between Political Exchange and Micro-Corporatism', in A. Ferner and R. Hyman (eds), *Industrial Relations in the New Europe*, Blackwell, Oxford, pp. 524-600.

Ferretti, M. (1996), 'Il trasporto intermodale', in Ministero dei Trasporti (ed*)*, *30 anni di trasporti in Italia*, Istituto Poligrafico e Zecca dello Stato, Roma, pp. 369-76.

Ferrovie dello Stato (1993), *Nuovo modello organizzativo delle Ferrovie dello Stato. Società di Trasporti e Servizi per azioni*. Supplemento 'linea news', Roma.

Ferrovie dello Stato (1996), 'Il gruppo ferrovie dello stato verso il nuovo piano di impresa', *L' amministrazione ferroviaria*, vol. 23, pp. 13-48.

Ferrovie dello Stato (1996a), *Ordine di servizio n. 5 del 4 Marzo 1996 di modificazione dell'assetto di vertice e di istituzione di nuove strutture organizzative*, CAFI, Roma.

Ferrovie dello Stato (1996b), 'Il contratto di programma 1994-2000', *L' Amministrazione Ferroviaria*, vol. 23, pp. 9-24.

Ferrovie dello Stato (2000), 'La "Politica Estera" delle Ferrovie dello Stato', *Documenti. Newsletter delle Ferrovie dello Stato*, vol. 3, p. 7.

Fiorentino, L. (n.d.), 'La riforma delle FF. SS. Legislazione e documentazione', *Rivista giuridica della circolazione e dei trasporti*, Quaderno no. 10.

FITA (Federazione Italiana Trasportatori Artigiani) (1996), *TrasNotizie No. 57*, 22.02.1996, Roma.

Fontanella, G. (1974), *Il sistema dei trasporti in Italia. Lineamenti generali*, CEDAM, Padova.

Fontanella, G. (1993), 'L'attività pianificatoria nel settore dei trasporti', *Uomini e trasporti*, vol. 12, pp. 20-21.

Fragolino, V. and Rossi, G. (1987), 'La nuova organizzazione strutturale dell'Ente FS', *L'Amministrazione Ferroviaria*, vol. 14, pp. 3-9.

Franchini, C. (1990), 'L' integrazione europea e il governo delle politiche comunitarie in Italia, organizzazione amministrativa e rapporti con le comunità europee', *Rivista di diritto europeo*, vol 1, pp. 17-32.

Franchini, C. (1993), *Amministrazione italiana e amministrazione comunitaria. La coamministrazione nei settori di interesse comunitario*, 2nd. edition, CEDAM Padova.

Gallori, E. (1996), *40 anni di lotte in ferrovia. Da sindacto a Cobas...*, Prefazione di Rossana Rossanda e Fausto Bertinotti, Ancora in marcia, Firenze.

Garrett, G., Kelemen, R. D. and Schulz, H. (1998), 'The European Court of Justice, National Governments, and Legal Integration in the European Union', *International Organization*, vol. 52, pp. 149-76.

Gelosi, G. (1995), 'Quando la notte si accorcia, l'offerta merci cerca di adeguarsi, non senza difficoltà, alla sensibile espansione della domanda ferroviaria', *FER-MERCI*, vol. 16, 22-25.

Gerken, L. (1995), 'Institutional Competition, An Orientative Framework', in L. Gerken, (ed), *Competition Among Institutions*, MacMillan, London, pp. 1-31.

Ghezzi, F., Magnani, P. and Siri, M. (1996), 'L'applicazione della disciplina Antitrust nei settori speciali, banche, assicurazioni e mass media. Questioni procedurali sostanziali alla luce dell'art. 20', *Concorrenza e Mercato*, vol. 4, pp. 179-228.

Giuliani, M. (1992), 'Il processo decisionale italiano e le politiche comunitarie', *Polis* vol. 6, pp. 307-42.

Giurisprudenza Commerciale (1991), 'Concorrenza e disegni di leggi *antitrust*', *Giurisprudenza Commerciale* vol. 18, I, pp. 1210-30.

Graser, A. (1998), Zum Stand der Diskussion zur Inländerdiskriminierung - Einige kritische Anmerkungen und ein Vorschlag zur prozessualen Behandlung, *Die Öffentliche Verwaltung*, vol. 51 pp. 1004-12.

Gobbo, F. and Salonico, T. (1995), 'Il potere dell'Autorità. Un primo bilancio sull'antitrust', *Il Mulino*, vol. 3, pp. 504-13.

Grande, E. (1996), 'Das Paradox der Schwäche. Forschungspolitik und die Einflußlogik europäischer Politikverflechtung', in, M. Jachtenfuchs and B. Kohler-Koch (eds), *Europäische Integration*, Leske + Budrich, Opladen, pp. 373-99.

Green-Cowles, M., Caporaso, J. and Risse, Th. (eds), (forthcoming), *Transforming Europe, Europeanization and Domestic Change*, Cornell, Ithaca.

Greenwood, J., Grote, J.R. and Ronit, K. (ed) (1992), *Organized Interests and the European Community*, Sage, London.

Gröhe, Christian (1996), *Kabotage im Güterkraftverkehr in Italien*, Luchterhand, Neuwied.

Gronemeyer, N. (1994), 'Die Entwicklung des EU-Kabotage-Rechts bis zur neuen Kabotage-Verordnung (EWG) Nr. 3118/93', *Transportrecht* vol. 17, pp. 267-71.

Grottanelli de' Santi, G. (1992), 'The impact of EC integration on the Italian form of government', in, Francioni, F. (ed), *Italy and EC Membership evaluated*, Pinter, London, pp. 179-90.

Guerci, C.M. (ed) (1996), *Telecommunicazioni e informatica per i trasporti. Tecnologia e mercato al 2005*, Il Mulino, Bologna.

Haas, P.M. (1998), 'Compliance with EU directives, insights from international relations and comparative politics', *Journal of European Public Policy* vol. 5, pp. 17-37.

Hall, P.A. (1993), Policy Paradigms, Social Learning, and the State. The Case of Economic Policymaking in Britain, *Comparative Politics* vol. 25, pp. 275-96.

Hall, P.A. and Taylor, R.C. (1996), Political Science and the Three New Institutionalisms, *Political Studies* vol. 44, pp. 952-73.

Haverland, M. (1999), *National Autonomy, European Integration and the Politics of Packaging Waste*, Thela Thesis, Amsterdam.

Héritier, A. (1993), 'Policy-Analyse. Elemente der Kritik und Perspektiven der Neuorientierung', in A. Héritier (ed), *Policy-Analyse. Kritik und Neuorientierung*, Politische Vierteljahresschrift Sonderheft, vol. 24, pp. 9-36.

Héritier, A., Kerwer, D., Knill, Ch., Lehmkuhl, D., Teutsch, M. and Douillet, A.-C. (forthcoming), *Differential Europe. New Opportunities and Restrictions for Policy making in the member states*, Rowman & Littlefield, Lanham.

Héritier, A., Knill, Ch. and Mingers, S. (1996), *Ringing the Changes in Europe. Regulatory Competition and the Transformation of the State*, de Gruyter, Berlin.

Hine, D. (1993), *Governing Italy. The Politics of Bargained Pluralism*, Clarendon, Oxford.

Hirschman, A.O. (1970), *Exit, Voice and Loyalty*, Harvard University Press, Cambridge.

Hirst, P. and Thompson, G. (1996), *Globalization in Question. The International Economy and the Possibilities of Governance*, Cambridge, Polity.

Hogwood, B. W. and Peters, B. Guy (1983), *Policy dynamics*, Wheatsheaf, Brighton.

Hollingsworth, J.R., Schmitter, Ph. C. and Streeck, W. (eds) (1994), *Governing Capitalist Economies. Performance & Control of Economic Sectors*, Oxford University Press, Oxford.

Hunt, M. (1990), *Die Praxis der Sozialforschung*, Campus, Frankfurt a.M.

Ingram, H. (1990), 'Implementation, A Review and Suggested Framework', in N.B. Lynn and A. Wildavsky (eds), *Public Administration. The State of the Discipline*, Chatham House, Chatham, pp. 462-80.

Jachtenfuchs, M. (1995), 'Theoretical Perspectives on European Governance', *European Law Journal*, vol. 1, pp. 115-33.

Jachtenfuchs, M. and Kohler-Koch, B. (1996), 'Einleitung: Regieren im dynamischen Mehrebenensystem', in M. Jachtenfuchs and B. Kohler-Koch (eds), *Europäische Integration*, Leske + Budrich, Opladen, pp. 15-44.

Jepperson, R.L. (1991), 'Institutions, Institutional Effects, and Institutionalism', in W.W. Powell, P.J. Di Maggio (eds), *The New Institutionalism in Organizational Analysis*, University of Chicago Press, Chicago, pp. 143-63.

Jessop, B. (1996), 'Veränderte Staatlichkeit. Veränderung von Staatlichkeit und Staatsprojekten', in D. Grimm (ed), *Staatsaufgaben*, Suhrkamp, Frankfurt a.M., pp. 43-73.

Jobert, B. (ed) (1994), *Le tournant néo-libéral en Europe. Idées et recettes dans les pratiques gouvernementales*, L'Harmattan, Paris.

Jobert, B. and Muller, P. (1987), *L'Etat en action. Politiques publiques et corporatismes*, Presse Universitaires de France, Paris.

Joerges, Ch. (1991), 'Markt ohne Staat? - Die Wirtschaftsverfassung der Gemeinschaft und die regulative Politik', in R. Wildenmann (ed), *Staatswerdung Europas? Optionen für eine europäische Union*, Nomos, Baden- Baden, pp. 225-67.

Kahn, A.E. (1970), *The Economics of Regulation, Principles and Institutions*, vol. 1, Wiley, New York.

Kahn, A.E. (1971), *The Economics of Regulation. Principles and Institutions*, vol. 2, Wiley, New York.

Kassim, H. (1996), 'Air transport', in H. Kassim and A. Menon (eds), *The European Union and National Industrial Policy*, Routledge, London, pp. 106-31.

Kaufmann, F.-X. (1994), 'Diskurse über Staatsaufgaben', in D. Grimm (ed), *Staatsaufgaben*, Nomos, Baden-Baden, pp. 15-41.

Keohane, R.O. and Milner, H.V. (eds) (1996), *Internationalization and Domestic Politics*, Cambridge University Press, Cambridge.

Kerwer, D. and Teutsch, M. (forthcoming), 'Elusive Europeanisation. Liberalising Road Haulage in the European Union', *Journal of European Public Policy*.

King, G., Keohane, R.O. and Verba, S. (1994), *Designing Social Inquiry. Scientific Inference in Qualitative Research*, Princeton University Press, Princeton.

Kingdon, J.W. (1984), *Agendas, Alternatives, and Public Policies*, Little, Boston.

Kiriazidis, Th. (1994), *European Transport, Problems and Policies*, Avebury, Aldershot.

Kitzmantel, E. and Moser, E. (1995), 'State competition with tax policy', in B. Unger and F. van Waarden (eds), *Convergence or Diversity? Internationalization and Economic Policy Response*, Avebury, Aldershot, pp. 135-43.

Knill, Ch. (forthcoming), 'Reforming Transport Policy in Britain, Concurrence with Europe but Separate Development', in A. Héritier et al., *Differential Europe. New Opportunities and Restrictions for Policy making in the member states*, Rowman & Littlefield, Lanham.

Knill, Ch. (1999), *The Transformation of National Administrations in Europe, Patterns of Change and Persistence*. Habilitationsschrift zur Erlangung der Venia Legendi im Fach Politikwissenschaft, FernUniversität-GesamtHochschule Hagen, Fachbereich Erziehungs-, Sozial-, und Geisteswissenschaften, Hagen.

Knill, Ch. and Lehmkuhl, D. (2000), 'An Alternative Route of European Integration, The Community's Railway Policy', *West European Politics*, vol. 23, pp. 65-88.

Krasner, S. (1988), 'Souvereignty, An Institutional Perspective', *Comparative Political Studies* 21, pp. 66-94.

Krislov, S., Ehlermann, C.-D. and Weiler, J. (1986), 'The Political Organs and the Decision-Making Process in the United States and the European Community', in M. Cappelletti, M. Seccombe and J. Weiler (eds) *Integration Through Law*. Volume 1, Methods, Tools and Institutions, Book 2, Political Organs, Integration Techniques and Judicial Process, de Gruyter, Berlin, pp. 3-109.

La Palombara, J. (1964), *Interest Groups in Italian Politics*, Princeton University Press, Princeton,

La Palombara, J. (1994), 'Clientela e parentela rivisitato', in M. Caciagli et al. (eds.), *L'italia fra crisi e transizione*, Laterza, Roma, pp. 23-43.

Lane, J.-E. (1995), 'The Public Sector. Concepts, Models and Approaches', Sage, London.

Lange, P. and Regini, M. (eds) (1989), *State, market, and social regulation. New perspectives on Italy*, Cambridge University Press, Cambridge.

Lavdas, K.A. (1997), *The Europeanisation of Greece. Interest Politics and the Crises of Integration*, MacMillan, London.

Lawton, Th.C. (1999), 'Governing the Skies, Conditions for the Europeanisation of Airline Policy', *Journal of Public Policy*, vol. 19, pp. 91-112.

Lehmbruch, G. (1987), 'Administrative Interessenvermittlung', in A. Windhoff-Héritier (ed), *Verwaltung und ihre Umwelt*. Festschrift für Thomas Ellwein, Westdeutscher Verlag, Opladen, pp. 11-43.

Lehmbruch, G. (1991), 'The Organization of Society, Administrative Strategies, and Policy Networks. Elements of a Developmental Theory of Interest Systems', in A. Windhoff-Héritier and R. Czada (eds), *Political Choice, Institutions, Rules, and the Limits of Rationality*, Westview, Boulder, pp. 121-55.

Lehmbruch, G. (1992), 'Bedingungen und Grenzen politischer Steuerung im Verkehrssektor', in Verband Deutscher Elektroingenieure (VDE) (ed), *Politik und Technik in der Verantwortung*, VDE, Frankfurt a.M., pp. 168-93.

Lehmbruch, G. (1997), *Discourse Coalitions and the Institutional Design of the Social Embedding of Capitalism*. Paper presented at 'Germany and Japan, The future of nationally embedded capitalism in a global economy. University of Washington-Seattle, April 10-12, 1997.

Lehmkuhl, D. (forthcoming), 'From Regulation to Stimulation, Dutch Transport Policy in Europe', in, A. Héritier, et al., *Differential Europe. New Opportunities and Restrictions for Policy making in the member states*, Lanham, Rowman & Littlefield.

Lehmkuhl, D. (1999), *The Importance of Small Differences. European Integration and Road Haulage Associations in Germany and the Netherlands*, Thela Thesis, Amsterdam.

Lepore, M.C. (1993), 'La circolazione delle merci su strada', *Rivista giuridica della circolazione e dei trasporti*, vol. 47, pp. 239-81.

Lepsius, M.R. (1991), 'Nationalstaat und Nationalitätenstaat als Modell für die Weiterentwicklung der Europäischen Gemeinschaft', in R. Wildenmann (ed), *Staatswerdung Europas? Optionen für eine europäische Union*, Nomos, Baden-Baden, pp. 19-40.

Lesquesne, Ch. (1993), *Paris-Bruxelles. Comment se fait la politique européenne della France*, Presse della fondation nationale de science politique, Paris.

Levitt, B. and March, J.G. (1988), 'Organizational learning', *Annual Review of Sociology*, vol. 14, pp. 319-40.

Lewanski, R. (1999), 'Italian Administration in Transition', *South European Society & Politics* vol. 4, pp. 97-131.

Lindberg, L.N. and Scheingold, S.A. (1970), *Europe's Would-Be Polity. Patterns of Change in the European Community*, Prentice-Hall, Englewood Cliffs.

Loraschi, G.C. (1984), *L'impresa pubblica, il caso delle ferrovie dello stato*, Giuffrè, Milano.

Lowi, Th.J. (1985), 'The State in Politics. The Relation Between Policy and Administration', in R. Noll (ed), *Regulatory Policies and the Social Sciences*, University of California Press, Berkeley, pp. 67-105.

Luhmann, N. (1977), 'Differentiation of Society', *Canadian Journal of Sociology*, vol. 2, pp. 29-52.

Luhmann, N. (1991), 'Soziologie des politischen Systems', in N. Luhmann, *Soziologische Aufklärung 1. Aufsätze zur Theorie sozialer Systeme*, 6th edition, Westdeutscher Verlag, Opladen, pp. 154-77.

Macchiati, A. (1996), *Privatizzazioni. Tra economia e politica*, Donzelli, Roma.

Majone, G. (ed) (1996), *Regulating Europe*, Routledge, London.

Majone, G. (1989), *Evidence, Argument and Persuasion in the Policy Process*, Yale University Press, New Haven.

Majone, G. (1991), 'Cross-National Sources of Regulatory Policymaking in Europe and the United States', *Journal of Public Policy*, vol. 11, pp. 79-106.

Majone, G. (1994), 'Comparing strategies of regulatory rapprochement', in OECD (ed), *Regulatory Co-operation for an Interdependent World*, OECD Paris, pp. 155-77.

Majone, G. (1994), 'The Rise of the Regulatory State in Europe', *West European Politics* 17, pp. 77-101.

Majone, G. (1996a), 'Redistributive und sozialregulative Politik', in M. Jachtenfuchs, Kohler-Koch, B. (ed), *Europäische Integration*, Leske + Budrich Opladen, pp. 225-48.

Majone, G. (1996b), 'The rise of statutory regulation in Europe', in Majone, G. (ed), *Regulating Europe*, Routledge, London, pp. 47-60.

Majone, G. (1996c), 'Regulation and its modes', in G. Majone (ed), *Regulating Europe*, Routledge, London, pp. 9-27.

Majone, G. (1997), 'From the Positive to the Regulatory State, Causes and Consequences of Changes in the Mode of Governance', *Journal of Public Policy*, vol. 17, pp. 139-67.

Malkin, J. and Wildavsky, A. (1991), 'Why the Traditional Distinction Between Public and Private Goods Should Be Abandoned', *Journal of Theoretical Politics*, vol. 3, pp. 355-78.

March, J.G. (1994), *A Primer on Decision Making. How Decisions Happen*, Free Press, New York.

March, J.G. and Olsen, J.P. (1989), *Rediscovering Institutions*, Free Press, New York.

Maresch, U. (1987), 'Verkehrsmarktordnungen in der Europäischen Gemeinschaft', *Internationales Verkehrswesen*, vol. 39, pp. 409-13.

Mattli, W. and Slaughter, A.-M. (1998), 'Revisiting the European Court of Justice', *International Organization*, vol. 52, pp. 177-209.

Mayntz, R. (1980), 'Die Entwicklung des analytischen Paradigmas der Implementationsforschung', in R. Mayntz (ed), *Implementation politischer Programme*, Athenäum, Königstein, pp. 1-17.

Mayntz, R. (1985), *Soziologie der öffentlichen Verwaltung*, Müller, Heidelberg.

Mayntz, R. (1988), 'Funktionelle Teilsysteme in der Theorie sozialer Differenzierung', in R. Mayntz (ed), *Differenzierung und Verselbständigung, Zur Entwicklung gesellschaftlicher Teilsysteme*, Campus. Frankfurt a.M, pp. 11-44.

Mayntz, R. (1992), 'Modernisierung und die Logik von interorganisatorischen Netzwerken', *Journal für Sozialforschung*, vol. 32, pp. 19-28.

Mayntz, R. (1993), 'Policy-Netzwerke und die Logik von Verhandlungssystemen', in, A. Héritier (ed), *Policy-Analyse. Kritik und Neuorientierung*, PVS Sonderheft 24, Westdeutscher Verlag, Opladen, pp. 39-56.

Mayntz, R. and Scharpf, F.W. (1995), 'Steuerung und Selbstorganisation in staatsnahen Sektoren', in R. Mayntz and F.W. Scharpf (eds), *Gesellschaftliche Selbstregelung und politische Steuerung*, Campus, Frankfurt a.M., pp. 9-38.

Mayntz, R. and Scharpf, F.W. (1995a), 'Der Ansatz des akteurszentrierten Institutionalismus', in R. Mayntz, and F.W. Scharpf (eds), *Gesellschaftliche Selbstregelung und politische Steuerung*, Campus, Frankfurt a.M., pp. 39-72.

Mazey, S. and Richardson, J. (1993), *Lobbying in the European Community*, Oxford University Press, Oxford.

McGowan, F. (1994), 'EC Transport Policy', in A.M. El-Agraa (ed), *The economics of the European Community*, Harvester Wheatsheaf, New York, pp. 247-64.

McGowan, L. and Wilks, S. (1995), 'The first supranational policy in the European Union: Competition policy', *European Journal of Political Research*, vol. 28, pp. 141-69.

McKenzie, R.B. and Dwight, L.R. (1991), *Quicksilver Capital. How the Rapid Movement of Wealth Has Changed the World*, Free Press, New York.

Meli, V. (1997), 'Attuazione della disciplina antitrust e regolazione amministrativa dei mercati', *Giurisprudenza Commerciale*, vol. 24, I, pp. 243-65.

Mendrinou, M. (1996), 'Non-compliance and the European Commission's role in integration', *Journal of European Public Policy*, vol. 3, pp. 1-22.

Mény, Y., Muller, P. and Quermonne, J.-L. (1996), 'Introduction', in Y. Mény, P. Muller and Quermonne, J.-L. (eds), *Adjusting to Europe. The Impact of the European Union on national institutions and policies*, Routledge, London, pp. 1-21.

Merlini, S. (1994), 'Il governo', in G. Amato and A. Barbera (eds), *Manuale di diritto pubblico*, Il Mulino, Bologna, pp. 419-61.

Militello, G. (1995), 'La natura e i programmi dell'Autorità garante della concorrenza e del mercato', *Giurisprudenza Commerciale*, vol. 22, I, pp. 909-15.

Millon, D. (1991), 'The Sherman Act and the Balance of Power', in Th.E. Sullivan (ed), *The Political Economy of the Sherman Act. The First One Hundred Years*, Oxford University Press, Oxford, pp. 85-115.

Ministero dei Trasporti (1977), *I Trasporti in Italia*, Libro Bianco, Roma.

Ministero dei Trasporti (1992), *Il Mercato dei Trasporti con l' estero*, Roma.

Ministero dei Trasporti (1994), *Le ferrovie in concessione e in gestione governativa*, Roma.

Ministero dei Trasporti (1996), *30 anni di trasporti in Italia*, Istituto Poligrafico e Zecca dello Stato, Roma.

Ministero dei Trasporti (2000), *Per l'avvio della liberalizzazione del trasporto ferroviario in Italia*, Roma, http//www.trasportinavigazione.it (visited 7 August 2000).

Ministero dei Trasporti (n.d.), *I trasporti in Italia. Efficacia, efficienza e produttività per superare la crisi*, Roma.

Ministero dei Trasporti (n.d.a), *L'autotrasporto merci. Analisi, Problemi, Prospettive*, Roma.

Ministero dell'Industria (1988), 'La concorrenza nel sistema economico italiano. Relazione conclusiva della Commissione istituita presso il Ministero dell'industria per lo studio della concorrenza nel sistema economico italiano (presidente Romani)', *Rivista delle Società*, vol. 33, pp. 559-71.

Moravcsik, A. (1991), 'Negotiating the Single European Act', in R. Keohane and S. Hoffmann (eds), *The New European Community. Decisionmaking and Institutional Change*, Westview, Boulder, pp. 41-84.

Moravcsik, A. (1993), 'Preferences and Power in the European Community, A Liberal Intergovernmental Approach', *Journal of Common Market Studies*, vol. 31, pp. 473-524.

Moravcsik, A. (1994), *Why the European Community Strengthens the State, Domestic Politics and International Co-operation*, mimeo, Harvard University.

Morisi, M. (1992), *L'attuazione delle direttive Ce in Italia. La 'legge comunitaria' in parlamento*, Giuffrè, Milano.

Muller, P. (1995), 'Les politiques publiques comme construction d'un rapport au monde', in A. Faure, G. Pollet and Ph. Warin (eds), *La construction du sens dans les politiques publiques. Débats autour de la notion de 'référentiel*, L'Harmattan, Paris, pp. 153-79.

Müller, W. and V. Wright (eds) (1994), *The State In Western Europe. Retreat Or Redefinition?*, West European Politics, Vol. 20, Special Issue.

Munari, F. (1991), 'The Legge 287/1990 on Protecting Competition in the Marketplace', *Europäische Zeitschrift für Wirtschaftsrecht*, vol. 2, pp. 489-96.

Munari, Francesco (1994), 'La Segnalazione dell'Autorità Garante della Concorrenza e del Mercato in materia di servizi di autotrasporto di merci', *Diritto dei trasporti*, vol. 7, pp. 903-18.

Mutimer, D. (1994), 'Theories of Political Integration', in H.J. Michelmann and S. Panayotis (eds), *European Integration. Theories and Approaches*, University Press of America, Lanham, pp. 11-42.

Necci, A.L. (1992), 'Per una politica di alleanze', *FER-MERCI*, vol. 13, pp. 4-5.

Necci, A.L. (1994), 'Il futuro delle ferrovie. L'armonizzazione delle condizioni di concorrenza. Intervento del presidente dell'Union de Chemin de Fer alla conferenza paneuropea dei trasporti', *L'amministrazione ferroviaria*, vol. 21, pp. 4-7.

Necci, A. L. and Normann, R. (1994), *Reinventare l'Italia*, Mondadori, Milano.

Ninni, A. (1995), 'Concorrenza per i mercati pubblici. Su due decisioni dell'Autorità Garante della Concorrenza e del Mercato in materia di rapporti tra Ferrovie dello Stato e industria ferroviaria', *Economia e Politica Industriale* vol. 86, pp. 43-53.

North, D.C. (1990), *Institutions, Institutional Change and Economic Performance*, Cambridge University Press, Cambridge.

Oberti, P. et al. (1995), 'Riforma della disciplina in materia di autotrasporto delle merci ed istituzione dell'Agenzia nazionale autotrasporto per conto terzi', *Camera dei Deputati, XII Legislatura, Disegni di Legge e relazioni*, No 3215, 4.10.1995.

Ohmae, K (1995), *The end of the nation-state, the rise of regional economies*, HarperCollins, London.

Olsen, J.P. (1991), 'Political Science and Organization Theory. Parallel Agendas but Mutual Disregard', in R. Czada and A. Windhoff-Héritier (eds), *Political Choice. Institutions, Rules and the Limits of Rationality*, Campus, Frankfurt a.M., pp. 87-119.

Olsen, J.P. (1996), 'Europeanization and Nation-State Dynamics', in S. Gustavsson and L. Levin (eds), *The Future of the Nation-State. Essays on Cultural Pluralism and Political Integration*, Routledge, London, pp. 245-86.

Olsen, J.P. and Peters, B. Guy (1996), 'Learning from Experience?', in J.P. Olsen, B. Guy Peters (eds), *Lessons from Experience. Experiential Learning in Administrative Reforms in Eight Democracies*, Scandinavian University Press, Oslo.

Organisation for Economic Co-operation and Development (OECD) (1990), *Competition Policy and the Deregulation of Road Transport*, OECD, Paris.

Ostrom, E. (1990), *Governing the Commons. The Evolution of Institutions for Collective Action*, Cambridge University Press, Cambridge.

Padoa Schioppa Kostoris, F. (1993), *Italy - the Sheltered Economy. Structural Problems in the Italian Economy*, Clarendon, Oxford.

Padoan, P.C. (1994), 'Le prospettive per l'economia italiana in un anno di grandi cambiamenti. Anno ventunesimo. Edizione 1994', in Istituto affari internazionali (ed), *L' Italia nella politica internazionale*, SIPI, Roma, pp. 23-37.

Parcu, P.L. (1996), *Stato e concorrenza. L'attività di segnalazione dell'autorità antitrust, contenuti, efficacia e prospettive*, Autorità garante della concorrenza e del mercato, Roma.

Pasquino, G. (1989), 'Unregulated regulators, parties and party government', in P. Lange and M. Regini (eds), *State, market, and social regulation. New perspectives on Italy*, Cambridge University Press, Cambridge, pp. 29-50.

Pavesio, C. (1989), 'Merger Control and Restrictive Practices in Italy', *European Competition Law Review*, vol. 9, 568-75.

Peters, B. Guy. (1992), 'Bureaucratic Politics and the Institutions of the European Community', in A.M. Sbragia (ed), *Europolitics. Institutions and Policymaking in the 'New' European Community*, Brookings Institution, Washington, pp. 75-122.

Pezzoli, A. (1995), 'Privatizzazione e riorganizzazione dei servizi di pubblica utilità: il trasporto ferroviario', *Rivista di Politica Economica*, vol. 85, pp. 221-44.

Pezzoli, A. and Venanzetti, A. (1996), *I trasporti e la concorrenza, una rassegna dei principali problemi a partire dagli interventi dell'Autorità Garante della Concorrenza e del Mercato*, mimeo, Convegno del Libero Istituto Universitario Carlo Cattaneo, Liberalizzazione e Regolazione nei Trasporti, Castellanza (Va).

Pinna, G. (1997), 'Intermodalità: svolta cruciale', *Lo Spedizioniere Doganale*, vol. 3, pp. 3-8.

Pizzorno, A. (1992), 'Lo scambio occulto', *Stato e Mercato*, vol. 34, pp. 3-34.

Pocar, F. et al. (1988), 'Italie', in H. Siedentopf and J. Ziller (eds), *Making european policies work. The Implementation of Community Legislation in the member states. National Reports*, Sage, London, pp. 449-517.

Polsby, N.W. (1984), *Political innovation in America. The politics of policy initiation*, Yale, New Haven.

Pontarollo, E. (1989), *Domanda pubblica e politica industriale, FS, SIP, ENEL,* Marsilio, Venezia.

Ponti, M. (1992), 'Il caso delle ferrovie dello stato', in M. Ponti (ed), *I trasporti e l'industria. Quinto rapporto CER/IRS sull'industria e la politica industriale italiana,* Il Mulino, Bologna, pp. 105-40.

Ponti, M. (1996), *Struttura del settore e politiche in atto,* mimeo, Convegno del Libero Istituto Universitario Carlo Cattaneo, Liberalizzazione e Regolazione nei Trasporti, Castellanza (VA).

Ponti, M, (1996a), '70mila miliardi in libera uscita', *Mondo Economico* 30.09.1996, pp. 18-20.

Powell, W.W. and Di Maggio, P.J. (1991), 'Introduction', in W.W. Powell and P.J. Di Maggio (eds), *The New Institutionalism in Organizational Analysis,* University of Chicago Press, Chicago, pp. 1-38.

Pressman, J.L. and Wildavsky, A. (1973), *Implementation. How Great Expectations in Washington are dashed in Oakland,* University of California Press, Berkeley.

Przeworski, A. (1987), 'Methods of cross-national research, 1970-1983: an overview', in M. Dierkes, H. Weiler and A.B. Antal (eds), *Comparative Policy Research. Learning from Experience,* Gower, Aldershot, pp. 31-49.

Putnam, R.D. (1988), 'Diplomacy and domestic politics: the logic of two-level games', *International Organization,* vol. 42, pp. 427-60.

Putnam, R.D. (1993), *Making Democracy Work. Civic Traditions in Modern Italy,* Princeton University Press, Princeton.

Radaelli, C.M. (1997), 'How does Europeanization Produce Domestic Policy Change? Corporate Tax Policy in Italy and the United Kingdom', *Comparative Political Studies,* vol. 30, pp. 553-75.

Radaelli, C.M. (2000), 'Whither Europeanization? Concept stretching and substantive change', *European Integration online Papers (EIoP),* vol. 4, http//eiop.or.at/eiop/texte/2000-008a.htm.

Rangone, N. (1995), 'Principi comunitari e disciplina interna della concorrenza: l'abuso di posizione dominante in un'analisi per casi', *Rivista italiana di diritto pubblico comunitario,* vol. 5, pp. 1305-53.

Regini, M. (1995), *Uncertain Boundaries. The Social and Political Construction of European Economies,* Cambridge University Press, Cambridge.

Regonini, G. (ed) (1995), *Politiche Pubbliche e democrazia,* Edizioni Scientifiche Italiane, Napoli.

Regonini, G. and Giuliani, M. (1994), 'Italie, au-delà d'une démocracie consensuelle?' in B. Jobert (ed), *Le tournant néo-libéral en Europe. Idées et recettes dans les pratiques gouvernementales,* L'Harmattan, Paris, pp. 123-99.

Reich, N. (1992), 'Competition Between Legal Orders, A New Paradigm of EC Law?', *Common Market Law Review,* vol. 29, pp. 861-96.

Reich, R.B. (1992), *The Work of Nations, Preparing Ourselves For 21st Century Capitalism,* Vintage, New York.

Reviglio, F. (1994), *Meno stato, più mercato. Come ridurre lo stato per risanare il paese,* Mondadori, Milano.

Rhodes, R.A.W. (1990), 'Policy Networks, A British Perspective', *Journal of Theoretical Politics*, vol. 2, pp. 293-317.

Richardson, J. (ed), (1982), *Policy Styles in Western Europe*, Allen & Unwin, London.

Rommerskirchen, St. (1985), 'Gestaltung und Kostenbedeutung der Abgabensysteme für Lastkraftfahrzeuge in ausgwählten ECMT-Ländern', *Zeitschrift für Verkehrswissenschaft*, vol. 56, pp. 216-36.

Ronzitti, N. (1987), 'European Policy Formulation and the Italian Administrative System', *The International Spectator*, vol 22, pp. 207-14.

Ronzitti, N. (1990), 'The Internal Market, Italian Law and the Public Administration', *The International Spectator*, vol 25, pp. 38-44.

Ross, J.F. (1994), 'High-Speed Rail: Catalyst for European Integration?', *Journal of Common Market Studies*, vol. 32, pp. 191-214.

Rossi, F. (1996), 'La 'legge comunitaria' per il 1994 e le nuove norme in materia di concorrenza', *Rivista italiana di diritto pubblico comunitario*, vol. 6, pp. 1355-73.

Rossi, G. (1995), 'L'Antitrust come libertà dei cittadini', *MicroMega*, pp. 113-24.

Russo Frattasi G.G. and Russo Frattasi, A. (1984), *Note di Economia e di pianificazione dei trasporti*, CLUT, Torino.

Sabatier, P.A. and Jenkings-Smith, H.C. (eds) (1993), *Policy Change and Learning. An Advocacy Coalition Framework*, Westview, Boulder.

Saja, F. (1991), 'L'Autorità garante della concorrenza e del mercato, prime esperienze e prospettive di applicazione della legge', *Giurisprudenza commerciale*, vol. 18, I, pp. 457-65.

Santoro, F. (1974), *La politica dei trasporti della Communità Economica Europea*, UTET, Torino.

Santoro, F. (1977), *Politica dei trasporti*, Giuffrè, Milano.

Sanviti, G. (1992), *Il Ministero dei Trasporti*, La Nuova Italia Scientifica, Roma.

Scassellati-Sforzolini, G. and Siragusa, M. (1992), 'Italian and EC competition law, a new relationship - reciprocal exclusivity and common principles', *Common Market Law Review*, vol. 1, pp. 93-132.

Scazzocchio, B. (1995), 'Tre questioni di vitale importanza. La parola ai vertici di UNATRAS', *Uomini e trasporti*, vol. 14, pp. 4-5.

Scharpf, F.W. (1987), *Sozialdemokratische Krisenpolitik in Europa*, Campus, Frankfurt a.M.

Scharpf, F.W. (1988), 'The Joint-Decision Trap - Lessons From German Federalism and European Integration', *Public Administration*, vol. 66, pp. 239-78.

Scharpf, F.W. (1996), 'Negative and Positive Integration in the Political Economy of European Welfare States', in G. Marks, F.W. Scharpf, Ph. C. Schmitter, and W. Streeck (eds), *Governance in European Union*, Sage, London, pp. 15-39.

Scharpf, F.W. (1997), *Games Real Actors Play. Actor-Centered Institutionalism In Policy Research*, Westview, Boulder.

Scharpf, F.W. (1997a), 'Introduction: the problem-solving capacity of multi-level governance', *Journal of European Public Policy*, vol. 4, pp. 520-38.

Schmitter, Ph.C. (1996), 'Examining the Present Euro-Polity with the Help of Past Theories', in: G. Marks, F.W. Scharpf, Ph.C. Schmitter, and W. Streeck (eds), *Governance in the European Union*, Sage, London, pp. 1-14.

Schmitter, Ph,C. and Grote, J.R. (1997), *The Corporatist Sisyphus, Past, Present and Future*, European University Institute, Working Paper SPS No. 97/4, Florence.

Schmuck, H. (1992), 'Die Eisenbahnen in der Gemeinsamen Verkehrspolitik der EG', *Transportrecht*, vol 15, pp. 41-53.

Scott, W. R. (1995), *Institutions and Organisations*, Sage, London.

Siedentopf, H. and Hauschild, Ch, (1988), 'The Implementation Of Community Legislation By the member states. A Comparative Analysis', in H. Siedentopf and J. Ziller (eds), *Making European Policies Work. Volume I, Comparative Synthesis*, Sage, London, 1-87.

Skocpol, Th. (1985), 'Bringing the State Back In: Strategies of Analysis in Current Research', in P.B. Evans, D. Rueschemeyer and Th. Skocpol (eds), *Bringing the State Back In*, Cambridge University Press, Cambridge, pp. 3-37.

Sleuwaegen, L. (1993), 'Road haulage', in P. Buigues, F. Ilzkovitz, J.F. Lebrun, and A. Sapir (eds), *Market Services and European Integration. The Challenges for the 1990s, European Economy, Social Europe*, Commission of the European Communities, Reports and Studies, Brussels, pp. 211-58.

Smelser, N.J. (1976), *Comparative Methods in the Social Sciences*, Prentice-Hall, Englewood Cliffs.

Sorace, D. (1994), 'Il governo dell'economia', in G. Amato and A. Barbera (eds), *Manuale di diritto pubblico*, Il Mulino, Bologna, pp. 783-841.

Spirito, P. (1995), 'Il processo evolutivo della normativa europea e l'impatto sulla riconfigurazione delle ferrovie', *L'amministrazione ferroviaria,* vol. 22, pp. 4-36.

Spirito, P. (1996), *Le ferrovie europee verso la liberalizzazione*, mimeo, Roma.

Spirito, P. (1996a),' La riforma del trasporto pubblico locale tra regionalizzazione ed incentivi alla efficienza gestionale', *L'Amministrazione Ferroviaria*, vol. 23, pp. 4-8.

Spulber, D.F. (1989), *Regulation and Marktes*, MIT Press, Cambridge.

Staw, B.M. (1981), 'The Escalation of Commitment To a Course of Action', *Academy of Management Review*, vol. 6, pp. 577-87.

Steinmo, S., Thelen, K. and Longstreth, F. (eds) (1992), *Structuring Politics. Historical Institutionalism in Comparative Analysis*, Cambridge University Press, Cambridge.

Stigler, G.J. (1971), 'The Theory of Economic Regulation', in G.J. Stigler, *The Citizen and the State. Essays on Regulation*, University of Chicago Press, Chicago, pp. 3-21.

Stocchi, L. and De Angelis, A. (1992), *Relazioni industriali nell'ente FS e regolamentazione dell'esercizio del diritto di sciopero nei servizi pubblici essenziali*, Edizione Collegio amministrativo ferroviario italiano, Roma.

Stornelli, R. and Battistoni, G. (1994), *Autotrasporto merci. Guida a leggi, decreti, e circolari*, FAG, Milano.

Strati, F., Franci, M. and Ferroni, M. (1996), *The Incorporation of the Environmental Dimension in Freight Transport. The Italian Case Study. Final Report*, Studio Ricerche Sociali, Firenze.

Streeck, W. and Schmitter, Ph.C. (1991), 'From National Corporatism to Transnational Pluralism, Organized Interests in the Single European Market', *Politics & Society*, vol. 19, pp. 133-64.

Strohl, M.P. (1993), *Europe's High Speed Trains. A Study in Geo-Economics*, Praeger, Westport.

Sun, J.-M. and Pelkmans, J. (1995), 'Regulatory Competition in the Single Market', *Journal of Common Market Studies*, vol. 33, pp. 67-89.

Suntum, U. van, 1986, *Verkehrspolitik*, Vahlen, München.

Sylos-Labini, P. (1995), *La crisi italiana*, Laterza, Roma.

Taylor, S.M. (1994), 'Article 90 and Telecommunications Monopolies', *European Common Market Law Review*, vol. 6, pp. 322-34.

Teutsch, M. (forthcoming), 'Regulatory Reforms in the German Transport Sector: How to Overcome Multiple Veto Points', in A. Héritier, et. al., *Differential Europe. New Opportunities and Restrictions for Policy making in the member states*, Rowman & Littlefield, Lanham.

Thelen, K. and Steinmo, S. (1992), 'Historical Institutionalism in Comparative Politics', in S. Steinmo, K. Thelen and F. Longstreth (eds) (1992), *Structuring Politics. Historical Institutionalism in Comparative Analysis*, Cambridge University Press, Cambridge, pp. 1-31.

Thomasberger, C. (1995), 'Financial market liberalization and monetary policy', in, B. Unger and F. van Waarden (eds), *Convergence or Diversity? Internationalization and Economic Policy Response*, Avebury, Aldershot, pp. 39-56.

Trachtman, J.P. (1993), 'International Regulatory Competition, Externalization, and Jurisdiction', *Harvard International Law Journal*, vol. 34, pp. 47-101.

Unger, B. (1995), 'European integration and fiscal policy options', in B. Unger, and F. van Waarden (eds), *Convergence or Diversity? Internationalization and Economic Policy Response*, Avebury, Aldershot, pp. 57-79.

Unger, B. and van Waarden, Frans (eds) (1995), *Convergence or Diversity? Internationalization and Economic Policy Response*, Avebury, Aldershot.

Unger, B. and van Waarden, F. (1995), 'Introduction: an interdisciplinary approach to convergence', in, B. Unger and F. van Waarden (eds), *Convergence or Diversity? Internationalization and Economic Policy Response*, Avebury, Aldershot, pp. 1-35.

Valdina, P.F. (1995), 'Antitrust e mercati regolati', *Giurisprudenza Commerciale*, vol. II, pp. 662-79.

Van den Bos, J.M.M. (1991), *Dutch EC Policy Making. A Model-Guided Approach to Coordination and Negotiation*, University Center for Sociological Theory and Methodology, Utrecht.

Van Schendelen, M. (1993), *National Public and Private EC Lobbying*, Dartmouth, Aldershot.

Van Scherpenberg, J. (1996), 'Ordnungspolitische Konflikte im Binnenmarkt', in M. Jachtenfuchs and B. Kohler-Koch (eds), *Europäische Integration*, Leske + Budrich, Opladen, pp. 345-72.

214 *Regulatory Reforms in Italy*

Viscusi, W.K., Vernon, J.M., and Harrington, J.E. Jr. (1995), *Economics of Regulation and Antitrust*, MIT Press, Cambridge.

Vogel, D. (1995), *Trading Up. Consumer and Environmental Regulation in a Global Economy*, Harvard University Press, Cambridge.

Vogel, S.K. (1997), 'International Games With National Rules, How Regulation Shapes Competition in "Global" Markets', *Journal of Public Policy*, vol. 17, pp. 169-93.

Volta, P. (1993), *Trasporto merci. Da costo a opportunità*, Il Sole 24 Ore, Milano.

Waarden, F. van (1992), 'The historical institutionalization of typical national patters in policy networks between state and industry. A comparison of the USA and the Netherlands', *European Journal of Political Research*, vol. 21, pp. 131-62.

Weidenfeld, W. (1992), 'Einführung: Verkehrspolitik im Europa von morgen', in K. Button (ed), *Europäische Verkehrspolitik - Wege in die Zukunft: Strategie und Optionen für die Zukunft Europas*, Bertelsmann Stiftung, Gütersloh, p. 11-26.

Weiler, J.H.H. (1991), 'The Transformation of Europe', *Yale Law Journal*, vol. 100, pp. 2403-83.

Wessels, W. (1992), 'Staat und westeuopäische Integration. Die Fusionsthese', in M. Kreile (ed), *Die Integration Europas*, PVS-Sonderheft 23, Westdeutscher Verlag, Opladen, pp. 36-61.

Wessels, W. (1996), 'Verwaltung im EG-Mehrebenensystem, Auf dem Weg zur Megabürokratie?', in M. Jachtenfuchs and B. Kohler-Koch (eds), *Europäische Integration*, Leske + Budrich, Opladen, pp. 165-92.

Whitelegg, J. (1988), *Transport Policy in the EEC*, Routledge, London.

Wildenmann, R. (ed) (1991), *Staatswerdung Europas? Optionen für eine Europäische Union*, Nomos, Baden-Baden.

Willeke, R. (1995), '40 Jahre Verkehrswissenschaft und Verkehrspolitik', *Zeitschrift für Verkehrswissenschaft*, vol. 66, 167-86.

Willke, H. (1995), 'The Proactive State. The Role of National Enabling Policies in Global Socio-Economic Transformations', in H. Willke, C. Krück, and Ch. Thorn (eds), *Benevolent Conspiracies. The Role of Enabling Technologies in the Welfare of Nations. The Cases of SDI, SEMATECH, and EUREKA*, de Gruyter, Berlin, pp. 325-55.

Willke, H. (1997), *Supervision des Staates*, Suhrkamp, Frankfurt a.M.

Wilson, J.Q. (1980), 'The Politics of Regulation', in J.Q. Wilson (ed), *The Politics of Regulation*, Basic Books, New York.

Wise, M.O. (1996), 'Overview, Deregulation and Antitrust in the Electric Power Industry', *Antitrust Law Journal*, vol. 64, pp. 267-78.

Witte, B. (1932), *Eisenbahn und Staat. Ein Vergleich der europäischen und nordamerikanischen Eisenbahnorganisationen in ihrem Verhältnis zum Staat*, Gustav Fischer, Jena.

Wolf, W. (1992), *Eisenbahn und Autowahn. Personen- und Gütertransport auf Schiene und Straße. Geschichte, Bilanz und Perspektiven*, Rasch und Röhring, Hamburg.

Woolcock, S. (1996), 'Competition Among Rules in the Single European Market', in: W. Bratton, J. McCahery, S. Piciotto and C. Scott (eds), *International Regulatory Competition and Coordination. Perspectives on Economic Regulation in Europe and the United States*, Clarendon, Oxford, pp. 289-321.

Young, A. (1994), *Ideas, Interests, and Institutions: The politics of liberalisation in the EC's road haulage industry*, Sussex European Institute, Brighton.

Zahariadis, N. (1996), 'Selling British Rail. A Idea Whose Time Has Come?', *Comparative Political Studies*, vol. 29, pp. 400-22.

Zefelippo, M.T. (1997), 'La freeway nord-sud è una realtà - passo importante dell'Europa ferroviaria delle merci', *Fermerci*, vol. 18, pp. 12-17.

Press Articles

Agence Europe, 22.03.1995, p. 13: Parliament takes stand for true liberalisation of rail infrastructure by amending council's common position that it considers too restrictive.

Agence Europe, 28.03.1991, p. 7-8: Transport Council: First steps towards free competition between railway companies, and a partial end to monopolies.

Economist, 31.05.1997: Disappearing Taxes. The tap runs dry.

Il Manifesto, 9.05.1997, p. 6: Amato fa accademia. Il presidente dell'Antitrust ha tenuto la sua ultima relazione.

Il Sole 24 Ore, 1.05.1992, p. 22: Fs, una Spa per linee in nero. Necci ha approvato e inviato al Cipe il progetto di trasformazione dell'Ente in società per azioni.

Il Sole 24 Ore, 17.05.1992, p. 15: Bernini dà luce verde alle Fs formato Spa. Inviato al Cipe con molte riserve il piano Necci.

Il Sole 24 Ore, 12.05.1995, p. 25: Per le authority alla Camera cammino ancora accidentato.

Il Sole 24 Ore, 13.05.1995, p. 18: Si accende la polemica sull'Authority-trasporti.

Il Sole 24 Ore, 09.08.1995, p. 23: Il TAR contro l'Antitrust. I giudici cancellano le multe da 20 miliardi comminate a 11 compagnie italiane.

Il Sole 24 Ore, 24.08.1995, p. 1: Trasporto merci, gli uffici doganali lasciano i porti.

Il Sole 24 Ore, 31.08.1995, p. 17: Confetra guida la crociata sulle dogane. Chiesto il rinvio della riforma.

Il Sole 24 Ore, 20.02.1996, p. 18: Gli sconti agli autotrasportatori 'dimezzano' bollo e pedaggi. Approvato dall'ultimo Consiglio dei ministri un decreto legge da 206 miliardi.

Il Sole 24 Ore, 01.05.1996, p. 9: Per l'autotrasporto aiuti nel mirino UE. Ultimatum di due settimane al Governo.

Il Sole 24 Ore, 10.05.1996, p. 25: 'Questo Antitrust va fuori campo'. Tutela della concorrenza: il padre della legge, Rossi, a duello con il garante, Amato.

Il Sole 24 Ore, 15.05.1996, p. 9: Caravale propone un'Authority anche sui trasporti.

Il Sole 24 Ore, 11.06.1996, p. 14: Computer selvaggio.

Il Sole 24 Ore, 03.09.1996, p. 13: Burlando, entro la fine del mese un altro vertice sulle tariffe.

Il Sole 24 Ore, 29.09.1996, p. 2: Comincia per le Fs la lotta agli sprechi.

Il Sole 24 Ore, 01.02.1997, p. 13: Prodi vara lo spezzatino ferroviario e 'mette a dieta' costi e personale.

Il Sole 24 Ore, 05.02.1997, p. 10: Una società unica per gestire i servizi. Il ministro Burlando conferma la disponibilità a modificare il progetto (ma non la TAV) e media sull'attuazione della direttiva Prodi.

Il Sole 24 Ore, 13.02.1997, p. 3: Bloccato il treno della riforma: Le condizioni poste dai sindacati rischiano di frenare il risanamento.

Il Sole 24 Ore, 20.02.1997, p. 9: FS, al via la nuova struttura, Conti e Forlenza alla direzione.

Il Sole 24 Ore, 15.03.1997, p. 9: Cimoli: 'Certezze dal Governo'. Senza indicazioni dell'azionista c'è il rischio di uno slittamento dei tempi del piano di impresa.

Il Sole 24 Ore, 09.05.1997, p. 3: Assalto all'impero dello statalismo. Dal presidente Amato raffica di critiche a un sistema normativo che imbriglia l'economia del paese.

Il Sole 24 Ore, 11.05.1997, p. 7: L'antitrust Ue riapre il dossier sul cartello delle assicurazioni. Bruxelles esamina il caso delle multe annullate da Tar e Consiglio di Stato.

Il Sole 24 Ore, 14.05.1997, p. 14: Esame Authority sull'intesa Enel-Eni. Partita con Testa e Tatò l'indagine conoscitiva.

Il Sole 24 Ore, 31.05.1997, p. 32: Dall'Authority cartellino giallo a Eni-Enel. Ranci lancia una serie di avvertimenti antimonopolio alla futura società comune.

Il Sole 24 Ore, 01.07.1997, p. 31: Indagine Antitrust pronta a fine mese.

Il Sole 24 Ore, 10.07.1997, p. 10: L'autotrasporto progetta la casa comune. Confronto sulla proposta Fai di rappresentanza unica.

Il Sole 24 Ore, 03.12.1997, p. 21: Ferrovie, c'è intesa sui tagli: azienda e sindacati firmano il protocollo sulla gestione degli esuberi.

Il Sole 24 Ore, 05.12.1997, p. 2: Ferrovieri, il no di Ciampi. Il ministro ha manifestato critiche e perplessità sulla gestione degli esuberi nel settore.

Il Sole 24 Ore, 19.12.1997, p. 11: Fs, deficit da 5mila miliardi. Prodi ribadisce la fiducia a Cimoli mentre viene rinviata ancora la decisione sugli aumenti tariffari.

Il Sole 24 Ore, 07.02.1998, p. 12: La deregulation viaggia sul Tir. Via al radoppio del parco-veicoli, abolite le licenze dal 2000, ridimensionato il ruolo dell'Albo.

Il Sole 24 Ore, 14.02.1998, p. 11: Tir alla ricerca di aiuti 'europei'. Bruxelles resta il vero arbitro della partita.

Il Sole 24 Ore, 22.04.1999: Autotrasporto, presto le tariffe liberalizzate (http://www.borsanoli.com/98-99/R33.html).

Il Sole 24 Ore, 24.05.1999: E la categoria minaccia il blocco (http://www.borsanoli.com/98-99/R58.html).

Il Sole 24 Ore, 27.05.1999: Tir, Roma ripresenta alla Ue il provvedimento sulle fusioni (http://www.borsanoli.com/98-99/R37.html).

Il Sole 24 Ore, 24.06.2000: De Palacio 'bachetta' le FS. Trasporti - Il commissario Ue denuncia i ratardi e chiede più impegno sulla liberalizzazione (http//www.ilsole24ore.it).

La Nazione, 25.04.1996, p.5: Autotrasportatori. Nuovo consorzio.

La Repubblica: Affari & Finanza, 18.09.1996, p.4: Cimoli e le Ferrovie dello status quo.

La Repubblica: Affari & Finanza, 23.09.1996, p.1-5: FS, il grande 'Progetto' finito negli scambi. Una gestione che ha rivoluzionato la vecchia struttura, nel bene e nel male, cercando sempre il consenso in ogni modo possibile.

La Repubblica, 21.06.2000, p. : Tir, sospeso il blocco. E il governo fa il decreto. (http://www.repubblica.it/online/cronaca/tir2/tir2/tir2.html).

L'Espresso, 30.03.2000: Intercity & Internet. Più puntualità. Sicurezza. Qualità dei servizi. Pulizia. Ma anche fibre ottiche e Web. Il manager delle FS è pronto al libero mercato (http://www.espressoedit.kataweb.it).

Mondo Economico, 15.07.1996, p.10-15: Vagoni di denaro.

Mondo Economico, 29.04.1996, p.86-88: Il treno viaggia senza controllore. Cosa nasconde il bilancio delle Ferrovie dello Stato.

Tuttotrasporti, September 1988, p.39: Blocco delle autorizzazioni: ogni decisione rinviata.

Interviews

Italian Parliament
Camera dei Deputati: April 1996, February 1997; Senato: May 1995.

Ministry of Transport
Albo nazionale degli autotrasportatori (National register of road hauliers): January 1996.
Cabinet: May 1996.
D.G.M.C.T.C. (Direzione Generale Motorizzazione Civile e Trasporti in Concessione): January 1996.
D.G.P.O.C. (Direzione Generale Programmazione, Organizzazione e Coordinamento): May 1995 (2 interviews), February 1996.

Ferrovie dello Stato
November 1996 (2 Interviews), December 1996 (2 interviews), February 1997, March 1997.

Regulatory Agencies
Autorità garante della concorrenza e del mercato: December 1995.
Commissione di garanzia: February 1997.

Trade Unions
COMU (Coordinamento dei Macchinisti Uniti): February 1997.
FISAFS (Federazione Italiana Sindacati Autonomi Ferrovieri Stato): March 1997.
FIT (Federazione Italiana Trasporti): May 1996, February 1997.

Interest Groups
ANITA (Associazione Nazionale Imprese Trasporti Automobilistici): March 1996, March 1998.
Confcooperative (Confederazione Cooperative Italiane): February 1996.
Confetra (Confederazione generale italiana del traffico e dei trasporti): May 1995, December 1995 (2 interviews), April 1996 (Brussels bureau).
Confindustria (Confederazione Generale dell'Industria Italiana): May 1996.
FAI (Federazione Autotrasportatori Italiani): February 1996.
Federtrasporto (Federazione Trasporto): November 1996.
FITA (Federazione Italiana Trasportatori Artigiani): March 1996 .
F&L (European Freight and Logistics Leaders Club): March 1997.

Industry
FIAT: March 1997.
Italcontainer: March 1997.
IVECO: March 1998.
Sticosped (freight forwarder, Naples): May 1995.

Research Institute
Studio Ricerche Sociali, Firenze: September 1994.

European Union
Community of European Railways, April 1996.
European Commission, DG VII: April 1996, March 1997 (2 interviews) .
European Parliament, March 1995 (2 interviews).

Legal acts quoted

Italy: Gazzetta Ufficiale della Repubblica Italiana
Legge 6 giugno 1974, n. 298 in: G.U. n. 200 del 31.07.1974.
Legge 30 luglio 1985, n. 404 in G.U. n. 189 del 30.07.1985.
Legge 10 ottobre 1990, n. 287 in: G.U. n. 240 del 13.10.1990.
Legge 5 febbraio 1992, n. 68 in G.U. n. 35 del 12.02.1992.
Legge 27 maggio 1993, n. 162 in: G.U. n. 123 del 28.05.1993.
Legge 5 gennaio 1996, n. 11 in: G.U. n. 9 del 12 .01.1996.
Legge 23 dicembre 1997, n. 454 in G.U. n. 303 del 31.12.1997.

Decreto-legge 29 marzo 1993, n. 82, in: G.U. n. 73 del 29.03.1993.
Decreto-legge 20 febbraio 1996, n. 67 in: GU n.42 del 20.02.1996.

Decreto-legge 14 marzo 1998, n. 85, in G.U. n. 83 del 09.04.1998.
Decreto-legge 20 dicembre 1999, n. 484, in G.U. n.298 del 21.12.1999.
Decreto-legge 28.03.2000, n. 70, in: G.U. n. 73 del 28-03-2000.

Decreto Presidente della Repubblica, 16.03.1999, n.146, in G.U. n. 119 del 24.05.1999.
Decreto Presidente della Repubblica, 8.07.1998, n. 277, in: Gazzetta Ufficiale n. 187 del 12.08.1998.

Deliberazione 5 novembre 1999 n. 180/99, in G.U. n. del 22.01.2000.

Ministero dei Trasporti, decreto 19.10.1990 in: G.U. n. 246 del 20.10.1990.
Ministero dei Trasporti, decreto 30.04.1990 in G.U. n. 99 del 30.04.1990.
Ministero dei Trasporti, decreto 15.02.1991 in: G.U. n. 42 del 19.02.1991.
Ministero dei Trasporti, decreto 23.12.1998, in G.U. n. 1 del 01.01.1999.

European Union: Official Journal
Council Regulation 1969/1191, O.J. L 156, 28.06.1969.
Council Regulation 1969/1192, O.J. L 156, 28.06.1969.
Council Regulation 1970/1107, O.J. L 130, 15.06.1970.
Council Regulation 1988/1841, O.J. L 163 of 30.06.1988, p. 1.
Council Regulation 1992/881, O.J. L 95, 09.04.1992, p. 10.
Council Regulation 1993/3118, O.J. L 279, 12.11.1993, p. 1.
Council Directive 1991/440, O.J. L 237, 24.08.1991, p. 28.
Council Directive 1992/82, O.J. L 316, 31.10.1992, p. 19.
Council Directive 1993/89, O.J. L 279, 12.11.1993, p. 32.
Council Directive 1996/26, O.J. L 124, 23.05.1996, p. 1.

Commission Decision of 9 June 1993 O.J. L 233, 09.06.1993, p. 10.
Commission Communication C 3/2, O.J. 06.01.1996.

European Court of Justice Decision of 17.11.1993, case C-185/91: Bundesanstalt für den Güterfernverkehr vs. Gebr, Reiff GmbH & Co. KG.
European Court of Justice Decision of 9.06.1994, case C-153/93 Federal Republic of Germany vs. Delta Schiffahrts- und Speditionsgesellschaft mbH.
European Court of Justice Decision of 5.10.1995, case C-96/94: Centro Servizi Spediporto Srl vs. Spedizioni Marittima del Golfo, Srl.
European Court of Justice Case C-280/95, O.J. 14.10.95.

Index